Visual Information Processing

A Series of Books in Psychology

EDITORS:

Richard C. Atkinson
Gardner Lindzey
Richard F. Thompson

Visual Information Processing

KATHRYN T. SPOEHR

STEPHEN W. LEHMKUHLE

Brown University

W. H. Freeman and Company
San Francisco

Project Editor: *Patricia Brewer*
Copyeditor: *Amy Einsohn*
Designer: *Brenn Lea Pearson*
Production Coordinator: *Linda Jupiter*
Illustration Coordinator: *Richard Quiñones*
Artist: *John Cordes*
Compositor: *Vera Allen Composition*
Printer and Binder: *The Maple-Vail Book Manufacturing Group*

Library of Congress Cataloging in Publication Data

Spoehr, Kathryn T., 1947-
  Visual information processing.

  (A Series of books in psychology)
  Includes bibliographies and index.
  1. Visual perception.   2. Human information pro-
cessing.   I. Lehmkuhle, Stephen W., 1951-   . II. Ti-
tle.   III. Series.
BF241.S72   152.1'4   81-22050
ISBN 0-7167-1373-X   AACR2
ISBN 0-7167-1374-8 (pbk.)

Printed in the United States of America

1234567890   MP   0898765432

Dedicated to Luther and Cindy

Contents

Preface

This book is for those who are interested in the full range of human visual processing phenomena and who wish to understand the visual system's individual parts as well as their interworkings. We have tried to cover all the normal visual activities in everyday life and to integrate the various approaches that psychologists have taken to the study of these phenomena. To do justice to so much material, we have chosen to present the visual system as an information processor and to look at both the processes and structures it uses in performing various tasks, from sensory processing to memory and thinking. The intent is to provide an integrated background in visual processing to students beginning their study of both sensory and cognitive psychology.

One of our primary considerations in writing this book was the apparent conceptual gap between the study of the visual system at the sensory level and more cognitive approaches within the field of psychology. The study of sensory psychology is incomplete if it fails to consider the uses to which sensory information is put or the relationship between sensory and cognitive issues. Conversely, cognitive psychologists should be aware of the types of information supplied by sensory processes to the memory and problem-solving systems. By putting into a single book the concepts and methods of these two approaches to the study of visual processing, we hope to provide a broad and integrated view of how the visual processing system works as a whole.

Another purpose of this book is to acquaint the reader with some of the methods employed in the study of visual processing. These range from neurophysiological recording techniques to memory and reaction time procedures. Because we think it is important for the reader to know both *what* is known about the visual system (the conclusions and findings of the experiments), and *how* those things are known (the experimental methods), we describe illustrative experimental procedures throughout the book. In many instances we discuss topics in sufficient detail to give the reader an understanding of the scientific reasoning and logic that govern the design of experiments in psychological research.

There are many unanswered questions about the visual processing system and just as many disputes over the causes of various visual phenomena. Although it might have been less distracting to the reader for us to have ignored or glossed over these issues, we chose to present them straightforwardly. Since such unresolved questions are the grist of any scientific discipline, we hope that our presentation of them will inspire further analysis, and possibly research as well, by the readers of this book.

No book of this type could be written by two authors alone, and many individuals contributed enormously to the preparation of this volume. We are grateful to Randy Blake, Naomi Weisstein, Jay McClelland, Howard Egeth, Bryan Shepp, Marilyn Adams, Keith Stanovich, Kathy Pezdek, Bill Whitten, John Jonides, and Molly Potter for comments on earlier drafts of the individual chapters. Our special thanks go to Jim Pomerantz for a serious, careful, and tremendously helpful review of the entire manuscript. We are also indebted to Janet Graham for the many hours she spent typing the manuscript, to Amy Einsohn for her care in editing the manuscript, and to Pat Brewer for guiding the manuscript through its production. Finally, we wish to thank our editor, W. Hayward Rogers, and our families, especially Luther Spoehr and Cindy Lehmkuhle, for their support and encouragement throughout the project.

December 1981

Kathryn T. Spoehr
Stephen W. Lehmkuhle

Visual Information Processing

Chapter 1

Introduction

Think about what you do in a typical day. From the moment you wake up and open your eyes, you carry out countless activities that require using your visual system. Some of these activites are quite simple, such as noticing that it is daylight and not nighttime outside. Others are slightly more complex, such as identifying common objects in the world around you and responding to them appropriately. Even more complex are situations in which you must remember something from the distant past, such as the face of an old friend whom you have not seen for a long time; or situations in which you must recognize complex scenes involving many objects and the relations between them. Finally, some of the most complicated things you do involve the visual system: reading, for example, requires a combination of visual and language skills, and your movements—your route to work or simply your going from the bedroom to the bathroom—involve your visual and motor skills.

Such common everyday activities involve many different parts of the visual system, which function in many different ways. Distinguishing light from dark calls for relatively simple responses by the visual receptor neurons on the retina of the eye. Identifying simple forms requires combining specific patterns of receptor activity from different parts of the eye, or often from both eyes. Most psychologists consider these activities as perceptual or sensory phenomena. When psychologists study how we analyze complex scenes and how we use information learned from experience to make decisions, they are examining human visual memory and the general problem-solving skills used by the visual information processing system. When psychologists study normal reading, they study a visual system that allows us not only to identify the visual forms of the letters but also to use that visual information to retrieve more abstract, language-related information about the words on the page.

If we want to understand human vision, we must not restrict our study of the visual system to the part that performs sensory analysis. In this book, therefore, we take a broad view of the entire human visual processing system and study how its parts are coordinated in normally functioning people. In some cases we discuss the exact mechanisms in the nervous system that allow people to do certain visual tasks, while in other cases we give only a general description of how the system works. In all cases, however, we will look at the evidence that psychologists and other visual scientists have accumulated from their experiments to examine how visual processing is studied and how conclusions are reached.

THE INFORMATION PROCESSING APPROACH

As the title of this book implies, we are taking a particular approach to the study of the visual system: the *information processing* approach. Visual information processing refers to the entire process by which human beings receive visual information and adjust their behavior on the basis of that information. Between the time the information enters the visual system through the eyes and the time a person responds to it in some way, the information is interpreted, identified, compared to information in memory, and so on. In other words, stimulus information is processed in some way, and our task is to examine that processing.

A Computer Analogy

To refine our understanding of information processing, let us consider the following analogy. Suppose aliens from space were to leave a mysterious computerized robot here on earth. Suppose further that careful tests showed that this robot could do all the visual tasks that humans can perform, tasks such as recognizing forms, analyzing scenes, remembering pictures, and reading books. Clearly, the computer controlling these activities must take in visual information, perhaps from a televison camera or some other electronic gadget. The output of the robot's computer could be printed lines on a piece of paper, the movement of an artificial arm, or some special set of sounds (perhaps even English speech!). In between the input and output, the robot's computer carries out a program that specifies how to manipulate the input and how to generate output. How can we find out what happens inside the computer while that program is being carried out?

There are two ways to proceed. We could try to determine which circuits are connected to which other circuits and how the electrical current flows while the computer carries out certain tasks. In this case we would be studying the computer's hardware. Unfortunately, the circuitry of such a sophisticated machine might be too complex to be thoroughly understandable. Moreover, it is likely that knowledge of the computer's electrical system will not give us a very clear idea of what the computer is programmed to do at each step.

A second approach to understanding the computer's functioning is to figure out what the program is like. In this approach, we are studying the computer's software, or program, the sequence of steps the computer executes, regardless of which combination of circuits carries out the work. For example, if the computer identifies a picture of a chair, we would examine whether its program required it to first determine component properties such as color and shape before identifying the whole object.

Just as we can analyze a computer either in terms of its hardware or software, we can analyze the brain, and the visual system in particular, in terms of either its neurophysiology (hardware) or its information processing mechanisms (software). Although we will briefly review the hardware of the visual system, most of our discussion focuses on the steps the visual system must surely execute in performing various visual tasks.

The Role of the System Itself

As we begin to consider the visual system as an information processor, we need to identify the points at which the system itself assumes an active role in relation to input. Simply, the information processing system must do something to the input it receives in order for an appropriate response to be generated. What types of things might the visual system do to information?

One effect the system has on information is to *transform* it from one form to another. For example, suppose that I see my friend Marilyn at work one day and see that she is wearing a green dress. I receive that information because energy, in the form of light, causes a certain pattern of stimulation on the retinas of my eyes. If someone later asks me what Marilyn had on, I can say, "Marilyn wore a green dress." My information processing system transformed the initial light information into neural impulses that allowed me to detect and remember some facts about the person I saw and what she looked like. Later, I transformed that information into a spoken description.

Another active role the information processing system has is to *reduce* information. Obviously, we do not remember every detail of all the sensory experiences we have everyday. Reduction is probably a necessary function for the system, since we would be subject to an information overload if we tried to make sense of everything we encounter. In some situations, however, the system must perform the opposite operation and must *elaborate* on information. Elaboration occurs when we fill out details on the basis of information stored in memory. Consider these words:

THE CAT

You probably read the phrase as "THE CAT" even though that reading required you to interpret the identical ambiguous character in the center of each word differently in the two cases. You used your knowledge of spelling combinations in English to elaborate the input and make sense of it.

Two final types of operations concern the use of memory. We are able to *store* information in and *retrieve* information from memory. These processes allow us to preserve information, remember experiences and things, and to use what we know when we need to.

Suppose you are shown the picture and sentence in Figure 1.1a, and you are asked to respond appropriately. What steps are necessary for you to respond correctly? Because the visual processing system can do so many tasks with even the simplest of stimuli, it is convenient to diagram the various information processing steps. Figure 1.1b is a flowchart of the steps involved.

Each stage or operation the system is presumed to perform is denoted by a rectangular box in the flowchart, and the direction of information flow is denoted by arrows from one box to another. Diamond-shaped boxes indicate points of choice or decision.

You probably identified the object first because it is on top, and it is possible that you did so by first spotting the component parts and then deciding that they make up a "chair." The processing of the sentence is somewhat more complicated. Of course, you must first identify individual line segments, then you must realize which letter is represented by the line segments you have identified. Simply recognizing the letters does not help you comprehend the sentence; you must combine the letters in order to determine the words and you must combine the meanings of the words, using the rules of English grammar stored in your memory. At this point you know what the sentence means, and you can compare the sentence to the object you recognized from the picture, decide whether they match, and make the proper response. Perhaps you processed the picture and the sentence at the same time, making the comparison decision at the completion of whichever operation took longer. This simultaneous processing is depicted in Figure 1.1c.

Our diagrams of the processes in Figures 1.1b and 1.1c are very general; each process is very complex and could be divided into sequences of more specific and simpler steps. Our flowchart, however, does illustrate several important assumptions of the information processing approach. First, notice that the sequential ordering of stages implies that the output from one stage serves as the input for the next stage. That is, at each stage the information is processed in such a way as to make it usable in the next stage.

If this is a picture of a chair, clap your hands.

a

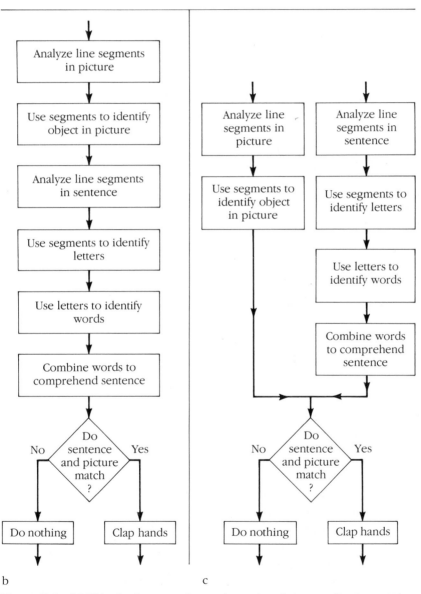

b   c

Figure 1.1   (a) This simple comparison task requires the respondent to complete a complex series of information processing operations to identify and analyze both the picture and the sentence. (b) The processing operations may occur in a serial sequence or (c) some may be performed simultaneously in a parallel fashion.

The information processing approach also makes some assumptions about the speed and accuracy with which certain tasks can be done. One assumption is that for a sequentially ordered task, the amount of time necessary to complete a task is the sum of the times needed to carry out each stage because each stage of processing is dependent on the output of the preceding stage. (In Chapter 9 we will, in fact, examine this proposition by analyzing two experimental tasks that differ only by one step, allowing us to measure the duration of a single processing stage.) Regarding accuracy, the information processing approach posits that the accuracy with which a particular task is accomplished depends on the accuracy of each of the component steps. Certainly we could not expect the correct answer to the task in Figure 1.1a of a subject who did not accurately identify the picture.

Let us make two important caveats about the information processing approach as we have presented it so far. First, although we denote each processing stage by a discrete rectangle in the flowchart, we are not implying that such operations take place in physically different locations in the brain nor that there are neurons specialized for each type of operation. In fact, we have relatively little knowledge of what cerebral mechanisms allow such operations to take place, and we do not know where they occur. The knowledge we do have, however, suggests that complex cognitive operations involve many areas of the brain working all the time, not isolated sections working at different times.

Our second caveat concerns the direction of information flow in the information processing system. The flowcharts in Figure 1.1 imply that information is received at one end of the system, travels in one direction, and provokes a response at the other end. Research, however, suggests that different stages affect one another. For example, the way in which a subject interprets the sentence in Figure 1.1a may influence how he or she goes about identifying the picture. If the sentence concerns a chair, the subject may disregard the color of the object in the picture as long as it has legs, a seat, and a back. In later chapters we examine this type of mutual influence, and we will place arrows between nonadjacent stages in our flowcharts to indicate the influence various stages have on one another.

MEMORY COMPONENTS IN THE INFORMATION PROCESSING SYSTEM

As we have seen, the human visual information processing system uses a number of different sensory and cognitive mechanisms. We divide these mechanisms into two qualitatively different types. In the previous section we primarily discussed one type: the operations, or *control processes*, used by the system. These include all the activities the system performs to process information; for example, identifying components and retrieving information from memory. To carry out such operations, the system must have a second type of component: *memory*. Memory can be thought of as the space set aside to store everything we need to remember and use during information processing.

Psychologists who study human information processing distinguish three kinds of memory storage: sensory information store, short-term memory, and long-term memory. The *sensory information store* in the visual system is a very short-lived type of memory that allows the system to maintain information about a visual stimulus for a few fractions of a second after it has disappeared. This kind of memory causes us to have the sensation that a briefly presented visual stimulus persists somewhat longer than it is actually present. Information held in the sensory information store has undergone little or no information processing, and it has not been interpreted. Since the sensory information store is capable of retaining information for less than a second, it is not a reliable or permanent memory storage system. (We discuss this store in detail in Chapter 5.)

Short-term memory refers to the type of memory that allows a person to retain information for several seconds or longer, as long as active attention is paid to keeping that information refreshed. A good example of short-term auditory memory is when someone tells you a telephone number for the first time. Unless you rehearse the number until you have committed the information to a more permanent form (either in your long-term memory or on paper), you are likely to forget the number. Although methods of visual rehearsal have not yet been specified by researchers, in Chapter 7 we present evidence for short-term, nonpermanent storage of visual information.

Finally, the information processing system has a *long-term memory store*. It is here that we keep relatively permanent records of scenes, objects, and events without the need for constant, active rehearsal of that information. Long-term memory is also responsible for maintaining abstract knowledge about the meanings of the things we see, our real-world knowledge about the way things are supposed to look and behave, and the rules and operations we use to process information.

These three types of storage systems are not physically localized or isolated in the brain. Rather, the distinctions between the three systems concern the different ways that information is stored at different times during processing. The type of storage depends on which processing operations have taken place. Specifically, the three types of memory differ in their information *representation*, that is, the way in which the information is recorded. For example, a photograph and a verbal description of an apple are two different representations of information about the apple. Similarly, the representation in the sensory information store is surely a visual representation, whereas information in the short-term memory has been transformed well enough to allow identification of various objects and their salient features such as color. In order to hold information in long-term memory, we need to generate a representation that retains abstract information on meaning. Thus, as we discuss various types of memory storage, we will examine the formation of various types of representations.

THE PLAN OF THIS BOOK

There are two important aspects to the study of the visual information processing system: the component physical structures (e.g., the retina, the visual cortex) and the operations they carry out (e.g., pattern recognition, storage in memory). In explaining the system's physical structure and processing operations, we will examine the laboratory evidence from which psychologists derive their knowledge. Thus, you will learn not only what psychologists know about human visual information processing but also how they came to know it. In Chapters 2 and 3 we discuss the sensory processing mechanisms that allow us to recognize simple forms and to interpret patterns. In Chapter 4 we describe some of the mechanisms that permit us to recognize individual patterns or parts of patterns as whole objects, whereas Chapter 5 concerns how we recognize and analyze several individual patterns at once.

The second half of the book is devoted to those aspects of visual processing that require the use of short- and long-term memory. In Chapter 6 we examine how visual processing interacts with verbal skills during the recognition of words during reading. Then, in Chapters 7 and 8, we turn our attention to issues concerning visual memory representation and processing. Finally, in Chapter 9, we consider how language and visual information interact in abstract long-term memory.

Sensory Processes
of the Visual System

Light that radiates from some source, such as the sun or a lamp, is reflected by objects in the world. The reflected light is focused in the eye onto a matrix of photoreceptors. The photoreceptors convert the light energy into electrical signals that carry all the sensory information about our external visual world, such as color, brightness, position in space, movement, and depth, and form the basis of all our visual perceptions. The way in which the visual system processes this sensory information has been studied by many kinds of scientists. Anatomists examine the neural paths through which sensory information flows in the visual system; physiologists concentrate on how single nerve cells process sensory information; and psychologists study how the sensory information is processed for the purposes of perception, recognition, and memory. Each approach contributes to our knowledge about sensory processing mechanisms, and in this chapter, we briefly discuss the major findings of each.

First, we consider the anatomy of the visual system, from the eye to the cerebral cortex. Then we discuss how individual cells located in different places in the visual system respond to light stimulation. We conclude by reviewing selected psychophysical research and considering some of the implications of this work for pattern perception. Our discussion is not a comprehensive one; it is intended as an introduction to anatomical, physiological, and psychophysical research in the area of vision. For each topic, we direct the reader to many excellent papers and books that provide a more thorough discussion of the issues.

STRUCTURE OF THE VISUAL SYSTEM

The hardware of the visual system can be grossly subdivided into the eye, neural pathways, neural structures, and individual nerve cells. The major function performed by the eye is sensory *transduction,* the converting of light energy into nerve impulses. The neural pathways, which are collections of nerve fibers of cells, then channel that information to different neural structures in the brain. Neural structures, sometimes called nuclei, are the processing centers of the visual system; under the microscope, these structures appear as collections of cell bodies. Such structures include the lateral geniculate nucleus, superior colliculus, and areas of the visual cortex. Individual nerve cells process specific bits of information. Their structure varies in a number of ways. Cells vary in the size and shape of their soma (cell body), in the number, orientation, and branching of their dendrites (the receivers of information), and in the size, length, and branching of their axons (the senders of information). Because these structures are so important to visual processing, let us examine some of them in more detail.

The Eye

In many ways the eye is like a camera. Both contain specialized parts to focus images of objects and to control the amount of entering light. A schematic of the eye is shown in Figure 2.1. The parts of the eye we normally

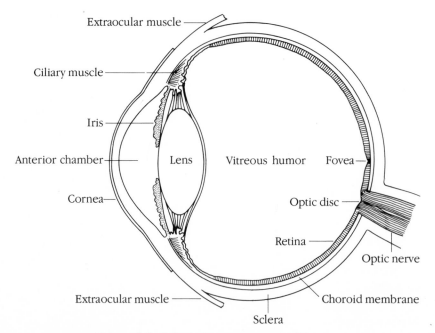

Figure 2.1 Schematic representation of the eye.

see are the *sclera* (the white of the eye), the *iris* (the colored part of the eye), and the *pupil,* the dark center of the iris that is the opening formed by the iris. The external parts of the eye that we normally do not see include the six muscles attached to the exterior of the globe of the eye that move the eye up or down, left or right, and rotate the eye to a very small degree in its socket. Another external part of the eye that we are normally unaware of is the *cornea,* a transparent covering on the front of the eye. The cornea serves to refract, or bend, light rays in order to focus them onto the back of the eye.

The interior of the eye contains many parts. The cavity behind the cornea is the *anterior chamber,* which contains the aqueous humor, a clear fluid absorbed by the cornea for nutrition. Any floating impurities in this chamber will cast shadows on the photoreceptors in the retina, causing the sensation of seeing spots before the eyes. Behind the aqueous humor and in front of the lens lies the *iris,* a circular muscle that controls the amount of light entering the eye by its contraction and relaxation. The interior of the eye is filled with vitreous fluid, a clear, jellylike substance that supports the eye and gives it its globelike or rounded shape. Attached to the back of the eye is the *retina,* which we describe later.

Most of the focusing of light onto the retina is done by the cornea. However, small adjustments in focusing needed to bring stimuli at different distances into focus are made by the *lens.* The lens is transparent and, like the cornea, contains no blood vessels; neither the lens nor cornea can contain blood vessels since both must transmit and focus light on the retina without blocking the image. However, unlike the cornea, the lens can change its shape in order to control the amount of refraction. This reflexive process of the lens changing its shape to keep fixated stimuli in focus is called *accommodation.* Accommodation is achieved by the lens either relaxing or contracting the ciliary muscles. The lens is suspended by a membrane called the *zonula* (not shown in Figure 2.1) that holds the lens under some tension. When the ciliary muscles contract, the tension on the lens is released, and the lens becomes more rounded. When the ciliary muscles relax, the lens becomes thinner.

The shape of the lens governs the refraction, or bending, of incoming light rays. In order for stimuli at different distances to be in focus, light rays must be refracted at different angles. The light rays reflected by stimuli close to the eye must enter the eye at a larger angle than those of the stimuli that are farther away. To image the light rays at the plane of the retina, which results in a focused image, the lens must bend light rays reflected by close stimuli more than the rays reflected by distant stimuli. The lens controls the amount of refraction by altering its shape. To focus on near stimuli, the lens becomes more rounded and bends the light rays more; to focus on distant stimuli, the lens becomes thinner and bends the light rays less.

Thus not all stimuli in our visual field of view are in focus simultaneously. As an example, place a pencil about an arm's length away and stare at it. You can read the writing on the pencil, but objects farther away than the pencil are blurred. When fixating on the pencil, the lens is very rounded and bends the light rays enough to focus the nearby pencil but too much to properly image distant objects. As a consequence, the image of the pencil is at the plane of the retina, but the images of the distant stimuli fall short of the retinal plane. Now stare at an object farther away than the pencil. The pencil is now blurred, but the distant object is focused. In this case, the amount of refraction for the distant object is correct, but the lens is too thin to refract the light rays reflected by the pencil in order to form an image at the plane of the retina. Instead, the image of the pencil is formed somewhere beyond the retinal plane.

Often the lens has a natural shape that is inappropriate for the length of the eye, and consequently either near or far stimuli cannot be adequately focused (see Figure 2.2). If the axial length of the eye is too long for the lens, the light rays reflected by distant objects are always refracted such that the image of the stimulus is formed before the retinal plane. However, close objects are properly imaged. This condition is called nearsightedness or *myopia*. In the opposite case, the axial length of the eye is too short for the lens, and the light rays reflected by near stimuli are always imaged beyond the retinal plane; however, distant stimuli are properly imaged. This condition is called farsightedness or *hypermetropia*.

Nearsightedness and farsightedness can be remedied with the aid of an appropriate lens in a pair of glasses or contact lenses. For nearsightedness, the overbending of reflected light rays can be compensated by a concave corrective lens. For farsightedness, the underbending of the light rays can be compensated for by a convex corrective lens. *Presbyopia,* a third optical abnormality of the eye, is the condition in which the lens loses its flexibility and is unable to alter its shape in order to accommodate. Consequently, it is difficult for an individual to focus stimuli that are very near and, in some

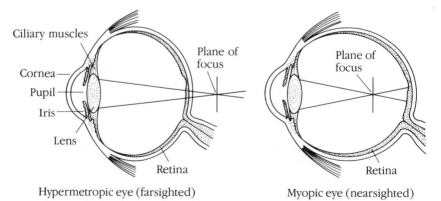

Figure 2.2 Schematic illustrations of the conditions of hypermetropia and myopia. In hypermetropia the length of the eye is too short for the lens; in myopia, the length of the eye is too long for the lens. The solid lines indicate where the image is focused by the lens.

cases, to focus stimuli that are very distant. Presbyopia is common in older people.

The Retina

In the retina are receptors that perform the crucial conversion of light to electrochemical energy, a translation necessary in order for the brain to interact with the external world. If one looks inside an eye with an ophthalmoscope, the light device an ophthalmologist uses to inspect the inside of the eye, three features of the retina are distinctive. First, one sees the many blood vessels that provide the nutrients for the cells in the retina. Second, one sees the *fovea,* a shallow depression in the retina containing many photoreceptors. The *fovea* is the most sensitive area of the retina for resolving fine detail. The third feature is the *optic disc,* the point of the retina at which all the nerve fibers exit the eye. The optic disc is an area on the retina that does not contain photoreceptors, which means that we cannot see with this part of our retina. However, this hole, or blind spot, in the visual field is not obvious in everday visual experience. In fact, a special effort must be made to become aware of the blind spot. To locate your blind spot, look at Figure 2.3. Fixate the cross with your left eye, closing your right eye. Hold the book about 12 inches away. If you move the book slowly back and forth, you should be able to find a distance at which the black disk disappears. At this distance the image of the black disk falls on the optic disc or blind spot.

Even an ophthalmoscope will not enable you to see the small cells that compose the retina. The retina contains many different cell types among which are two types of photoreceptors, *rods* and *cones.* Rods and cones can be distinguished by their shapes and by the types of photopigments they contain. The photopigment absorbs light energy and converts that energy into electrochemical nerve impulses. The pigment in rods is much more efficient at converting light to electrochemical energy, and as a consequence, rods are most useful for night vision or at low-luminance levels. The rods are concentrated outside the fovea. Cones are concentrated in and near the fovea. Although the pigment in cones is not as efficient at converting light to electrical energy, the pigment contained in cones does vary in its ability to absorb light containing different wavelengths or colors. Some cones contain pigment that is much better at absorbing light containing wavelengths that

Figure 2.3 Demonstration of the retina's optic disc, or blind spot. Close your right eye. Fixate the cross while holding the book about 12 inches away. Slightly move the book back and forth, until the black disk disappears. The disk disappears at that distance because its image falls on your retina's optic disc.

look red to us. Other cones contain pigment that is much better at absorbing wavelengths that appear green to us, and still other cones contain pigment that is much better at absorbing wavelengths that appear blue. The three types of cone pigment and their differing ability to absorb wavelengths of light form the basis for our perception of color. Color blindness occurs when some, or all, of these cone pigments are missing in the retina.

The output of the photoreceptors enters a complex matrix of retinal cells, where a considerable amount of processing of the photoreceptor signals takes place before the output reaches the last type of cell in the chain, the *ganglion cells*. The nerve fibers of the ganglion cells depart the eye through the optic nerve at the optic disc. The three types of ganglion cells, referred to as X-, Y-, and W-cells, differ in a number of ways. Y-cells have large cell bodies and thick axons. They conduct electrical nerve impulses very quickly. X-cells have smaller cell bodies and axons, and they conduct impulses more slowly than Y-cells. W-cells have very small cell bodies, and their axons conduct very slowly. Y-cells are concentrated in the periphery of the retina, X-cells are concentrated in and around the fovea, and W-cells are located mainly outside the fovea.

The photoreceptors in the retina are pointed away from incoming light such that they point to the back of the eye and face the *choroid membrane*. Therefore, in order for light to strike the photoreceptors it must penetrate the neural tissue in front of the photoreceptors, including the ganglion cells. The human choroid membrane is dark and thus absorbs the extra light that is not absorbed by the rods and cones. In some animals, especially those adapted for nocturnal life, the back of the eye is covered by a shiny surface known as a *tapetum*. The tapetum acts as a mirror and reflects the light back up to the receptors, which gives the receptors another chance to absorb the light. Cats have a tapetum, and this is why you can often see the reflected light of a cat's eye at night. Because the retina is inverted, light is somewhat scattered by the neural tissue before it is absorbed by the receptors. Such light scatter causes a decrease in the sharpness of vision everywhere in the retina except the fovea. At the fovea, the neural tissue is swept aside, causing a depression on the retina. Thus, the foveal photoreceptors are more directly exposed to incoming light rays, and we have our keenest vision at this point on the retina.

After the Retina

The axons of the ganglion cells depart the eye through the optic nerve, leaving through the blind spot described earlier. The axons that originate from cells located in the nasal halves of the two retinas (that is, the half of the retina closer to the nose) cross at the *optic chiasm* and travel to the opposite side of the brain (see Figure 2.4a). Thus axons of the ganglion cells in the nasal retina of the left eye terminate in the right hemisphere of the brain, and the axons of ganglion cells in the nasal retina of the right eye terminate in the left hemisphere. The axons of ganglion cells in the temporal halves of the retinae (that is, the half closer to the temple) do not cross at the optic chiasm but instead stay on the same side of the brain. The result of this partial crossing of ganglion cell axons in the optic chiasm is that the right half of our visual world is represented in the left hemisphere, and the left half in the right hemisphere. For example, if you go to a baseball park and stand on homeplate facing centerfield, then left and left centerfield will be represented in your right hemisphere and right and right centerfield will be represented in your left hemisphere.

Thus all the axons of cells that are responsible for the same parts of our visual field are routed to the same hemisphere. Returning to the baseball example, if you stand on homeplate facing centerfield, the image of the first baseman falls on the temporal retina of your left eye and on the nasal retina of your right eye. The axons of the ganglion cells activated by the image of the infielder are both routed to the left hemisphere, and the information provided by the ganglion cells of the two eyes are then systematically combined in the visual cortex.

After these fibers leave the optic chiasm, the information that they carry eventually reaches the visual cortex, which is located toward the back of the head. Visual information travels to the cortex by one of two routes: the geniculo-striate pathway or the tectocortical pathway (Figure 2.4b). In the geniculo-striate pathway, ganglion cell fibers connect onto a collection of cells referred to as the *lateral geniculate nucleus.* The fibers of the lateral geniculate nucleus in turn project onto cells in the visual cortex. In the tectocortical pathway, ganglion cell fibers terminate on a nucleus referred to as the *superior colliculus;* the cells of the superior colliculus in turn project to the pulvinar nucleus; and these cells then project to the visual cortex. Both pathways carry considerable information from the eyes to the brain, and if one is destroyed some vision remains. When both are destroyed, however, blindness results (Diamond, 1976). It does seem, though, that the geniculo-striate system plays an important role in processing information carried by small spatial details, important in coding information about shapes, and probably plays a very important role in depth perception (Berkley and Sprague, 1979).

THE RESPONSE OF SINGLE CELLS
TO LIGHT STIMULATION

How do nerve cells in the brain process light information? One method of determining how the brain processes visual information is to record the electrical activity of single nerve cells, called *action potentials,* and note their response to light stimulation. When this kind of experiment is performed in animals, it becomes clear that cells have a baseline level of activity, referred to as spontaneous activity, and visual information is encoded by the cells by

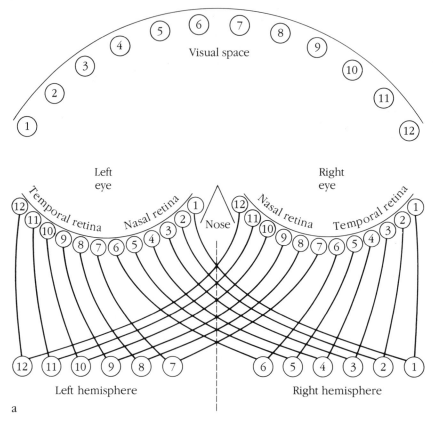

Figure 2.4 (a) Schematic illustration of the crossing of ganglion cell fibers. The visual field is shown divided into 12 regions: the low numbers represent the extreme left visual field; the middle numbers represent the central visual field; and high numbers represent the extreme right visual field. The right visual hemifield (7–12) falls on the nasal retina of the right eye and temporal retina of the left eye. The left visual hemifield (1–6) falls on the nasal retina of the left eye and the temporal retina of the right eye. Note that the fibers departing the temporal retinas of both eyes remain on the same side of the brain whereas the fibers departing the nasal retinas of both eyes cross and terminate in the opposite side of the brain. Thus the fibers representing any one part of visual space terminate in the same side of the brain. (b) Schematic illustration of the geniculo-striate and tectocortical pathways, which carry visual information from the retinas to the visual cortex. The geniculo-striate pathway includes the retina and the lateral geniculate nucleus. The tectocortical pathway includes the retina, superior colliculus, and the pulvinar nucleus.

either increasing or decreasing the frequency of this activity. For example, a ganglion cell may elicit a great number of action potentials only when a large spot of light is shown on the fovea of the retina of the right eye, whereas another ganglion cell will elicit a great number of action potentials only when the light is shown in the periphery of the retina of the right eye. In general, each ganglion cell is responsive to light when a certain region of

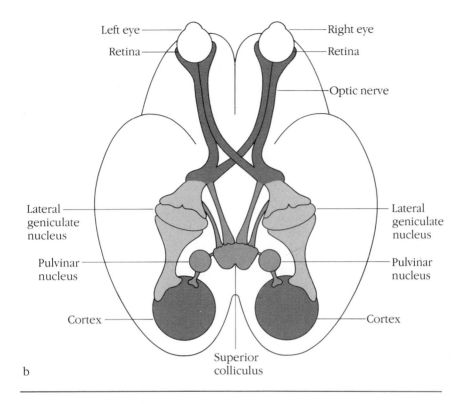

Left eye

Retina

Right eye

Retina

Optic nerve

Lateral
geniculate
nucleus

Lateral
geniculate
nucleus

Pulvinar
nucleus

Pulvinar
nucleus

Cortex

Cortex

Superior
colliculus

b

the retina is stimulated, and different ganglion cells respond when various regions of the retina are stimulated by light. A cell's response region is called its *receptive field.*

By using very small spots of light, one can discover more specifically how cells respond to light (Kuffler, 1953). For instance, recordings from ganglion cells show that some cells increase their activity when a small spot of light is turned on, but only when the light falls within a small circular region on the retina. When the light stimulus is presented immediately outside this circular retinal region the cell will increase its activity only when the light is turned off. When the light is moved outside of this surrounding region, the cell will respond neither to the light being turned on nor to the light being turned off. This type of cell is referred to as an on-center, off-surround cell. Ganglion cells that respond in the opposite way are called off-center, on-surround cells. A light placed in the center region of the receptive field of such a cell will activate the cell only when the light is turned off, whereas when the light is moved into the surrounding region the cell will respond when the light is turned on. Receptive field maps of both types of cells are shown in Figure 2.5a.

Cells respond or encode light information in many different ways. Some cells respond better or become more active to lights placed in their receptive fields that consist of a certain wavelength (that is, light of a certain color). Others respond best when the spots are small, and others respond best when the spots are large. Some cells emit sustained activity throughout the entire time the light is present within their receptive field, while others emit only a transient burst of activity when the light is first turned on or off.

Most ganglion cells in the retina and cells in the lateral geniculate nucleus respond in the ways just described, and have circular receptive fields. However, the cells in the visual cortex of the brain respond much differently.

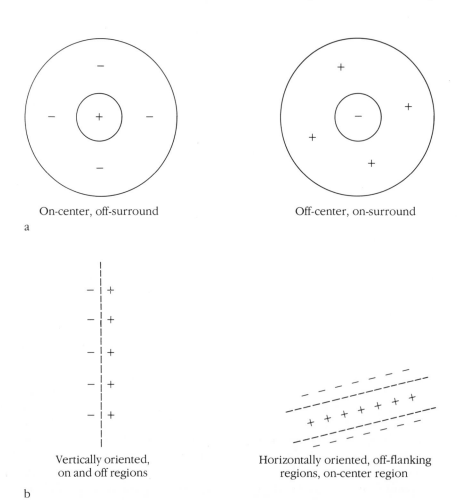

Figure 2.5 (a) Receptive fields of ganglion or lateral geniculate cells. (b) Examples of cortical receptive fields. The receptive fields of ganglion and lateral geniculate cells are circular with center and surround regions. The receptive fields of cortical cells are elongated in shape. The plus signs indicate areas in which the cell responds when light is turned on in this region of the receptive field. The minus signs indicate areas in which the cell responds when light is turned off in this region.

Rather than preferring spots of light, they respond best to slits of light or lines that are properly oriented; such cells have elongated, not circular, receptive fields. Moreover, some cortical cells respond best to lines moving in a certain direction, while other cortical cells respond best to lines of a certain length (Hubel and Wiesel, 1962). Representative maps of cortical receptive fields are shown in Figure 2.5b.

Another major difference between cortical cells and those of the retina and lateral geniculate nucleus is that most cortical cells respond to stimulation from either eye. If a line of a certain orientation, moving rightward across the fovea of the right eye, excites a cortical cell, then most likely a line of the same orientation moving in the same direction across the fovea of the left eye will also activate the same cell. Some cortical cells are equally excited by the visual stimulation of either eye; other cortical cells are more excited by the stimulation of one eye than that of the other. All these cells are *binocular* cells, since they respond to at least some degree to stimulation of either eye. Ganglion cells and lateral geniculate cells are *monocular* in that they are activated by stimulation of only one eye and not the other. Thus the input from the two eyes is not combined until the information received by each eye reaches the visual cortex.

Cortical cells preferentially respond to other aspects of the visual stimulus as well. Some cortical cells respond to the information contained in the stimulus that is important for depth perception (Pettigrew, Nikara, and Bishop, 1968), some cortical cells respond best when the stimulus is a certain color (Hubel and Wiesel, 1968), and some cells respond best when the stimulus has certain spatial properties which are important for form vision (De Valois and De Valois, 1980). Electrophysiologists are only beginning to understand the way in which cortical cells respond and presumably encode visual information. At present, researchers cannot explain how the receptive field properties of cells relate to the way in which we see.

PATTERN RECOGNITION

Although the recording from single cells in animals may tell us a lot about how individual nerve cells encode visual information, at present this work does not tell us anything about how a visual percept is formed. It is simply impossible to predict from work on single cells in animals how a physical pattern on the retina will appear to a human observer. Today our best approach to studying perception in human beings is to use behavioral, psychophysical approaches.

Sensitivity

At first glance, pattern perception may seem a trivial problem. For example, if one presents to an observer two sets of bars, one set oriented obliquely

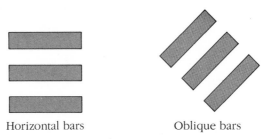

Horizontal bars   Oblique bars

Figure 2.6   Horizontal and oblique sets of bars.

and another set oriented horizontally (see Figure 2.6), not surprisingly the observer will indicate that he or she saw a horizontal and an oblique set of bars. This simple experiment indicates only that bars with such spatial arrangements of luminances imaged on the retina produce reports of horizontal and oblique. The experiment does not reveal how these stimuli are processed by the visual system in order to produce the different perceptions. If we ask the observer to describe whether the different orientations were treated the same or differently by the visual system, the introspective response would probably be uninformative.

However, if we measure the sensitivity of an observer to stimuli of different orientations, our psychophysical experiment would reveal properties about visual processing of which we are otherwise unaware. For example, if the contrast of the oblique and horizontal sets of bars is decreased (the difference in the luminance between the light and dark bars is reduced), observers are able to identify the horizontal bars at much lower contrasts than the oblique sets of bars, a perceptual outcome dubbed the *oblique effect.* Such a sensitivity experiment yields a difference between the two orientations that suggests that our visual system processes oblique and horizontal bars differently.

We can learn a lot about visual processing by measuring sensitivity to different stimuli. By taxing the sensitivity of a visual system, experimenters can uncover differences that simple introspection does not reveal. For this reason, measurement of sensitivity, or visual threshold, is often used to explore the operation of the human visual system. In threshold experiments, some dimension of the stimulus is varied, such as stimulus illuminance (a measure of the amount of light reflected by a stimulus), stimulus contrast, stimulus size, and so on. Then some response of the observer is measured. The observer may be asked to simply indicate whether or not the stimulus is visible. Or the stimulus may be presented in one of several time intervals or presented in one of several locations, and the observer must indicate on each presentation when or where the stimulus occurred. To the extent that sufficient information is available, the observer will guess above a chance level. A third method gives the observer control of some aspect of the stimulus, and he or she adjusts the stimulus until threshold is reached.

Threshold measurement, however, is subject to two kinds of error. First, the method employed to measure threshold influences the estimates of threshold. For example, when the observer adjusts the stimulus, the estimate of the threshold is usually much higher than when the observer is forced to guess in which interval of several the stimulus occurred. Second, an observer's threshold for a stimulus is not fixed but is somewhat variable. That is, there is no one value of the dimension of the stimulus above which one always sees the stimulus and below which one never sees the stimulus. We each have a range of stimulus values for which we sometimes report seeing the stimulus and other times report not seeing the stimulus. Therefore, as observers we each must adopt a criterion to help us decide when the stimulus is present and when it is not. When an experimenter obtains different thresholds from two observers, the difference may reflect a difference in the sensitivities of the observers, or a difference in their selection of the criterion for threshold. In Appendix A, we describe the psychophysical techniques that can separate the absolute threshold from the observer's criterion.

Reaction Time

Other ways to measure the sensitivity of the visual system do not require the researcher to change a dimension of the stimulus. One method is to measure a subject's *reaction time*—how quickly a stimulus is seen, or how long it takes to completely process and recognize the stimulus. To measure reaction time, the experimenter can present a stimulus that is well above threshold and have the observer report its presence. The experimenter then measures the time elapsed between the onset of the presentation of the stimulus and the response of the observer. Recall the earlier experiment with the horizontal and oblique bars that suggested that the visual system is more sensitive to horizontal bars. Reaction time experiments show that reaction time to horizontal bars is faster than reaction time to oblique bars, even when luminance, contrast, and size are held constant (Olson and Attneave, 1970).

Thus the results of both reaction time experiments and threshold experiments suggest that horizontal bars and oblique bars are processed by different neural mechanisms having different sensitivities. However, had we not observed a sensitivity difference, we could not draw any conclusion. For example, identical sensitivity to horizontal and vertical lines could be produced either by a single neural mechanism for both horizontal and vertical orientations or by two separate mechanisms that have the same sensitivity. In fact, we would tend to favor the latter hypothesis because physiological data show that different cortical cells are maximally sensitive to different orientations. Fortunately, other psychophysical methods can be used to explore more fully the question of whether different neural mechanisms process different attributes of the stimulus. These methods, for instance, confirm that horizontal and vertical orientations are processed by different neural mechanisms even though the sensitivities are the same. Three of the most commonly used methods are visual masking, selective adaptation, and subthreshold summation; let us examine each in turn.

Visual Masking

Visual masking refers to the destructive interaction that can occur between two stimuli that are presented in proximity in space and time (Werner, 1935). Consider the following experiment: An observer is shown two stimuli: a mask and a target. The mask is formed by two bars, separated by some distance, that flank the target stimulus (see Figure 2.7). The mask is presented for a relatively long duration, usually well above the threshold of the observer. The second stimulus, the target, is a single contour that is presented either alone or between the two flanking contours of the mask. The exposure duration of the target alone is first adjusted to just above threshold. When the target is presented alone, the observer can detect the stimulus about 70 to 80 percent of the time. When the mask and target are presented together, detectability of the target is greatly reduced, maybe even down to chance levels. Visual masking refers to this interfering effect that the mask has on the target. The more interference, as measured by a detection decrement, produced by the presentation of the mask, the greater the amount of visual masking.

The amount of visual masking is dependent on a number of variables, such as mask contrast, spatial proximity, configurational similarity, and temporal separation of the target and mask. For example, when the contrast of the mask is reduced, the amount of visual masking decreases. When the target is presented above the mask, the amount of masking decreases greatly. If the target is changed from a line contour to a circle, then the amount of masking also decreases. If the mask is presented $\frac{1}{100}$ of a second either before the target or after the target, it interferes with detection of the target. But if the mask is presented 1 second before or after the target, it does not interfere with the target detectability.

Mask   Target   Mask and Target

Figure 2.7 Examples of mask and target stimuli used in a masking experiment. When the target and mask are presented simultaneously, it is difficult to identify the target if it is presented very briefly.

When the mask is presented before the target, the interference it produces is called *forward masking* since the mask's effect impairs detection of the target that follows. An example of forward masking is the temporary blindness that occurs after the presentation of a bright light such as a camera flash or lightning. When the mask is presented after the target, the resultant interference is called *backward masking* since the mask impairs detection of the preceding target. Although we may not be aware of backward masking, a camera or lightning flash will blank our field of view even before we perceive the bright flash of light.

Researchers interpret the temporal properties of visual masking as evidence of the limitations on the rate at which information can be processed by different mechanisms. If a lot of information is presented in a very short period of time, the visual system simply loses some of that information. Simultaneous presentation of the target and mask activates the observer's visual mechanism and overloads it with information. As a consequence some information is lost, as reflected in the reduced detectability of the target.

Let us return to the question of whether horizontal and vertical orientations are processed by different neural mechanisms and consider a visual masking experiment that addresses this question. This experiment uses two masks: a set of horizontal contours and a set of vertical contours. The target is always a set of vertical contours. If masking occurs when the target has the same orientation as the mask (vertical) and is absent when the target and mask orientations are orthogonal, then we would assume that different mechanisms process horizontal and vertical orientations. If the amount of masking is the same, irrespective of the similar orientations of the target and mask, then we would assume that the same mechanisms process both horizontal and vertical orientations. Experiments show that the amount of masking is much greater when the target and mask have the same orientation than when the target and mask have different orientations (Houlihan and Sekuler, 1968; Gilinsky, 1967). The implication of this finding is that the mask greatly interferes with the detectability of the target when the two stimuli are processed by the same mechanisms, such as mechanisms for vertical orientation. When the target and mask stimulate different mechanisms, one processing vertical information and another horizontal, there is no overload and no masking.

Selective Adaptation

Selective adaptation is another psychophysical technique that permits inferences about whether the same or different mechanisms process some stimulus attribute. Like visual masking, selective adaptation causes a reduction in sensitivity if the same neural mechanisms are activated; but unlike visual masking, which is transient, selective adaptation operates over longer time periods. Selective adaptation experiments require the observer to stare at or fixate a stimulus that is well above threshold for a given length of time, for example, 1 to 10 minutes. After this inspection, the observer's threshold for a second stimulus that is similar or dissimilar to the first is measured. The long inspection period is intended to fatigue the neural mechanisms active during processing the first stimulus. If the second stimulus activates the fatigued mechanisms, then the threshold will be higher than that for mechanisms not fatigued by previous adaptation. Thus, if the threshold is not higher after inspection, we can assume that different mechanisms are activated by the first and second stimuli; the mechanisms that process the second stimulus were not active during the inspection period.

The results of selective adaptation experiments also suggest that horizontal and vertical contours are processed by different neural mechanisms (Blakemore and Campbell, 1969). After inspection of a set of high contrast, vertical contours, an observer's threshold for vertical contours is much higher than his threshold for horizontal contours. During inspection of the vertical contours, the mechanisms that are maximally activated by vertical orientations become fatigued and less sensitive; thus the threshold for vertical contours is elevated. But the mechanisms that are maximally activated by horizontal contours are not fatigued during the inspection period, and thus their sensitivity is unchanged, and the threshold for horizontal contours does not increase after the inspection of vertical contours.

Subthreshold Summation

A third technique often used by psychophysicists to isolate mechanisms of visual processing is subthreshold summation. This technique uses as a dependent measure the increase in sensitivity (that is, a reduction of threshold), unlike the techniques of visual masking and selective adaptation, which measure sensitivity loss. The observer is presented with a background stimulus that is below threshold along with a second target stimulus. The threshold of the target stimulus is then measured. Although the background stimulus is below threshold and cannot alone generate a sufficient amount of activity in any given mechanism, it could enhance the detection of the target stimulus if both the background and target stimulus activate the same mechanism. In other words, the information from the target and background stimulus is summed by the mechanism, and the threshold for the target stimulus is lower than when the target is presented alone. If the background stimulus is processed by a different mechanism than the target stimulus, then the threshold for the target stimulus is not affected by the presence of the background stimulus.

Consider again our example of the vertical and horizontal contours. Let the background stimulus be either a set of horizontal or vertical contours, and let the target stimulus be a set of vertical contours. When the orientations of the two stimuli are the same, the background stimulus enhances the detectability of the target; when the stimuli have different orientations, target detectability is not facilitated (Kulikowski, Abadi, and King-Smith, 1973).

Again, these results imply that separate mechanisms process horizontal and vertical orientations.

Locus of Processing

Electrophysiologists study how visual information is processed at different sites in the visual system by placing an electrode in the desired site and recording responses of cells to light stimulation. For instance, recordings from cells in the lateral geniculate nucleus show that these cells are generally monocularly activated and are insensitive to changes in the orientation of a stimulus. Most cells in the cortex, however, respond to the stimulation of either eye, and all cortical cells are sensitive to changes in the orientation of a stimulus. By using an electrode to measure receptive field properties, one can study how visual processing differs at various places in the visual system.

Behavioral work does not afford the experimental advantages of electro-physiology. In psychophysical work with human subjects, we cannot isolate the activity of a selective site in the visual system and we cannot remove the influences of other visual structures on the one we want to study. All we can do in psychophysical experiments is to grossly subdivide the visual system by inference. By making assumptions about both the anatomy of the visual system and the basic receptive field properties of cells at different stages in the visual system, we can make some reasonable guesses about the site at which certain visual effects occur. Unfortunately, these inferential psychoan-atomical techniques are rather imprecise. They allow only such divisions of the visual system as that between peripheral and central stages of processing. *Peripheral* stages include all subcortical sites, such as the retina and the lateral geniculate nucleus, and *central* stages include all cortical areas.

A number of techniques enable us to identify whether a given visual effect is the result of central or peripheral mechanisms. One common method is to test whether the visual effect under study is significantly influenced by changes in orientation. As we noted earlier, cortical mechanisms are sensitive to changes in orientation whereas peripheral mechanisms, such as the lateral geniculate nucleus and ganglion cells, are not. For example, consider the following selective adaptation experiment. After inspecting a high-contrast grating pattern (a set of equally spaced light and dark bars) of a certain bar width, an observer's threshold for a grating pattern of the same bar width is elevated. Where in the visual system does this adaptation effect take place? Is the elevation due to the fatiguing of ganglion cells or lateral geniculate cells, or does it involve the fatiguing of cortical mechanisms?

One way to partially answer these questions is to measure the influence of orientation on the magnitude of adaptation. If there is no threshold elevation for a test grating that is orthogonal to the inspection grating, one could conclude that grating adaptation effects most likely originate at the more central, cortical level. At the cortical level, only those cells responsive to the orientation of the inspection grating are fatigued during the inspection period, and thus the threshold for the orthogonal grating is not elevated. If there is an elevation of threshold for the test grating independent of its orientation, then one could conclude that the adaptation effect originates at more peripheral stages. Since cells at more peripheral stages of the visual system are not sensitive to orientation, any adaptation effects at this level of the visual system would not be influenced by changes in the orientation of the grating. Research shows that grating adaptation is strongly dependent on the similarity between the orientations of the adapting and test gratings, and thus this effect is presumed to originate at central stages in the visual system (Blakemore and Campbell, 1969).

Other psychophysical tests can test the centrality of a visual effect. For example, we know that the input from the two eyes is not combined until the input reaches the visual cortex, the central stage of the visual system. Thus, if a visual effect occurs when the stimulus that induces the effect is presented separately to each eye, we can assume that some aspect of the effect involves central mechanisms. We can test whether the grating adaptation effect described earlier occurs when the inspection grating is viewed by the right eye and the test grating is viewed by the left eye to determine if the effect exhibits interocular transfer. If the inspection grating fatigues only those cells that receive input from one eye, such as lateral geniculate or ganglion cells, then the cells activated during the test period differ from those fatigued during the inspection period, and there is no interocular transfer. However, if inspection of the grating fatigues a mechanism that receives input from both eyes, such as cortical cells, then the adaptation effect should transfer since the same cells are fatigued and activated during inspection and test periods. The grating adaptation effect does exhibit interocular transfer and is thus presumed to involve the fatiguing of central mechanisms (Blakemore and Campbell, 1969).

We can apply similar logic to infer whether visual masking and subthreshold summation effects involve central binocular mechanisms. For instance, a patterned mask presented to the right eye does interfere with the detectability of a target stimulus presented to the left eye; therefore, this type of visual masking is thought to involve central mechanisms (Turvey, 1973). Similarly, the threshold for a grating pattern presented to the right eye is lowered when a subthreshold grating pattern of the same orientation and bar width is presented to the left eye (Blake and Levinson, 1977). Thus detection of grating patterns must involve central binocular mechanisms.

Another psychoanatomical technique that capitalizes on the binocular properties of the visual system employs random dot stereograms (see Figure 2.8). A separate pattern of random dots, neither of which contains an apparent pattern, is presented to each eye. In order to see the stimulus pattern the two eyes must interact, and the visual system then must extract some correlation between the two eyes' views. Since the stimulus present in these displays can be seen only when two eyes are used and cannot be seen with the use of only one eye, it is called a *cyclopean stimulus* (Julesz, 1971).

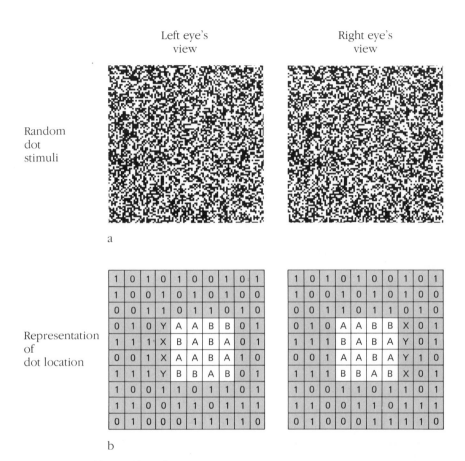

Figure 2.8 (a) A random dot stereogram is made from a matrix of many small dots for each eye. The placement of the dots in each eye's matrix is identical except for a subset of dots which is shifted laterally in one eye's view. When either dot matrix is viewed alone, all that is seen is a flat textured surface. When the matrices are viewed binocularly, one presented to each eye, the shifted dots in one eye's view generates a *binocular disparity* between the eyes, which produces a sensation of depth called *stereopsis* and, as a consequence, this shifted subregion stands out in depth. Binocular disparity refers to the stimulation of noncorresponding regions of the retinas of the two eyes. When you fixate a stimulus, this stimulus is imaged on the fovea of each eye. A second stimulus that is at a different distance from the observer than the one fixated necessarily falls on different, noncorresponding regions of the retinas of the two eyes. The stimulation of noncorresponding retinal regions is called binocular disparity. The capacity to utilize binocular disparity as a cue for depth and distance is called stereopsis. (b) If the dot stimuli were fused in a stereoscope, the square region denoted by A's and B's would stand out in depth. All the elements—1's for filled elements, 0's for unfilled elements—are the same in the two eyes' views except for a vertical rectangular region in the left eye vacated due to the shift of the square. This region, denoted by X's and Y's, generates a binocular disparity that makes the square stand out in depth. [From B. Julesz, *Foundations of cyclopean perception.* Reprinted by permission of The University of Chicago Press. © 1971 by The University of Chicago.]

Responses to a cyclopean stimulus originate in that part of the visual system where the two eyes interact to produce stereoscopic depth, and they cannot occur until the central stages of processing. Since the stimulus is not internally formed until this stage, in a sense the cyclopean stimulus skips or bypasses the peripheral stages. If a visual effect is induced by random dot stereograms, then the effect can be induced by activating only central mechanisms. For example, visual masking occurs for cyclopean stimuli formed from random dot stereograms, which implies that visual masking effects can occur without stimulation of peripheral mechanisms, that is with stimulation of only central mechanisms (Vernoy, 1976). If an effect cannot be induced by random dot stereograms, then either the site of the mechanism responsible for the effect resides in the peripheral stages or the effect requires the cooperation of central and peripheral systems.

SENSORY CONSIDERATIONS FOR PATTERN RECOGNITION

In the previous section, we discussed different psychophysical procedures for measuring visual thresholds. Those procedures give us some idea about how sensitive a human observer is to different types of visual stimuli. Such measurements of sensitivity also provide some insight into how and where visual information is processed. Obviously, our sensitivity to various aspects of a visual stimulus plays an important role in perception—if we are insensitive to a certain aspect of the stimulus then this aspect would not significantly affect our perceptions. For example, if our visual system were insensitive to different wavelengths of light, our perceptual world would not be richly colored. But our visual system can discriminate different wavelengths, and this wavelength information contributes to our visual world. A knowledge of normal sensory limits is important to our understanding of the kinds of information available for perception. Our knowledge of normal sensory limits helps us restrict the range of stimuli we need to study.

Spatial Limits

One sensory limit that obviously restricts the spatial information our visual system processes in recognizing patterns is *visual acuity,* the ability of an observer to resolve small stimuli. Optometrists measure acuity by asking us to read the smallest line of letters on an eye chart. Clinically, normal visual acuity is defined as the ability to resolve a stimulus of 1 minute of visual angle; the visual angle is the angle subtended at the retina by the stimulus. Figure 2.9 shows how this measure is calculated. Notice that light reflected by the edges of a large stimulus forms a large angle at the retina, whereas the edges of a small stimulus form a small visual angle. Of course, visual angle is influenced by viewing distance in that a near stimulus forms a larger

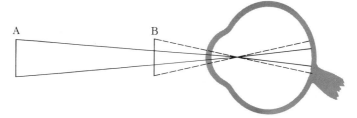

Figure 2.9 Visual angle. Stimulus A and stimulus B, although they have the same physical size, have different visual angles. The visual angle of A is smaller than the visual angle of B since A is farther away. A rough approximation of visual angle can be calculated from the formula:

$$\text{V.A. (degrees)} = \frac{57.3 \times \text{Size of object}}{\text{Distance between object and observer}}$$

angle at the retina then does the same stimulus viewed farther away. Thus stimulus size and viewing distance determine visual angle. A 1-inch diameter circle viewed at a distance of about 287 feet subtends a visual angle of 1 minute of arc; the same circle viewed from a distance of 1 foot subtends a visual angle of about 4.75 degrees of arc.

Visual acuity measures only the ability to resolve small stimuli—the ability to see fine spatial details. Of course, other spatial aspects of a stimulus are important for perception; for example, such aspects of the stimulus as overall size, orientation, and contrast. A measure of spatial sensitivity that characterizes our ability to see small details as well as larger aspects of the stimulus is the spatial *contrast sensitivity function* (CSF). The spatial CSF measures contrast sensitivity to grating patterns of varying bar widths. In order to explain spatial CSFs, we must define three terms: sinewave gratings, contrast, and spatial frequency. In a *sinewave grating,* the luminance across the pattern varies in a sinusoidal fashion; in other words, the bars of the gratings do not have sharp edges, but rather the transition from a bright to a dark bar is gradual, as shown in Figure 2.10. The term *contrast* refers to the difference between the light and dark points of the grating. The larger the difference between the light and dark bars, the greater is the contrast. Finally, *spatial frequency* refers to the width of the bars of the grating. It is measured by the number of cycles, or number of light and dark bars, per degree of visual angle. A grating with narrow bars has a high spatial frequency; a grating with broad bars has a low spatial frequency.

A spatial CSF is a measure of the sensitivity of contrast for different spatial frequencies. Sensitivity at each spatial frequency is defined as the reciprocal of the contrast threshold at that frequency. The CSF is therefore a measure of the resolving power of the visual system not only for small spatial details but also for broader, larger spatial aspects of the visual stimulus. A demon-

a

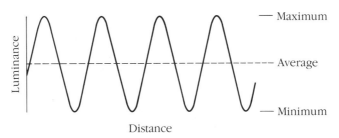

b

Figure 2.10 (a) An example of a sinewave grating. There is a gradual change in the brightness of the neighboring light and dark bars. (b) The luminance profile of a sinewave grating. The bright bars of the grating are represented by the peaks in the graph, and the dark bars by the troughs. Note that the changes from maximum to minimum luminances are gradual.

stration of the spatial CSF is depicted in Figure 2.11a. In this figure, spatial frequency increases from right to left, and contrast decreases from top to bottom. You can estimate your contrast threshold by viewing the figure at arm's length and following a particular bar starting at the bottom and moving upward until you reach a point on the bar at which you can no longer distinguish the bar from a homogeneous field. This point on the bar is an estimate of your contrast threshold. The farther you can see up the bar, the lower your threshold and the higher your sensitivity.

If an observer were equally sensitive to all spatial frequencies then his or her contrast threshold would be the same at all spatial frequencies; that is, the point at which the bars fade out in Figure 2.11a would be the same for all the bars. However, human beings are most sensitive to the intermediate spatial frequencies. We can follow the medium bar widths higher up on the figure than the broader or narrower bars. When we look at the narrower bars (increased spatial frequency) or the broader bars (decreased spatial frequency), we stop at a lower point on the bar. If we mark the points at which the bars fade into the background at the different spatial frequencies and connected these points, we would produce a graph of our spatial CSF like that shown in Figure 2.11b. The advantage of measuring spatial sensitivity using a spatial CSF rather than a measure of visual acuity such as an eye

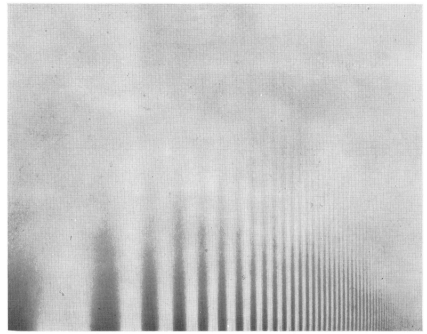

a

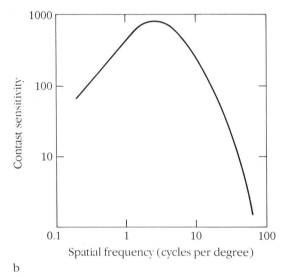

b

Figure 2.11 (a) Demonstration of the spatial contrast sensitivity function. Spatial frequency increases from left to right, and contrast increases from top to bottom. For a particular spatial frequency, one can estimate one's contrast threshold by following a given bar from the bottom up. The point at which the bar fades into the background is an estimate of the contrast threshold. The higher up the bar you see, the lower the threshold or the higher the sensitivity to this spatial frequency. (b) An example of a contrast sensitivity function. Contrast sensitivity (the reciprocal of the contrast threshold) is plotted on the ordinate, and spatial frequency (cycles per degree of visual angle) is plotted on the abscissa. The function shows that we are more sensitive to intermediate spatial frequencies (around 5 cycles per degree) and less sensitive to low spatial frequencies (around 1 cycle per degree) and to high spatial frequencies (around 10 cycles per degree). [(a), courtesy of Jay M. Enoch.]

chart is that the spatial CSF characterizes sensitivity for stimuli of all sizes, whereas visual acuity only measures the ability to resolve small stimuli.

This advantage of the spatial CSF is reported to have clinical relevance (Hess and Howell, 1977; Hess and Woo, 1978; Bodis-Wollner, 1972). For instance, patients with cataracts, a condition in which the lens of the eye is clouded, have low visual acuities. However, some of these patients complain of poor vision through the eye with the cataract, whereas other patients with the same visual acuity report fair vision with the cataract eye. Visual acuity tests fail to distinguish these two groups of patients. When one measures the spatial CSFs of these patients, those who complain of poor vision demonstrate reduced sensitivity at low spatial frequencies, but those who do not complain of severely impaired vision demonstrate normal sensitivity at low spatial frequencies. Thus, the spatial CSF distinguishes these two types of patients and can be used as a diagnostic test. Spatial CSF measures have also been performed for patients with visual impairments attributed to neural problems, such as amblyopia—a loss of vision not attributed to optical abnormalities—and multiple sclerosis. Clinical observations suggest that both low and high spatial frequencies are important for pattern perception.

Any visual stimulus can be analyzed in terms of the spatial frequencies contained in the stimulus. The high spatial frequencies in the stimulus are the sharp edges and the small, fine details. The low spatial frequencies in the stimulus are the more global, coarse spatial features of the stimulus. The different kinds of spatial information carried by low and high spatial frequencies can be demonstrated by viewing a visual stimulus that has been either defocused or diffused. Defocusing is accomplished by simply blurring a stimulus. If you wear glasses, removing those glasses will defocus an image. By defocusing or blurring a stimulus, we reduce the contrast of the high spatial frequencies of the stimulus but do not affect the contrast of the low spatial frequencies of the stimulus. When we look at a blurred stimulus, we do not see sharp edges or fine details. If the stimulus is a picture of a tree, we would not see the very fine branches, the edges of the leaves, or the individual blades of grass beneath the tree. However, we would recognize that the blurred stimulus is a tree; we would be able to distinguish the trunk, the larger limbs, and clumps of leaves. Clearly, the low spatial frequencies of a stimulus carry a lot of important information for pattern recognition.

By diffusing a visual stimulus, one reduces the contrast of both the low and high spatial frequencies. Pattern recognition of a diffused stimulus is often very difficult. Diffusion is best demonstrated by looking through wax paper, looking through a fogged windshield, or looking at your reflection in a mirror that is steamed. In all cases low and high spatial frequencies are filtered and pattern recognition is difficult. Recall, for example, how poor visibility is when you are driving in a fog.

The differences between the effects of diffusion and defocus on pattern perception seem to illustrate the importance of both low and high spatial frequency information to pattern perception. Indeed, a patient with cataracts who has contrast sensitivity losses at all spatial frequencies has a diffused retinal image. The patient views the world as if through a piece of wax paper, and pattern perception is surely impaired. A patient with cataracts who has contrast sensitivity losses only at high spatial frequencies has a defocused retinal image. Although this patient cannot resolve the fine spatial detail of a stimulus, the patient can clearly see the larger, more global aspects of the stimulus, and pattern perception is much less impaired.

The role of low spatial frequencies in pattern perception is clearly demonstrated by quantized pictures (Harmon, 1973). A quantized picture is formed by measuring the luminances of small blocks of a picture and calculating the average luminance for each area (see Figure 2.12). A quantized picture is formed by displaying in the correct spatial arrangement only the average luminances of each block. The quantization procedure thus removes all spatial detail, or high spatial frequency information, yet preserves the more global low spatial frequency information. One artifact of this procedure is to introduce new edges or high spatial frequency information into the quantized picture that are not present in the original picture. The blocked appearance of the quantized picture somewhat impairs recognition. However, if one defocuses the quantized picture by squinting, one softens the artificial edges without affecting the original low spatial frequency information. Look at Figure 2.12 and squint to blur the image and recognize the face.

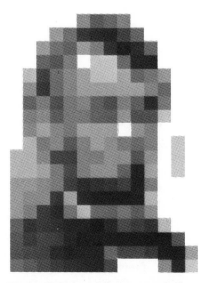

Figure 2.12 Quantization picture of a famous person. [Courtesy of Leon D. Harmon.]

Movement

Up to now, our discussion about the limits of spatial vision has not distinguished between stationary and moving stimuli. In the real world, however, stimuli often move. How does movement influence the limits of spatial vision and influence pattern recognition? Obviously, the speed of the stimulus movement affects recognition. If a stimulus moves exceptionally fast, an observer can discriminate the passage of the stimulus but cannot identify very many spatial characteristics of the stimulus. If the stimulus moves slower, an observer can discriminate many spatial characteristics of the stimulus, although not the small spatial details of the stimulus.

To demonstrate how visual acuity is reduced when the stimulus moves, fixate on your finger and then place next to your finger a pencil with the manufacturer's name toward you. Note your ability to read the writing on the pencil. Now, continue to fixate on your finger and move the pencil up and down. Note again your ability to read the writing on the pencil. It is much more difficult to read the writing when the pencil is moving. However, you can still recognize the moving object as a pencil, identify its orientation, and determine if the pencil is sharpened. Although you cannot resolve any of the small details of a moving stimulus, you can recognize many of its other spatial properties.

From your observation of a moving pencil, you probably can guess how movement affects the spatial contrast sensitivity function. Movement of the gratings reduces sensitivity at high spatial frequencies (the small spatial details) but does not reduce sensitivity at low spatial frequencies (Kulikowski and Tolhurst, 1973).

Depth and Distance

Another important aspect of pattern recognition is distance or depth. Our perceptions of patterns are three-dimensional, but only two of these dimensions, the horizontal and vertical axes, have a geometrical basis in the flat image of the world formed on the retina. The depth dimension is not geometrically represented on the retina. Nonetheless, the flat retinal image provides some cues concerning depth. One cue is derived from the slightly different views our two eyes have of the world, our stereoscopic depth perception. Other depth cues are present in the monocular view. These include the cue of interposition (a near object partially covers a far object), the cue of shadows or shading (the direction of shadows registers the relative positions in depth), the cue of aerial perspective (far objects contain less detail), the cue of linear perspective (physically parallel edges converge with increasing distances), the cue of texture gradients (surface density increases at further distances), the cue of familiar and relative size (objects at far distances appear smaller), and in the case of moving stimuli or moving observers, the cue of motion parallax (the relative directions and velocities of movement register the relative depths of objects in space).

Many kinds of stimuli have the capacity to evoke the impression of depth and distance, and such impressions seem to influence pattern perception in a number of ways. First, they govern the perceived size of a pattern. The size of a person is perceived to be constant regardless of how far away this person is from the observer. This constancy of perceived size across different viewing distances occurs even though the size of the retinal image of the person is different at each viewing distance. The visual system seems to scale the size of the retinal image according to the perceived distance of the stimulus from the observer. The perceived size of a stimulus remains constant although the retinal image size changes with viewing distance, because either the perceived size of a close stimulus is scaled down or the perceived size of a far stimulus is scaled up, or both.

The size scaling performed by the visual system can be tricked by a variety of size-distance illusions. One famous size-distance illusion is the moon illusion: The perceived size of the moon seems much larger at the horizon than it does at the zenith although, of course, the actual size of the moon and its retinal image do not change. The change in perceived size seems to result from the observer's differing perceptions of the moon's distance at the horizon and at the zenith. The horizon appears farther away than does the sky directly above. Since the retinal image size of the moon is the same at the horizon and the zenith and since perceived distance to the horizon is farther than the perceived distance to the zenith, size scaling causes the moon at the horizon to appear larger than the moon at the zenith.

Depth perception seems to influence pattern perception in other ways as well. In a series of experiments on simultaneous contrast, Gilchrist (1977) reports that perceived depth can influence the perceived brightness of a pattern. *Simultaneous contrast* refers to a change in the perceived brightness of a stimulus of moderate intensity (gray) when it is surrounded by or next to a second stimulus of either much greater intensity (very bright) or much less intensity (very dark). A gray stimulus is perceived as dark when its neighbor is bright and as light when its neighbor is dark. Gilchrist shows that the perceived brightness of a gray stimulus depends on the perceived depth, not the actual distance, of the gray stimulus. When the gray stimulus appears farther away and adjacent to a dark stimulus, it is perceived as light; but when the gray stimulus appears closer and adjacent to a light stimulus, it is perceived as dark. Thus the perceived depth of stimulus plays an important role in our perception of the brightness of a pattern.

Visual masking is also influenced by depth perception. Lehmkuhle and Fox (1980) found that when the mask appears to be behind the target, the amount of masking decreases; if the mask appears to be far behind the target, the mask does not interfere with the detection of the target. When the mask appears to be in front of the target, the amount of masking is as large as when the target and mask appear next to each other in the same depth plane. Since visual masking effects are believed to be a product of the mechanisms that recognize patterns, the finding that depth influences the amount of masking implies that depth plays an important role in pattern recognition. Indeed, the perception of pattern in random dot stereograms (see Figure 2.8) suggests that the perception of depth can even create the perception of pattern (Julesz, 1971).

In summary, depth and distance seem to influence the perceived size, perceived brightness, and even the recognition of patterns. Perceived depth may influence pattern perception in still other ways; perceptual psychologists are only beginning to understand how depth and pattern interact.

SUMMARY

In this chapter we reviewed, in a very general way, three approaches to research on the visual processing of sensory information and briefly summarized the major findings.

Anatomical studies show that visual information travels along one of two major routes from the eye to the cortex, on the geniculo-cortical and the tectocortical pathways. Anatomical studies have also identified major structural divisions of the visual system; examples are the lateral geniculate nucleus, the superior colliculus, and areas of visual cortex.

Electrophysiological investigations of the visual system that measure the response properties of individual cells show that ganglion cells and lateral geniculate cells have receptive fields that are circular in shape and are monocularly activated. Cortical cells, in contrast, have receptive fields that are elongated in shape and are mainly binocularly activated. Because of the elongation of their receptive fields, cortical cells are sensitive to the orientation of the stimulus. They are also sensitive to the direction of movement, length, width, and wavelength composition of the stimulus.

We also briefly reviewed some results of psychophysical investigations and examined some of the interpretations drawn from the results of these experiments. We noted that sensitivity experiments, such as the measurement of threshold or reaction time, provide some insight into the nature of visual processing. Visual masking, selective adaptation, and subthreshold summation were presented as psychophysical techniques to isolate and study the dynamics of visual mechanisms. We also noted that the visual system can be grossly subdivided into central and peripheral stages through the use of orientation manipulations, binocular stimulation procedures, and random dot stereograms. Our discussion of sensory considerations relevant to human pattern recognition highlighted the importance of spatial frequency, movement, and depth.

Each of these approaches emphasizes a different aspect of the visual system. Anatomy emphasizes structure, electrophysiology emphasizes response dynamics, and psychophysics emphasizes function. Each approach contributes to our overall knowledge of the visual system. Any substantive explanation of how the visual system converts light energy into visual perceptions must incorporate the findings of all three fields of study.

SUGGESTED READING

As we mentioned at the beginning of this chapter, our discussion serves as an introduction to and not a comprehensive examination of the visual system. Many important points about the anatomy, physiology, and psychophysics of the visual system have not been covered in this chapter. For a comprehensive examination of many of these topics, see Kaufman (1974), Gregory (1966), Polyak (1957), or any of the *Scientific American* offprints on the visual system, among the most recent of which are Campbell and Maffei (1974), Johansson (1975), Julesz (1975), and Pettigrew (1972).

Chapter 3

Pattern Recognition in Humans

In the preceding chapter, we discussed three approaches to studying the visual system. Anatomical experiments indicate the routes used for the processing of visual information; physiological experiments indicate how nerve cells encode visual information; and human psychophysical experiments provide us with some ideas about how the visual world is analyzed and processed. Although each approach tells us something about where and how information is processed in the visual system, visual scientists still have only a vague idea about how the stimulus on the retina is finally represented in the brain and how this internal representation leads to the perception or recognition of the stimulus by the observer. In this chapter, we present some of the models of pattern perception that attempt to describe how our visual world is internally represented and how this representation gives rise to perception. This chapter, as compared to others, contains more theory and fewer experimental results because at present only a few hypotheses about pattern perception are sufficiently well formed to be subject to experimental tests.

The explanatory models of pattern recognition fall into three categories: template models, prototype models, and feature models. These models can be compared in terms of their ability to explain our perceptions of a stimulus subjected to variations and distortions. A model of pattern recognition must explain why we can recognize and identify a stimulus presented in a number of situations and distortions. According to *template models,* the visual system forms a picture of the presented visual scene, and recognition of that scene is the result of finding a match between the present visualization and a picture stored in memory that has been labeled from experience. As we will see, this kind of model cannot adequately explain why certain distortions of the visual stimulus do not impede pattern recognition. *Prototype models,* designed to surpass the limitations of the template models, are more flexible and can deal with variability within single classes of patterns. Some experimental evidence supports prototype models.

The third category of pattern perception models is *feature models.* An attractive aspect of feature models is that this class of models, at least at a first glance, corresponds more closely with the physiology and the psychophysics of vision. Feature models posit that the visual system analyzes various features of the stimulus, such as orientation, spatial frequency, color, and so on. Pattern recognition is the result of a match between the features of the present stimulus and a stored set of features. Although feature models are flexible enough to explain stimulus variability, they—like template and prototype models—cannot explain how the context in which the stimulus is present directs and facilitates the processing of this stimulus.

In the final part of this chapter, we discuss some computer simulation research. Experimenters have tried, so far with limited success, to devise a computer program that would enable a computer to recognize simple patterns of light. The designers of such "reading machines" have run into the same kinds of problems as have theorists of pattern recognition in humans; computer simulation studies illustrate in a concrete fashion the problems of pattern recognition. The computer simulation of pattern recognition also reveals some of the limitations of the assumptions of the template, prototype, and feature models.

TEMPLATE MODELS

The complexity of the problem of pattern recognition can be demonstrated by considering template models. A template model assumes that the brain forms a "picture" of the stimulus imaged on the retina of the eye much in the same way a piece of exposed film has a representation of the light imaged on it through the lens of a camera. The brain's representation does not, of course, resemble a photograph, but it does bear some relationship to the visual stimulus; for example, the spatial arrangement of the components of the visual stimulus is assumed to be preserved. How do we recognize our brain's representation of a stimulus? Template models assume that a vast assortment of pictures or visual representations, usually referred to as templates, are stored in memory. These stored templates have been labeled, acquiring their names from the observer's experience with the internal representation of the visual stimulus. For example, three contours each connected at their endpoints produce an internal representation that, with repeated exposure, is stored in memory and labeled as a triangle. Pattern recognition is the result of a search to match a present internal representation and a template in the memory.

A template model is a simple but necessarily incomplete theory of pattern recognition. The main inadequacy of template models is that they explain our ability to recognize different patterns only by positing that an almost infinite number of templates are stored in memory. Our everyday experience tells us that we can recognize and identify stimuli under a large variety of stimulus situations and distortions. For instance, when we read, we can change our viewing distance or our orientation to the page without impairing pattern recognition or reading. A change in viewing distance changes the size of the letters on the retina, and head movements change the orientation of the letters on the retina—yet such dramatic changes in the stimulus do not impair recognition. Similarly, we recognize the pattern of letters in various type styles and handwriting styles, and even in texts turned upside down. For a template model to account for our ability to recognize patterns under a large number of distortions, it has to postulate an almost infinite number of templates stored in memory, each corresponding to every possible size, orientation, and style of letter or pattern. Although the brain contains many nerve cells, the neural structure is finite and probably does not have the capacity to store all the templates that would be needed to accomplish everyday pattern recognition.

An advocate of a template model might argue that the match between the internal representation and the stored template need not be perfect, or that the brain executes a normalization process that rearranges the internal representation into a standard position, size, and so on, before the search for a match begins. Although both arguments reduce the requirements on memory storage capacity, other problems arise, such as mismatches. Consider the example of recognizing the letters A and R. We can distort the letter A (see Figure 3.1) so that it closely resembles the template for the letter R. However, almost everyone identifies the distorted A as an A and not an R. This example illustrates the inadequacy of template models for pattern recognition.

Internal representation of distorted A

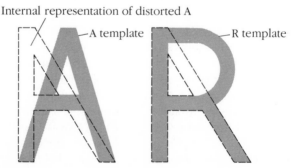

Figure 3.1 Distorted character matched to templates of A and R.

The hypothesis that a neural normalization process reconceives the internal representation to match a standard template also seems inadequate. Such a normalizing mechanism would have to have some information about the stimulus in order to reconceive the internal representation. Consider again the distorted A in Figure 3.1. In order to normalize that character to match a standard template of A rather than one for R, the brain would have to have information that the character was an A and not an R. Thus we again confront our original problem of identifying the letter. Although some kind of normalization process may exist, one that interprets the context in which the stimulus appears to "clean up" a distorted stimulus, normalization would not dramatically remedy the inadequacy of template models.

For these and other reasons, researchers have never seriously considered a strict template model as a paradigm for pattern recognition. Template models are inadequate and inaccurate in explaining actual human performance; they are simply too inflexible to explain our recognition of varied stimuli. We now turn to prototype models, a class of models designed to explain human pattern recognition without recourse to assumptions of almost infinite memory requirements.

PROTOTYPE MODELS

Strict template models treat each stimulus as an isolated case regardless of any similarities or features that this stimulus may share with other stimuli. For instance, although C and Ɔ share a number of features, according to a template model, knowledge of the attributes of C do not have any influence on recognition of Ɔ. Strict template models posit two templates, one for C and one for Ɔ, and recognition of each stimulus is independent. This separate and independent treatment of every stimulus requires the enormous memory capacity of template models.

Prototype models do not treat each stimulus independently but assert that the similarities among related stimuli are essential to pattern recognition. Prototype models emphasize that any stimulus is a member of a class of stimuli, and that each stimulus reflects the shared attributes of a class as well as the variance between itself and the average, or *prototype,* of a class. According to a prototype model, C and Ɔ belong to the same class of stimuli (a rounded figure with a gap on one end) much in the same way that all the characters in Figure 3.2 belong to a class.

What defines a class of stimuli? According to prototype models, schema delineate different stimulus classes. *Schemata* are rules that describe the essential characteristics of a prototype of a class. A schema for the prototype class of C may be simply an incomplete circle with a break on the right side. Stimuli that belong to the class vary in the extent to which they adhere to or follow these schema rules. A Ɔ contains an incomplete circle and a gap, but the gap is on the left. A handwritten letter may not be circular, but contains some curvature with a break in the line on the right side of the character.

Figure 3.2   Various representations of C—yet, in all cases, we recognize the symbols as C.

Pattern recognition, according to prototype models, is a process not only of extraction of information but also of abstraction of information. Pattern recognition depends on the abstracting or cataloguing of the essential attributes of the stimulus and the search for the schema rule that characterizes these attributes with the lowest variability. Once the best schema is found, pattern recognition is categorized both by the name of the prototype of the class and the nature and amount of deviation of the stimulus from the prototype of the class. The stimulus Ɔ is recognized as a mirror-reversal distortion of C.

Prototype models thus are more efficient and require less memory storage than template models. Consider again the distorted character in Figure 3.1. According to a prototype model, the distorted character is recognized as an A and not an R since the schemata of a prototype A (two lines that intersect at their endpoints and a third line that connects the other two) fit the distorted character better than the schemata for the prototype R (a semicircle connected to the top of a line and a second line protruding downward from the semicircle). The size of the memory load assumed by prototype models is far less than that assumed by template models because a few prototypes with simple schemata are stored rather than many templates. But do prototype models have any experimental validity? Does pattern recognition proceed in a way similar to that described by prototype models?

Some experimental evidence suggests that prototypes do exist. An experiment conducted by Attneave (1957) shows that experience with a prototypical stimulus can enhance identification of a related group of stimuli. A number of different prototype shapes (irregularly shaped contours) were constructed by connecting random points, and variations of these prototypical shapes were made in one of two ways (see Figure 3.3). First, eight variations of the prototype were made by repositioning *certain* points such that the prototype was the average or central tendency of the class of variations. Second, eight variations were made by repositioning *different* random points; however, the prototype still represented the average of the class of variations. Two groups of subjects were used: One group was given pretraining with the prototype stimuli; the second was given pretraining with an irrelevant set of shapes. The pretraining for both groups consisted of repeated presentations of the shapes interspersed with attempts by the subject to reproduce a shape. After pretraining both groups were given a paired associate learning task in which one of the eight variations of the prototype was shown and, at the same time, a letter of the alphabet was given aloud. This procedure was repeated for each of the eight stimulus variations. After the learning trials, the observers were shown one of the eight variations of the prototype and were asked to write down the letter associated with the stimulus variation.

Attneave reports that the group given pretraining with the prototypes made fewer errors in the paired associate recall task than did the group given pretraining with the irrelevant shapes. Attneave suggests that both groups of subjects probably learned three characteristics of the class of the stimuli used in the paired associate task: (1) the average of the eight; (2) how the eight

Figure 3.3 Example of stimuli used in Attneave's experiment. The top two rows show the 10 shapes used as prototypes. The bottom two rows show a set of eight variations of one of the prototypical shapes. [From Attneave, 1957. Copyright 1957 by the American Psychological Association. Reprinted by permission of the publisher and author.]

differed; and (3) how much they differed from one another. The pretraining with the prototypes enhanced the first group's learning of these characteristics, and thus that group made fewer errors in the paired associate recall task.

Attneave also reports that subjects made fewer errors when they performed the paired associate learning task with the set of stimuli in which the same points were the ones varied. In other words, pretraining with the prototype was more beneficial when the same parts of the figure were varied. This finding suggests that observers use their knowledge of the prototype to aid them in locating the distinguishing attributes of the members within a class. Note also that a template model would not predict this result. According to a template model, the amount of distortion from the template formed during pretraining would be the same whether the same or random points were varied and, therefore, there would be no difference in performance between these two conditions.

Posner and Keele's (1968) experiment with random dot patterns also suggests that observers construct prototypes for classes of related stimuli. In this experiment, the prototype stimuli were random dot patterns, and each prototype was varied to yield a set of patterns such that the dispersion of dots in the prototype was the arithmetic average of the set. An example of a set of such stimuli is shown in Figure 3.4. Subjects were shown four variations of each of three prototypes—but not the actual prototypes—and were asked to classify those patterns into three categories. Since they were not shown the prototypes, subjects initially made many errors. But they were given feedback about the correctness of each of their responses and thus with repeated trials learned to correctly classify the twelve patterns. They were then presented with a new set of stimuli and asked to classify each stimulus into one of the three prototype categories. Some of the new stimuli were identical to those seen before (old distortions), other stimuli were new variations of the prototype (new distortions), and others were the actual prototypes.

Posner and Keele found that subjects classified the prototypes and the old distortions equally well and with fairly high accuracy, but they classified the new distortions with lower accuracy. These results suggest that in learning a class of stimuli, one learns the prototype or average of the class as well. The subjects learned not only the variations of the prototype that were presented but also the prototype of the class, which was not shown during training.

One of the most elaborate demonstrations that stimuli are abstracted and prototypes are constructed is offered by Franks and Bransford (1971). They constructed prototypical patterns by combining several geometrical forms and then systematically altered these prototypes by deleting a form, substituting a new form, changing the size of the component forms, and so on. An example of a prototype and transformations used in their experiment is shown in Figure 3.5. Observers were first presented a series of stimuli that

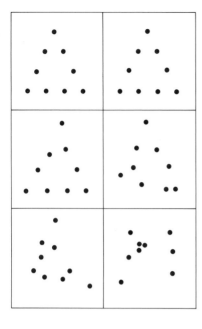

Figure 3.4 Example of stimuli used by Posner and Keele. The prototype is in the upper left-hand box. The other patterns are sample distortions of the prototype. [From Posner, Goldsmith, and Welton, 1967. Copyright 1967 by the American Psychological Association. Reprinted by permission of the publisher and the author.]

were transformations of various prototypes, but the observers were not shown the prototypes. Observers were then presented another series of stimuli and were asked to rate how confident they were that they had seen these stimuli during the initial presentation. Some of the stimuli in the second series were transformations shown during the initial presentation; some stimuli were distortions not shown earlier; and some were the prototypes that also had not been shown.

Franks and Bransford report two major findings. First, the observers were most confident they had seen the prototypes even though the prototypes were not shown during the initial presentation. Second, the greater the number of transformations from the prototype, the lower the confidence ratings of the observers. In other words, a stimulus they had seen before was rated no more familiar than a stimulus they had not seen before if the two stimuli contained the same number of transformations from the prototype. These findings suggest, as do the findings of Attneave, and Posner and Keele, that an observer forms a prototype when presented a class of related stimuli. Even when the observers are not shown and have no experience with the prototype, these experiments seem to indicate that a prototype is formed. Moreover, the experiment of Franks and Bransford suggests that when presented new stimuli, observers use knowledge of the prototype (i.e., schema rules) to classify and identify new stimuli. This proposition follows from the result that the amount of transformation of a prototype influenced recognition regardless of whether the stimulus had been seen before.

Base

Transformations

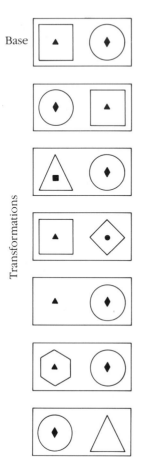

Figure 3.5 Example of base stimulus (prototype) and transformations used by Franks and Bransford. [From Franks and Bransford, 1971. Copyright 1971 by the American Psychological Association. Reprinted by permission of the publisher and the author.]

Thus experimental research provides some evidence that observers form and use prototypes to recognize artificial stimuli in the laboratory. If indeed human beings form and use prototypes for pattern recognition outside the laboratory, one might ask about the nature of such natural prototypes. Are they an average of a class or a central tendency? Rosch et al. (1976) attempt to enumerate the characteristics of natural prototypes by studying objects that can be assigned a number of different names and determining a hierarchy of increasing generality for the names. For example, observers could give a number of names in response to a picture of an automobile: automobile, car, vehicle, red sportscar, and so on. These names can be ranked in terms of generality. Vehicle is the most general name; car or automobile are more specific; and red sportscar is the most specific.

Rosch et al. (1976) found that the names used most often in response to an object were neither the most specific nor the most general but those in the middle of the hierarchy. They call this kind of name the basic-level name. For example, the basic-level name for a picture of a collie is *dog,* rather than *collie* or *animal,* and that for a picture of a tulip is *flower* rather than *tulip* or *plant.* The experimenters labeled the more specific names (e.g., red sportscar, collie, tulip) as subordinate-level names, the more general names (vehicle, animal, plant) as superordinate-level names.

Rosch et al. also found that basic-level names are more descriptive of the stimulus class or category in that observers could list more common characteristics of the category when presented the basic-level name than when presented a subordinate or superordinate name. Moreover, as Rosch and Mervis (1975) showed, basic-level names of different categories tend to share very few characteristics. Therefore, basic-level names not only delineate the common attributes of a stimulus category but also distinguish that category from other categories.

The basic-level name might be the name of a prototype for a class, which would imply that a prototype is not necessarily an arithmetic average or central tendency of the class. Some evidence to support this idea is offered by Rosch et al.: When observers were asked to name a stimulus, they were quicker to give a basic-level name than a subordinate or superordinate name. Under the assumption that we have faster access to the prototype of a class than to distortions of the prototype, this experimental result implies that the basic-level names reflect the prototype of the class.

In summary, according to prototype models, pattern recognition is the completion of a search process that locates the best-fit schema rules, and stimuli are labeled as a prototype with a distortion. Prototype models can account for the accuracy of pattern recognition under a great variety of stimulus situations and variations without positing almost infinite memory storage. Prototype models are appealing for these reasons, yet these models do not necessarily explain how a stimulus is internally represented nor how prototypes are stored in memory. For instance, are there templates of prototypes? Feature models of pattern recognition address this question by positing that stimuli are internally represented as a set of features, such as size, length, orientation, color, curvature, and so on. Feature models further assume that prototypes are stored in memory as networks of discrete features.

FEATURE MODELS

In Chapter 2, we presented some physiological evidence that eloquently demonstrates that individual nerve cells of the visual cortex maximally respond to specific aspects of the stimulus. Visual cortical cells are maximally responsive to a narrow range of line orientations. Some cortical cells respond best to vertical orientations; some respond best to oblique orientations, and others to horizontal orientations. Within each of these groups, some cells respond best to stimuli of a certain length and width. Within each of those groups, some respond only to stimuli moving in a certain direction or to stimuli of a particular color. In other words, one can locate a cell in the visual cortex that would respond to a very specific stimulus, such as a stimulus that is oriented horizontally, 2 degrees of visual angle long and 1 degree wide, green on a red background, and moving rightward.

The response specificity of single nerve cells provides the physiological basis for feature theories of pattern recognition. Feature theories, capitalizing on these recent electrophysiological discoveries, assume that a stimulus pattern on the retina is analyzed for its component features and that the stimulus is internally represented as a list of features rather than as an isomorphic representation, which is assumed in template models. In feature theories, pattern recognition is the result of finding a match between a list of features for the stimulus and a list of features stored in memory. In recent years feature theories have gained support mainly because they apply some of our notions of the physiology of the visual system to yield a psychological model.

The Pandemonium Model

One feature theory used to analyze visual pattern recognition is the pandemonium model (see Selfridge, 1959). The pandemonium model describes recognition as a series of processing stages, using the term *demon* to describe the functional elements of each stage. The model posits image demons, feature demons, cognitive demons, and a decision demon (see Figure 3.6).

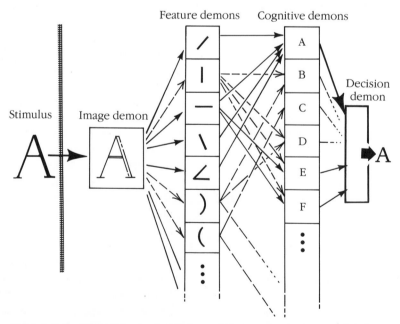

Figure 3.6 Schematic representation of the pandemonium model. [From R. L. Klatzky, *Human memory,* 2nd ed. Copyright © 1980 by W. H. Freeman and Company.]

Image demons convert the light information that is imaged on the retina by the optics of the eye into electrical nerve impulses, the language of the brain. The physiological counterparts of image demons are the neural machinery of the retina, especially the rod and cone receptors that transduce light energy into electrochemical energy. The image is further processed and converted into electrical impulses by other cells of the retina. Undoubtedly, some of these cells do more than just convert the stimulus into an internal image; some of these cells process basic information such as color, brightness, and so on. Cells that process information contained in the image are considered feature demons.

Feature demons analyze the internal representation of the visual stimulus. Each feature demon searches for a particular stimulus characteristic contained in the representation. For instance, some feature demons search for certain orientational information; others look for a certain length or width, color, angle, curve, and so on. Indeed, the specificity of the responses required for feature demons would seem, at first glance, to describe the responses of visual cortical cells. However, the responses of ganglion and lateral geniculate cells do extract some basic stimulus information, and they filter and channel the appropriate information to each of the cortical cells. Thus ganglion and geniculate cells are also considered feature demons, although in a feature model their function is less important than that of the cortical cells.

Cognitive demons monitor the responses of feature demons. Cognitive demons search for a particular combination of features contained in the internal representation. For example, a cognitive demon for A would search the internal representation for the combination of two oblique contours bisected by third horizontal contour. There could be a cognitive demon that is maximally responsive to the set of features contained in a table, or in a human face, or in a tree, and so on. The greater the number of features contained in the internal representation that match the list of features possessed by the cognitive demon, the more excited the demon, or the more activity it generates. The physiological analogue of a cognitive demon is a highly specific cortical cell. For example, there might exist a cell or cells that respond maximally when activated by an A. In fact, Gross, Rocha-Miranda, and Bender (1972) report that cells in higher visual cortical areas, such as the inferotemporal cortex, seem to respond to very specific combination of features.

The last processing stage is the decision demon. The major function of the decision demon is to decipher the activity of the cognitive demons and decide which cognitive demon is most active. This decision results in the recognition of the pattern. This stage of processing is difficult, at least at this time, to explain in physiological terms. The model requires that the output from almost all visual cells eventually flow to a central weigh station or comparator. Our present understanding of the anatomy of the visual system simply does not include such a central comparator. But the model requires such a comparison process to disentangle the responses of the cognitive demons, especially since almost any stimulus contains some of the features in many cognitive demons' list of features. For example, consider the features contained in the letters A, R, and C. The first two share the feature of oblique contours, whereas the latter two share the feature of curvature. Thus an R would activate to some extent the cognitive demons for both A and C, while maximally exciting the cognitive demon for R. At this point in the process, a decision demon is required to locate the most active, and thus the appropriate, cognitive demon.

Feature models, such as the pandemonium model, combine attractive aspects of both template and prototype models. Like template models, feature models address the question of the nature of the internal representation stimulus. Template models assume that the stimulus is represented as an internal replica of our visual world; feature models assume the stimulus is represented as a catalogue of features. Most prototype models, however, are not as explicit about the nature of the internal representation of a visual stimulus. But, like prototype models, feature models are flexible enough to explain why pattern recognition is fairly immune to simple distortions of the stimulus. Another attractive aspect of feature models is that they describe a model of pattern recognition that seems to be consistent with the physiology of the visual system and the operating characteristics of single visual cells. However, as we will see later in this chapter, there are some inconsistencies between descriptions of the feature detectors in feature models and the response properties of single nerve cells in the visual system.

The apparent similarity between feature models and visual physiology is often used as indirect support for the validity of the models. However, more direct experimental support derived from psychological experiments on pattern recognition also exists. One set of experiments analyzes the nature of errors made by observers shown letter stimuli that were so near the exposure threshold for the letter that often perception of the stimulus was incomplete (Kinney, Marsetta, and Showman, 1966). The analysis shows that observers make systematic errors in identifying letter stimuli, that is, they tend to make the same kind of errors when certain letter stimuli are presented. For example, when R is presented very quickly, identification errors tend to be P or F rather than X or W. Indeed, P, R, and F share many features. If the processing at the level of the feature demons is incomplete because of the brief presentation, then the cognitive demons for R, F, and P might respond with equal vigor; these cognitive demons would have a greater opportunity for activation than those associated with X or W, which have no features in common with P. Thus, the pattern of errors made by observers is consistent with the notion that visual stimuli are encoded by features.

Gibson, Shapiro, and Yonas (1968) measured the length of time it took observers (adults and seven-year-olds) to decide whether two stimuli were the same or different. They report that an observer's response latencies vary considerably across pairs of different letters, and these latencies seem to be related to the number of features the letters share. It took longer for an observer to decide that P and R were different than to decide that G and W were different. Analysis of the response data identified several distinctive features of letters such as linearity versus curvilinearity, obliqueness, vertical versus horizontal, intersection, and closed versus open.

Although both indirect and some direct support exists for feature models, two major problems confront their adherents. First, evidence fails to confirm these models' conceptualization of cortical functioning and their implicit assumption that visual cortical cells act as feature detectors. Second, feature theories, like template and prototype theories, are unable to account for contextual effects. For example, an R is more easily recognized when presented in the context of a word than when presented in the context of a nonword. These two problems are discussed in the next sections.

Are Cortical Cells Feature Detectors?

At first glance, there seems to be a remarkable similarity between feature detectors or demons, as described by the pandemonium model, and the selectivity of the responses of visual cortical cells. This apparent similarity between the hypothetical units and physiological observations makes feature models quite appealing. However, closer examination reveals that the hypothetical operation of feature detectors is not similar to the way in which cortical cells respond to visual stimuli. In fact, the difference between hypothetical feature detectors and cortical cells is sufficient to bring into question the validity of feature models.

A feature detector, as described by the pandemonium model, extracts certain information contained in the visual stimulus. For example, a feature detector may respond when the visual stimulus contains contours with a horizontal orientation. Furthermore, this horizontal-feature detector extracts this information independent of the presence of other information contained in the stimulus, such as color, width, size, contrast, direction of movement, and so on. In other words, the function of a feature detector is to signal the presence of a particular stimulus attribute regardless of the presence of other attributes. This provision is a necessary assumption of a feature model; it provides the flexibility to account for the accuracy of pattern recognition under a variety of stimulus variations and distortions. The stimulus A is recognized as such even though the stimulus moves left to right, moves up or down, is red or green, or is large or small, because for all these stimulus conditions the same core group of feature detectors are activated and encode the stimulus as an A.

However, visual cortical cells do not respond in this way. A visual cortical cell is selectively responsive to, for instance, a horizontal contour, but its response is not independent of the presence of other stimulus attributes. That is, a visual cortical cell does not signal the presence of a horizontal feature separate and independent of the influence of other stimulus attributes. A cortical cell that responds preferentially to a horizontal contour placed in its receptive field will exhibit a greatly diminished response to a horizontal contour that is too wide or small, too long or too short, the incorrect color, or moving in an inappropriate direction. Thus visual cortical cells cannot be the physiological counterparts of feature detectors.

Furthermore, experiments using the psychophysical technique of adaptation fail to confirm the existence of feature detectors. (The adaptation paradigm is described in Chapter 2.) The logic of such adaptation experiments is that if one could selectively fatigue a feature detector, such as a horizontal-feature detector, then the effects of this fatiguing should occur under a variety of stimulus conditions and should be independent of the presence of other stimulus attributes. For instance, adaptation to a horizontal set of contours should elevate the threshold for a test stimulus of horizontal contours, and the amount of threshold elevation should be independent of the relative spatial frequencies of the adapting and test stimuli, their color, and their relative directions of movement. As noted in Chapter 2, experiments do not yield result. The amount of adaptation depends for the most part on the overall similarity between the adapting and test stimuli and not on the presence of a single feature in both stimuli.

One psychophysical finding, nevertheless, may suggest the existence of orientation feature detectors. Campbell and Maffei (1971) and Parker (1972) report that the magnitude of the tilt aftereffect is not dependent on the relative spatial frequencies of the adapting and test stimuli. The *tilt aftereffect* refers to the change in the perception of orientation for vertical test contours induced by staring at, or adapting to, a set of contours of a different orientation for an extended period of time. For example, if one stares at a set of contours oriented 15 degrees counterclockwise from vertical for a period of 3 minutes, then a vertically oriented set of contours will appear tilted 5 to 6 degrees clockwise from vertical.

Campbell and Maffei (1971) and Parker (1972) report that the magnitude of this tilt aftereffect (the amount of distortion in the perception of orientation) is not influenced by the relative spatial frequencies of the adapting and test contours. These authors interpret this finding to mean that the adaptation of orientation detectors can occur without the adaptation of spatial frequency detectors. This interpretation is consistent with the view that the visual system contains feature detectors, at least for orientation. However, a more recent experiment (Ware and Mitchell, 1974) suggests that the magnitude of the tilt aftereffect *is* dependent on the similarity between the spatial frequencies of the adapting and the test stimuli. Thus the question of whether the magnitude of the tilt aftereffect is dependent on the similarity between the spatial frequencies of the adapting and test stimuli is unresolved.

The bulk of the psychophysical evidence, nonetheless, fails to uncover in the human visual system the existence of feature detectors as defined by feature models. Rather, these psychophysical findings are more easily explained in terms of the response properties of cortical cells as revealed by electrophysiologists. At this time, neither the electrophysiological nor the psychophysical evidence supports the proposition that feature detectors exist and form the basis for all pattern recognition in human beings.

Another apparent similarity between feature models and visual physiology that excites many pattern recognition theorists is the serial, hierarchical manner in which information flows in both systems. Feature theories assume that processing proceeds in a serial fashion: the formation of an image is followed by feature extraction and combination, and then the recognition of the visual pattern. Moreover, the processing is hierarchical in that the cognitive demons receive input from the combination of a certain set of lower-level feature demons. Early physiological investigations of the visual system seemed to show that visual processing did indeed proceed in a serial, hierarchical fashion.

For example, Hubel and Weisel (1962) reported that the output of lateral geniculate cells terminate on a group of *simple cells,* that the output of these simple cells form *complex cells,* and that these complex cells terminate on still another group of *hypercomplex cells.* They described these hypercomplex cells as responding to a much more specific combination of stimulus features than either complex or simple cells. For example, a typical simple cell responds best to a horizontal contour placed in a particular part of its receptive field; a complex cell is most active when a horizontal contour moving rightward is placed anywhere in its receptive field; and a hypercomplex cell responds best when this horizontal contour is moving rightward and is 2 degrees of visual angle in length.

More recent physiological and anatomical investigations challenge this view of visual processing. Some of these investigations suggest that a great deal of nonserial processing of information occurs in the visual cortex, that not all complex cells are constructed from the output of simple cells, and that not all hypercomplex cells are made from the output of complex cells. (For a recent review of this topic, see Lennie, 1980.) At the minimum, this more recent evidence suggests that visual processing is not as simple as electrophysiologists initially believed or as is suggested by many feature models.

Contextual Effects

Feature models are also challenged by experimental findings that show that the context of the stimulus influences an observer's ability to identify or recognize the stimulus. The effects of context have, for example, been reported for simple line stimuli. Weisstein and Harris (1974) compared the detection of a line embedded in a briefly flashed three-dimensional form with that of a line embedded in a briefly flashed less coherent form. Observers were to judge which one of four possible line targets, which varied in orientation and position, was presented. The four targets and sample contexts are shown in Figure 3.7.

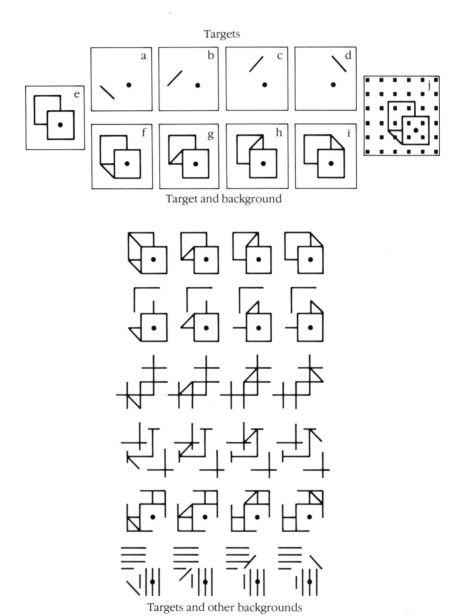

Figure 3.7 Stimuli used in experiments by Weisstein and Harris: target lines, target lines embedded in three-dimensional forms, and target lines embedded in forms that vary in coherence and in three-dimensionality. [From Weisstein and Harris, *Science,* 1974, *186,* 752–755. Copyright 1974 by the American Association for the Advancement of Science.]

The main finding in this experiment is that target detection is highest when the target lines are part of a three-dimensional form, and that target detection declines as this form becomes more incoherent and flat. Weisstein and Harris label this context effect the *object-superiority effect* (an analogue to the word-superiority effect, see Chapter 6). This finding suggests that the context of overall structure and form influences feature extraction.

Template, prototype, and feature theories cannot explain this powerful influence of context on pattern recognition. For example, feature theories have difficulties accounting for context effect because the target line, whether part of a three-dimensional form or part of an incoherent, flat display, would activate the same feature detector. Feature theories make no provisions for the nature of processing to be affected by context; thus they cannot account for the superiority of detection of features within meaningful contexts. One could argue that the visual system identifies the context before feature extraction occurs, but the assumptions made by feature models concerning the machinery of visual processing contradict this argument. Feature models posit that feature extraction occurs prior to the construction of the form and structure of the pattern, that feature demons precede cognitive demons.

In summary, the effects of context provide some major difficulties for feature models as well as for template and prototype models. Context effects do not disprove the basic tenets of any of these models, but they demonstrate that pattern recognition is more complex than these relatively simple models and suggest that pattern recognition may involve both serial and parallel processing of information. For example, there may exist two channels through which visual information travels in parallel. In one channel, very gross feature information is processed quickly in order to ascertain basic form information. In the other channel, more detailed feature information is processed at a slower rate. Context effects could be the result of the fast channel exerting influence on the slower channel to reroute or accentuate certain types of information so as to give preferential treatment or processing to certain sets of features in the slower channel. This two-channel model is an idea on the drawing board, like the template, prototype, and feature models. All these models require further elaboration and modification, and confirmation is dependent on the outcome of experimentation.

PATTERN RECOGNITION BY COMPUTERS

Pattern recognition in human beings is usually automatic and effortless. We are able to quickly recognize forms and shapes under a variety of distortions and situations and are able to capitalize on the context of the stimulus in order to provide more coherence to our visual world. We are quite good at pattern recognition considering the complexity of the task. Our competency in pattern recognition appears even more remarkable when researchers attempt to design a machine to simulate human pattern recognition or to design a new scheme for recognition using modern electronic and computer technology. Some researchers have been successful, and their machines are used everyday in banks and retail stores. Banks have machines that read check numbers, and retail stores have machines at cash register checkouts that automatically encode prices, stock item numbers, and inventory. Such reading machines are more or less reliable and fast.

However, these reading machines are inflexible because they operate according to the principles of template models. They produce an isomorphic internal representation of the code on the price tag or of the number on a check (that is, electrical impulses that vary in duration and spacing that directly correspond to the width and separation of the black bars or "zebra stripes" on the tag), and this internal representation is matched with representations for numbers and letters stored in the machine's memory. When a match is located, the machine labels the input. However, if the cash register operator runs the light probe across the item ticket in a perpendicular orientation, or if the item ticket is wrinkled, the machines will be unable to or will incorrectly label the input. It is the same problem of inflexibility that led many to reject template models for pattern recognition in human beings.

Reading machines designed according to the principles of a template model are simple and useful in situations in which the input is rigidly fixed and invariable. In these situations, the machines are fast, reliable, and economical. But what about reading machines that can handle more varied input, such as letters printed by different type styles, letters of different sizes, and possibly even handwritten letters? A reading machine with this capability would be extremely useful in many different situations; for example, such a machine could read for the blind. To achieve this flexibility in recognition by machine, researchers have abandoned the template matching scheme and are trying schemes involving feature extraction.

Recognition of Letters by Feature Extraction

As discussed earlier, flexibility in pattern recognition can be achieved by encoding the visual input in terms of features. Although the stimulus may be varied in many ways, a core group of features remains and can be used to identify the stimulus. Several researchers have attempted to design input devices and write computer programs based on the fundamental principles of feature models of pattern recognition. Selfridge and Neisser (1960) describe a system that has two levels. The first level encodes the features of the input (i.e., generates an internal representation of the input); and the second level matches the encoded features with sets of features, stored in the memory of the computer, that label different letters. The success of these systems depends heavily on the skills of the designer, who must select the set of features that uniquely define each letter under a variety of stimulus situations.

As an example, the letters A, H, V, and Y can be differentiated by the presence or absence of three features: concavity above, crossbar, and vertical line. These three features can be searched for in either a serial or parallel manner (see Figure 3.8). In serial processing, the feature concavity above would be searched for first. If it is absent, the input is labeled as an A. If present, the next feature searched for is the crossbar. If a crossbar is present, the input is identified as an H. If a crossbar is not present, then there is a search for a vertical line. If a vertical line is absent, the input is a V; if it is present, the input is a Y. Notice that the order of the tests and the set of possibilities are critical. The crossbar test will not positively identify H unless A has been previously eliminated as a possibility by a previous feature test. In a parallel processing approach, the search for each of the three features occurs simultaneously and matches are made on the basis of combined findings.

Although parallel processing is more complex and generally demands the manipulation of more information, parallel processing has several advantages over serial processing. One problem with serial processing is that a mistake at an early stage leads to certain error and misguided processing unless elaborate provisions are made for checking earlier decisions. A mistake on one feature has a less devastating effect in a parallel processing system. Another important advantage of parallel processing is that it can be applied to situations in which some features of stimuli cannot be represented in a dichotomous fashion. For instance, does B contain a crossbar? One way to approach this problem is to represent features in a quantitative manner. An O would be represented as having less of the crossbar feature than a B; and B would be represented as having less of the crossbar feature than A. A quantitative description of features can be achieved more easily with parallel processing.

A third advantage of parallel processing is that the amount of attention or weight assigned each feature can be varied. This approach is desirable because for certain recognitions the presence of one feature is much more important than the presence of another feature. Moreover, programs can be written so that the weights of the features assigned to each letter can be altered as the result of experience. That is, the program can improve its recognition accuracy through interactions with the input letter.

A machine designed according to such principles can do quite well in recognizing different letters, although it does less well recognizing hand-written script (see Selfridge and Neisser, 1960). An addition that would considerably improve the proficiency of such a machine would be a program to generate its own feature set. At present, the machine's success relies solely on the ingenuity of the designer to program the correct set of features. Another limitation of such a machine is that it is limited to recognizing individual letters. Is it possible to design a machine that could recognize words, objects, and even complex scenes? To do so, designers must first solve the problem of segmentation.

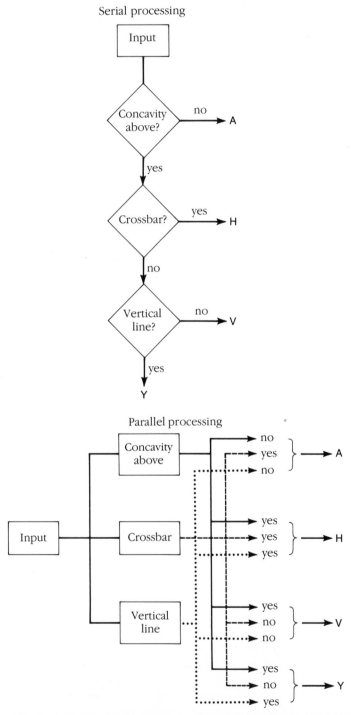

Figure 3.8 Serial and parallel searches for features in the letters A, H, V, and Y.

Problem of Segmentation

The problem of segmentation is a problem of grouping. It is the problem of discerning which letters belong to which words; in a scene of a forest, it involves deciding which limb belongs to which tree; and in general, segmentation is the process of assigning each contour to the appropriate pattern. In written texts, features such as the spacing of letters, capital letters, and punctuation guide the reader's grouping. If letters were printed evenly spaced and without punctuation, our reading would be impaired. For example, try to read the next line of unsegmented text:

i t i s d i f f i c u l t t o r e a d b u t t h e m e a n i n g o f t h e w o r d s c e r t a
i n l y h e l p s s e g m e n t

The problem of segmentation in real world scenes is overwhelming. Look at the picture of a set of blocks in Figure 3.9. We automatically and effortlessly segment this scene into a coherent picture of blocks of different sizes and shapes, but this segmentation would seem to be an insurmountable problem for a computer programmer. It would be a very difficult task, if not impossible, to program a computer to decide which edges and which surfaces belong to which block. In this picture of blocks, once the problem of segmentation is resolved then pattern recognition easily follows.

Winston (1970) and Guzman (1969) thoroughly study the blocks world as a paradigm to explore the problem of segmentation in real-world scenes. The solution to the problem of segmentation in the blocks world can be solved by elaborate computer programs that first identify different types of vertices where edges meet. Figure 3.10 shows the types of vertices Guzman

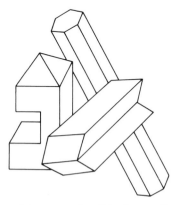

Figure 3.9 Example of block stimuli used by researchers in designing computer programs to identify patterns. The computer must be programmed to recognize the various edges, vertices, and surfaces and to assign each to the appropriate block.

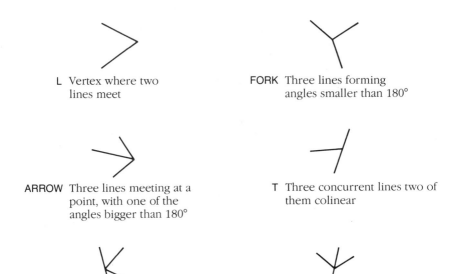

L Vertex where two
lines meet

FORK Three lines forming
angles smaller than 180°

ARROW Three lines meeting at a
point, with one of the
angles bigger than 180°

T Three concurrent lines two of
them colinear

K Two of the vertices are colinear
with the center, and the other
two fall in the same side of such
a line.

X Two of the vertices are
colinear with the center
and the other two fall on
opposite sides of such a
line.

Figure 3.10 Types of vertices identified by Guzman in studying the blocks world.

considers important. Next the concavity and convexity of these vertices are determined by the physical constraints imposed by neighboring junctions. For example, a convex edge at one junction cannot become a concave edge at a neighboring junction. These constraints, which permit surfaces and edges to be identified and labeled, impose order upon the blocks-world scene. Thus work with the blocks world demonstrates the complexity of the problem of segmentation even in simple scenes. Indeed, this work serves to increase our appreciation of the ability of our visual system to segment visual scenes with ease. Moreover, rules for segmentation of the blocks world are valid only for the blocks world. The problem of segmentation in more natural scenes is even more complex.

Marr (1976) reports some success in designing systems that analyze and segment natural-world scenes. His approach is to impose structure on a feature description of the input by applying grouping principles that resemble Gestalt principles of organization derived from human perceptual research (see Chapter 4). Marr's strategy is presented in schematic form in Figure 3.11 with a demonstration of the processing of a teddy bear image. The actual input of a teddy bear is shown in Figure 3.11a. Figure 3.11b shows the input image, which is formed by displaying the average luminance of some prescribed area. In this example, the luminance was averaged over

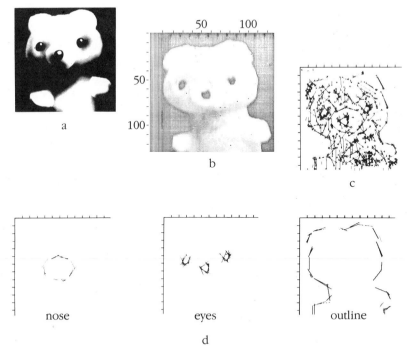

Figure 3.11 Example of Marr's system for analyzing and segmenting a complex visual scene: (a) actual input; (b) quantization of input; (c) feature description; and (d) segmentation of input. [From Marr, 1976.]

very small areas. (The quantization of Abraham Lincoln, Figure 2.12, was formed in the same manner, but the luminance was averaged over larger areas.) The computer then analyzes this input image in terms of a number of features (line, edge, slit) at a variety of orientations across a number of different positions in the picture. The feature description of the image is a representation of this orientational analysis. The feature description of the teddy bear, shown in Figure 3.11c, is simply a collection of line segments, so much of the information actually gathered is lost in this depiction. Using the feature description, Marr's program groups together clusters of features according to a number of rules. The grouping features appropriately segment many of the parts of the input image; for example, feature clusters segment the outline of the teddy bear, its eyes, and its nose (Figure 3.11d).

Marr's computer simulations of pattern recognition provide many insights into the process of segmentation of real-world scenes. Unfortunately, his programs are not able to appropriately segment all visual scenes. Some scenes present ambiguities in segmentation that can be solved only by using information about the object in the scene. For instance, a teddy bear is known to have eyes, a nose, and ears, but such information is derived from higher-level processes that are not easily programmed in a computer. Undoubtedly similar higher-order processes operate during human pattern recognition and give rise to context effects.

Pattern recognition by machine is rapidly advancing with the advent of new computer technology. For instance, a reading machine for the blind (Kurzweil reading machine) now exists, which uses feature analysis to recognize letters printed in a large number of type fonts, on different grades and colors of paper, and also under certain amounts of smudging and brokenness. But even with new advances in computer technology, pattern recognition remains a formidable problem. If we could build a machine that has the efficiency and flexibility of human pattern recognition, we would have a basis from which to build a model for pattern recognition in humans. Such a model would generate new hypotheses about the visual system that could be tested by physiological and psychological research. In the same light, current physiological and psychological findings provide insight into how to design machines capable of pattern recognition. This partnership between psychological and physiological research, on the one hand, and computer and technological research, on the other, makes exciting the prospects for solving the problem of pattern recognition.

SUMMARY

In this chapter, we reviewed three models (template, prototype, and feature) of human pattern recognition. These models differ in their characterizations of the internal representation of the visual stimulus and in the processes by which recognition of the internal representation is achieved.

None of these models can account for all human abilities to recognize visual patterns. However, feature and prototype models seem to have more validity than template models, which are severely limited due to their inflexibility and their enormous memory requirements. Although some empirical evidence supports prototype models, these models fail to adequately characterize the nature of the internal representation. Feature models offer an appealing mechanistic explanation, which is why machines built to recognize patterns often operate according to the principles of feature models. Yet the mechanistic nature of feature models is too constrained to account for the influence of stimulus context on pattern recognition.

SUGGESTED READING

For a more complete discussion of pattern recognition, see Winston (1977), Reed (1973), and Frisby (1980).

Chapter 4

Organization and Visual Processing

When you look at a tree, what do you see? You might describe a tree as composed of a trunk, branches, leaves, and perhaps blossoms or fruit. Each of these parts is a pattern that you would easily recognize by itself in the absence of the other parts. Yet when you look at an entire tree you are not immediately conscious of each individual part, rather you are aware of the overall object. The parts are of only secondary importance even though you can clearly see them. Indeed, if we first had to make a complete inventory of all the parts of something as visually complex as a tree, it would take us a very long time to identify that tree.

Viewing a tree is an example of a very common visual phenomenon: Individual patterns are often organized into larger, meaningful wholes that have visual properties in their own right. Consider this figure:

```
            K
        K       K
      K             K
      K             K
        K         K
          K   K   K
```

Most people would say that they see a circle made up of K's. None of the individual elements, namely the K's, are the least bit circular in themselves, yet the overall configuration has the property of circularity. These properties that emerge from the organization of individual elements, called *emergent features,* lead to problems of pattern recognition that are very different from the ones we have discussed so far. In this chapter we examine such organizational factors.

Three sets of issues regarding organization and perception concern us in this chapter. First, we want to know which aspects of a stimulus allow individual patterns to be seen as being part of an overall configuration. The examples we have noted so far suggest that physical arrangement influences our ability to organize patterns; thus we want to examine which aspects of physical arrangement produce the organization.

Second, we discuss how the organization of the stimulus affects our recognition of the component patterns. As noted in Chapter 3, Weisstein and Harris (1974) report that the presence of an organized, three-dimensional figure aids an observer in recognizing the individual components of the figure. Even though the single-line feature components of Weisstein and Harris' figures are somewhat simpler than the K's in the circular arrangement, in both cases observers must carry out some sort of pattern recognition process to identify the components. How does overall configuration influence the recognition of the individual components? That is, does pattern recognition proceed from individual components to the larger configuration, or is the overall configuration processed before the individual elements? A related question is whether recognition of the individual elements proceeds independently or if it is influenced by analysis of the whole configuration.

Third, we consider the role of attention in processing large organized patterns. When you look at the circle of K's, you may be more aware of either the overall circular pattern or the individual letters. By concentrating on one or the other, you can control which aspect of the stimulus receives the majority of your attention. However, later in this chapter we examine situations in which certain aspects of the stimulus virtually force attention to be paid either to the components or to the overall configuration. In these situations we are concerned with how much control a subject can exert on the aspects of the stimulus he notices and processes. In addition we want to know what characteristics of the stimulus affect attentional control.

GESTALT PRINCIPLES OF ORGANIZATION

Among the earlier studies of how individual elements can be organized into figures are those undertaken in the 1920's by a group of psychologists known as the Gestalt psychologists, a group that includes such well-known scientists as Kurt Koffka, Wolfgang Köhler, and Max Wertheimer. One of their principal interests was how individual stimuli are grouped together during perception into wholes or *Gestalts.* Such Gestalts possess features of their own that are not obvious from an examination of their individual parts. Our

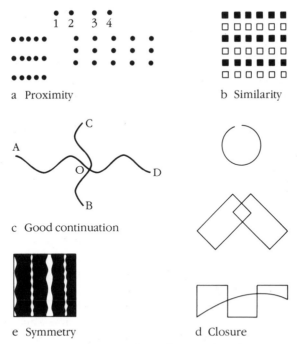

Figure 4.1 Illustrations of Gestalt principles of organization.

circle of K's is an example of a particular Gestalt, or whole, that has the *emergent feature* of circularity not present in the component letters.

One of the principal aims of the Gestalt psychologists in the area of visual perception was to specify the principles by which individual items are combined into larger, organized wholes. They also sought to find the principles by which these wholes are perceptually segregated and separated from other organized wholes. By asking subjects to view various patterns and describe what they saw, the Gestalt psychologists were able to discover many general "laws" of perceptual organization that determine an observer's perceptual experience. Let us examine some of these principles as described by Wertheimer (1958).

The first principle suggested by Wertheimer is the *principle of proximity,* which states that grouping of individual elements occurs on the basis of nearness or small distance. Figure 4.1a shows several examples of the principle of proximity at work. At the top of this figure are four dots numbered 1, 2, 3, and 4. When a subject looks at this configuration, dots 1 and 2 appear to cluster together, while dots 3 and 4 cluster with each other. Dots 2 and 3 appear to fall into two different clusters, and the probable explanation of this is that the distance between them is quite large relative to their distances from other immediately neighboring dots. Thus spatial proximity forces the grouping of 1 and 2, and the separation of 2 and 3. This proximity rule can be extended, as shown in the two dot matrices in the lower portion of Figure 4.1a. Each of the two matrices contains 15 dots, yet the one on the left appears to contain 3 rows of 5 dots each, while the one on the right appears to contain 5 columns of 3 dots each. The difference is, of course, that the grouping by rows is induced by the close horizontal proximity of the dots, while the grouping by columns is induced by the close vertical proximity of the dots.

The *principle of similarity* is illustrated in Figure 4.1b. Since the horizontal and vertical distances between squares in this matrix are equal, proximity should yield no impression of rows or columns. However, because the squares across alternate rows are physically similar, they form good perceptual groups. Thus the obvious organization by rows is produced by similarity of form.

Suppose that an arrangement of individual elements already forms a good perceptual unit through the operation of either of these two principles. What would happen to the apparent grouping if some of the elements were simultaneously shifted in position? For example, if dots 2 and 3 in Figure 4.1a were suddenly to begin moving downward simultaneously, would the subject still perceive the same grouping of dots? In this case, probably not. Although dots 2 and 3 are not originally part of the same group, their simultaneous motion gives them a "common fate," the directionality of motion. Under the organizational *principle of common fate,* dots 2 and 3 would be grouped together, possibly as endpoints of an imaginary moving line, while dots 1 and 4 share the common fate of remaining stationary.

From the preceding three examples one might surmise that continuous lines are tremendously important to organization. This importance is captured by the *principle of good continuation,* which states that elements will be organized into wholes that yield few interruptions or changes in continuous lines. Moreover it is clear that lines need not be straight in order for good continuation to operate. In Figure 4.1c, one could describe the arrangement of curvy lines as four line segments, A, B, C, and D, radiating from the single, center point O. However, the more common, and seemingly more accurate, grouping is to describe the figure as consisting of two curvy lines that cross at point O. Thus segments D and C are perceived as being continuations of segments A and B respectively.

Related to the principle of good continuation is the *principle of closure.* This law states that our organization of elements tends to form them into simple, closed figures, independent of their other continuation similarity, or proximity properties. Such closed figures are often referred to as *good figures.* Figure 4.1d gives several illustrations of closure at work. We describe the figure on the top as a circle even though the small gap technically makes it an unclosed curve; closure helps us to fill in missing information to organize the information that is present. We describe the middle figure as two overlapping rectangles, not as a small diamond surrounded by two rectangles with a corner cut out of each, because the overlapping-rectangles organization allows us to group the information into simple, closed figures instead of incomplete ones. In the figure on the bottom in Figure 4.1d, closure works to counteract good continuation. Good continuation would produce the organization of a curve and a squared zig-zag line. However, because closure is a powerful principle, subjects report seeing three closed figures that touch at the corners.

The principles of good continuation and closure explain why we sometimes have difficulty performing embedded figures tasks. Several numerical digits are embedded in the simple figure shown in Figure 4.2a, yet some are harder to find than others. The 1 stands out because its one vertical stroke is not continued in a smooth and unbroken fashion into other parts of the figure. However, the 5 is harder to spot because several of its parts are continued into other parts of the figure even though the continued sections are extraneous to the form of a 5. Other digits are embedded in this figure as well. Similarly, in Figure 4.2b the hexagon is difficult to spot in the figure on the right because of the closure properties of the figure in which it is embedded. The diagonals necessary to form the points of the hexagon are included as integral parts of the closed diamond pattern in the background distractor.

The principles we have discussed so far are the major ones that describe how individual elements are grouped together under various circumstances. Other Gestalt principles describe the factors that cause one pattern to be segregated from another. Such factors have a large influence on how the perceptual system segregates a figure from the background against which it is shown. Figure 4.2b illustrates one major principle for figure-ground segregation, the *principle of area,* which states that the smaller of two overlapping figures is more likely to be viewed as the figure, and the larger as the ground. The two overlapping regions are the white square in the center and the textured grid pattern that appears to be in back of it. Because the grid pattern is larger, the figure is perceived as a white square against a textured background. A second principle of segregation, the *principle of symmetry,* states that the more symmetrical a figure is the more likely it is to be seen as a closed figure. Symmetrical contours thus define a figure and isolate it from the ground, (Figure 4.1e).

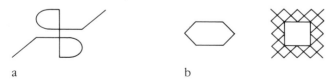

a   b

Figure 4.2 The Gestalt principles of good continuation and closure help explain why it is difficult to see many of the numerical digits embedded in (a), or to find the hexagon in the drawing on the right in (b).

Experimental Validation of Gestalt Principles

The Gestalt principles of organization are very general descriptions of what subjects report they see when looking at various types of patterns. A number of researchers have conducted experiments to determine in a more exact and quantitative way how these laws operate. Some researchers, for example, sought to measure the relative strengths of several of the principles in order to predict which law would govern visual organization in any particular case. Hochberg and Silverstein (1956) compared the effects of similarity and proximity. In the control condition of the experiment, subjects were shown a matrix of dots similar to the matrix of squares shown in Figure 4.1b. The dots were all equidistant, yielding no proximity cues for a preferred grouping. However, since the alternate rows of dots were black and light gray, subjects tended to group the matrix by rows.

The subjects were then given the opportunity to decrease the vertical spacing between the dots while maintaining the horizontal spacing. If the vertical spacing is small enough, the dots no longer appear to form rows but, instead, fall into columns of alternating black and gray dots. The subject's task was to find the adjustment of vertical spacing that made organization into rows and columns appear equally likely. This task thus pits the principles of proximity and similarity against each other. By having the subject make the distance adjustment, the experimenters could quantitatively determine the circumstances under which the two principles are equally strong.

Not surprisingly, Hochberg and Silverstein found that the vertical spacing had to be reduced quite a bit in order for proximity to counteract the similarity effect. However, a more interesting test of the relative effects of these two principles is a matrix whose rows of dots are black alternating with a dark gray. In this case the initial similarity grouping is not strong because the dots within a row are not exceedingly more similar to each other than to dots in adjacent rows. Since the similarity is not strong, we would expect that subjects would have to move the rows only slightly closer together to counteract the weak similarity effect by a proximity effect. Hochberg and Silverstein's results confirm our expectation: The weaker the similarity grouping, the less vertical contraction necessary to counteract it.

A second group of studies on the Gestalt laws attempt to specify the precise characteristics of patterns that yield grouping according to the various principles. Beck (1966), for example, examined the role of orientation and overall shape of individual components in producing similarity groupings. All of Beck's stimuli were simple elements containing two lines placed at right angles to one another (e.g., T, ⅄, ⊢, ⌐, V, X and +). When he asked subjects to make ratings of the similarity between various pairs of these items, they rated as very similar pairs that were identical except for orientation; for example, pairs such as T⊢, T⅄, and + X. Other pairwise comparisons of the stimuli yielded low similarity ratings.

The pattern of results changed markedly, however, when subjects were shown whole groups of these stimuli rather than just two. In the second task subjects viewed an entire field divided into three noticeable, but contiguous, sections. Each section contained 36 of one of the stimulus elements. Thus, for example, a subject might see:

The task in this case was to divide the field into two regions by indicating a boundary where "the most natural break occurs." For our example, we might expect subjects to group the T and the ⋏ together since they had been rated as being highly similar. However, almost all subjects placed the boundary so that the tilted ⋏'s were separated from the upright T and upright ⌐ . This judgment appears to be based on the orientations of the line segments of the individual elements and not on pairwise similarity. For a series of such separation tasks, the only major exceptions to this rule occurred when the three elements had segments in the same orientation but differing in whether the segments crossed. For example, in a figure with T, ⊢, and +, subjects separated the +'s from the others because they contained crossing lines while the other two element types did not.

Beck's study illustrates that the repetition of individual elements makes subjects sensitive to certain properties that are not so important when only a few elements are present. One of these properties is the orientation of line segments. Olson and Attneave (1970) extended Beck's result to show that similarity grouping depends not only on the overall orientation of the elements but also on the slope of their component line segments relative to a horizontal-vertical reference system. Olson and Attneave obtained a more quantitative measure of similarity grouping by presenting a circular field of line elements. Three of the quadrants of each circle contained the same type of element; for example, ı, −, or V . One of the quadrants contained another type of element. The experimenters measured how long it took a subject to determine which of the four quadrants contained the different elements.

The subjects responded most quickly to fields that required them to distinguish horizontal from vertical line elements, and almost as quickly to fields in which tilted lines had to be distinguished from either horizontal or vertical lines. The slowest reaction times were for fields whose disparate quadrant contained elements that, although different overall, had the same line slopes as the elements in the other three sections; for example, ∧ versus V . Olson and Attneave suggest that grouping depends on the subject's ability to generate an adequate internal description of the relationships between elements in the field. The easiest descriptions to make are those for elements that are, or contain, segments perpendicular to the horizontal and vertical axes. Next easiest are descriptions when some elements, but not all, have horizontal or vertical components. The most difficult cases are those in which the descriptions of all the elements relative to Cartesian axes are identical, and other distinguishing features must be found.

Olson and Attneave also showed that the results of the reaction time experiment change when the orientation of the entire stimulus field is changed relative to the observer. They had their subjects view the stimulus arrays either normally or with their heads tilted at a 45° angle. In the tilted condition, the reference axis system changes so that lines previously horizontal or vertical are diagonal. Similarly, lines that are diagonal when the head is upright become horizontal or vertical when the head is tilted. The results of the experiment show that the best grouping still occurs for the horizontal-vertical discriminations, where vertical is defined as being the same orientation as the head. Thus, discriminations that are easy when the head is upright are difficult when the head is tilted, and vice versa.

Hochberg and McAlister (1953) sought to specify the physical characteristics of stimuli classified as good figures. They argue that the processing system organizes input into the simplest interpretation possible, and that the Gestalt principles such as closure (or good figure) are simply statements about which interpretations of a multielement stimulus are the simplest. Moreover, they propose a way to quantify figural simplicity.

Consider, for example, the three line drawings representing a three-dimensional cube shown in the top row of Figure 4.3. Drawings from some angles of view give a very strong impression of showing a three-dimensional object, such as view 3. View 1, however, is more easily seen as a two-dimensional hexagon containing interior line segments. View 2 sometimes appears to be three-dimensional, but then "flips" perceptually and appears to be two-dimensional for awhile. Hochberg and McAlister's approach suggests that those versions of the cube that are good figures (i.e., more simply described) in three dimensions are easily perceived as three-dimensional objects, while those versions that are simpler planar figures are seen as two-dimensional.

Hochberg and McAlister experimentally examined several physical characteristics of the drawings that might be good measures of planar simplicity or goodness: number of line segments, number of angles, and number of points of intersection contained by each figure when viewed as a two-dimensional drawing. Thus, for example, view 1 contains 12 individual line segments, while view 3 contains 16 because many of the "edges" of the three-dimensional cube break into two segments at the interior intersection points in the two-dimensional interpretation. Therefore view 1 ought to be seen as two-dimensional more often than view 3 because when both are given a two-dimensional interpretation view 1 is simpler than view 3. Similar arguments can be made using number of angles and number of intersections as measures of simplicity.

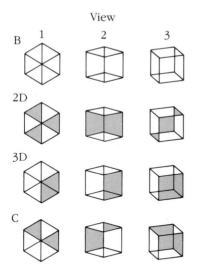

View

Figure 4.3 The simplicity of the figures at the left when interpreted as planar, two-dimensional objects is greater than those at the right. However, shading can make it more or less likely that a figure will appear two- or three-dimensional. [From Hemenway and Palmer, 1978. Copyright 1978 by the American Psychological Association. Reprinted by permission of the publisher and the author.]

Hochberg and McAlister's subjects viewed each of the three cube drawings for nearly 2 minutes and recorded whether the figure looked two- or three-dimensional at various points during the interval. As predicted, view 1 appeared two-dimensional 60 percent of the time and view 3 only 1 percent of the time. View 2, being intermediate in two-dimensional simplicity, was seen as a planar figure 49 percent of the time.

Hemenway and Palmer (1978) further studied how organization affects dimensional perception with this type of stimulus. Clearly one of the main problems in deciding on the dimensionality of a line drawing in which the "back" surfaces show through, is to decide whether two adjacent regions are part of the same surface or not. Color cues help us resolve the initial ambiguity since regions that are part of the same surface of a three-dimensional object have the same color. Hemenway and Palmer's subjects were therefore shown some drawings that had no color cues (the B condition in Figure 4.3) and others that were shaded to give the impression of two dimensionality (the 2D and C conditions) or the impression of three-dimensionality (the 3D condition).

In two experiments Hemenway and Palmer measured both the likelihood that the subjects perceived the drawings as three-dimensional and the amount of time, measured from the onset of the stimulus, for the subject to report obtaining a three-dimensional perception. For the unshaded drawings, the likelihood was that subjects would report an initial three-dimensional organization and a decreasing latency for doing so in going across from view 1 to 3. The 2D and control shadings significantly increased the likelihood that subjects initially reported seeing a two-dimensional configuration, and significantly increased the latency for forming a three-dimensional organization. The 3D shading patterns increased the initial three-dimensional organization and decreased subjects' times to report three-dimensional organization. Thus even view 1 was easily seen as three-dimensional with the proper coloration cues. Apparently, shading significantly alters the simplicity, or goodness, of the two- and the three-dimensional interpretations of these drawings. It therefore influences how subjects organize the stimulus input.

The principle of good continuation has been examined by Prytulak (1974). The principle predicts how individual points will be organized when they fall on a straight line, and Prytulak wanted to determine how good continuation is applied to ambiguous situations, such as when two lines meet at an angle. Clearly the organization will depend on the angle between the two segments and on the nature of any surrounding segments or elements. The stimuli in Prytulak's experiment were all arrow dot patterns that contained a shaft of four dots, and two arms radiating from a single common dot at the end of the shaft. For example:

The subjects viewed dot patterns that varied in the angular arrangement of the arms, and they were to decide which of the two arms appeared to be grouped most strongly with the shaft. Prytulak found that three stimulus characteristics govern which arm is perceived as a continuation of the shaft. First, rectilinearity: The arm that is closest to forming a 180° angle with the shaft will be judged as the better continuation. Second, orientation: An arm that lies along the horizontal or vertical will be grouped with the shaft more often than an arm that falls at an oblique angle. Third, enclosure: The rectilinearity principle will be stronger if the two arms fall on different sides of the shaft than if they fall on the same side of the shaft.

All the studies we have reviewed, both those done by the Gestalt psychologists and by later investigators, show that the configuration of individual elements in a stimulus lead to strong organizational effects that affect the interpretation or identification given to that stimulus. The Gestalt psychologists were successful in specifying what those organizational principles are, but only more recent research has specified the precise aspects of the stimulus that lead to these effects. While these studies are moderately successful in determining the factors underlying perceptual organization, they are not the only approach to this problem. We now examine an alternative approach, that of information theory.

Information Theory Account of Gestalt Principles

Every visual stimulus or arrangement of individual items gives the viewer some information that helps to identify it. To identify a stimulus is to distinguish that stimulus from anything else that could appear. If very few cues are provided, the viewer has little information about which stimulus has been shown, and will not easily identify it. However, a full and complete stimulus, one that contains lots of information, is easy to identify. One of the goals of information theory is to specify which aspects of a stimulus convey information about the identity of that stimulus. Although it is possible to quantitatively specify the amount of information contained in any particular stimulus, we will describe the informational approach to the study of form in a more general, qualitative way. The interested reader is referred to Attneave (1959) for a more mathematical discussion of these concepts.

To show what information is, we borrow an example from Attneave (1954), shown in Figure 4.4. Consider a 50-by-80 grid of squares, each of which is colored either white, black, or brown in the manner shown in the figure. The squares are colored to represent a picture of a black ink bottle sitting on a brown platform against a white background. Suppose you are given a blank 50-by-80 grid and asked to determine the color of each of the 4000 squares by guessing. You are to start at the far lower left of the grid and work across an entire row before going up to the next row, and you are allowed to keep track of your answers by coloring in the squares on your blank grid. If you guess the wrong color on your first try on a particular square, you are allowed to guess a second time between the two remaining possibilities.

If you were to guess at random for each square, you would make approximately 4000 errors before correctly identifying the colors of all the squares (2666 errors on the first guess and 1333 on the second). However, as you start across the first row you undoubtedly notice that a pattern of white squares is developing. Although you might make a mistake at position 20 of the first row, where the color suddenly turns to brown at the edge of the platform, you will probably make no further errors after the first few brown squares. In fact, if you generalize the pattern from row 1 to the next 19 rows, you can guess those rows without any errors at all. When you get to the top of the platform and begin on the inkwell you will probably make a few mistakes in guessing black squares in the first few rows, but once you notice the symmetrical pattern of the inkwell, you will again guess correctly nearly

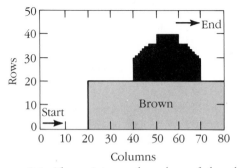

Figure 4.4 The points on the edges of the objects contain the most information about the forms that are present. [From Attneave, 1954. Copyright 1954 by the American Psychological Association. Reprinted by permission of the publisher and the author.]

all the time. Attneave reports that the average subject can accomplish this task making only 15 to 20 errors altogether.

As you perform this task, the feedback you get from each of your guesses gives you some information about the stimulus, in this case information about the color of each individual box and thus about the location and shape of the desk and the ink bottle. However, notice that the feedback from guesses about some boxes is more helpful than the feedback from guesses about others. When told that your guess that some box in the interior of the platform is brown is correct, you learn very little that you have not already surmised from the structure of the stimulus. In the terminology of information theory, the feedback you get from these guesses is *redundant* or predictable from other information. Thus not much information is obtained from being told the colors of these boxes.

However, when you get feedback about squares that lie along the edges of the objects, you are getting more information since the edge contours are not entirely predictable. Thus although you might do fairly well in predicting the transition from white to brown along the left vertical edge of the platform, you obtain a great deal of information about color and shape both at the top corner and at the jagged and less predictable boundaries of the ink bottle. A quantitative computation of the amount of information conveyed at each box in this figure confirms our intuitive conclusions. Specifically, information about the organization of a figure is concentrated at the contours, particularly at the points where the direction of an edge changes abruptly.

Attneave (1954) points out that if we consider the Gestalt principles of similarity, proximity, good continuation, and common fate in the light of information theory, we find that each refers to a situation of high redundancy. That is, the Gestalt laws posit that elements that share the same information are grouped together perceptually. We can restate Hochberg and McAlister's concept of simplicity as the defining characteristic of good figures by saying that good figures are those that have both the fewest points of high informational content and the most redundancy. Thus the most perceptually simple interpretation of a line drawing is that in which there are fewest individual line segments and angles.

Summary

Our discussion of the Gestalt principles of organization has offered a qualitative description of how figures can be organized for visual analysis. Although some of the original principles lacked precision, both information theorists and other later investigators of perceptual processing have shown some specific ways in which we can predict the strength of various organizations and the applicability of the different principles. We now turn our attention to examining how those organized structures are related to one another and how the processing of organized wholes and their component elements affect one another.

HIERARCHICAL STRUCTURE AND GLOBAL VS. LOCAL PROCESSING

In order to understand the effects of the organization of individual elements on pattern recognition and how such recognition processes are carried out, let us first look at the results of a few experiments that further investigate Gestalt organizational principles. Good continuation is explored in an experiment done by Prinzmetal and Banks (1977). On each trial of the experiment, the subject's task was to determine whether a T or an F was present among a group of characters that looked very similar to T's and F's. Two types of stimulus arrangements were used:

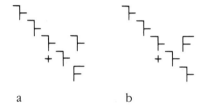

a   b

The main difference between these two arrangements is that in (a) the target letter appears as part of the linear portion of the stimulus, while in (b) the target appears next to the line.

Each stimulus was shown briefly, and the reaction time for the subject to decide whether a T or an F had been presented was recorded. The subjects were significantly faster in reporting the correct target letter when the target appeared next to the linear array rather than when it appeared as part of the line. The apparent effect of good continuation is to organize all the elements in the line into a single pattern, such that its component parts are relatively hard to identify. The lone element, in contrast, is organized into a pattern all by itself and is therefore identified quickly.

Banks and Prinzmetal obtained a similar set of results using nonlinear good configurations. The task for the subject was again to decide whether an array of characters of the type used in the previous experiment contained a T or an F. The following arrangements were used as stimuli:

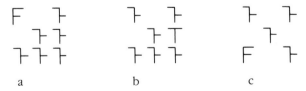

a   b   c

In (a) the distractor characters occupy a triangular good figure, while the target is physically separate. We would expect the target to stand out and be identified quickly because the distractor elements can be grouped into an organized triangular pattern excluding the target. In (b) the target is part of the triangular arrangement, while the separate position is filled by a distractor. This target should be relatively more difficult to spot and identify because it does not stand out from the distractors as readily. In (c) the target and distractor elements also form a good figure, but there are fewer elements overall in the pattern. This pattern should take longer to process than (a) but less time than (b) because there are fewer elements overall. The data confirm these predictions.

The results of these two experiments suggest that pattern recognition occurs in a *global-to-local* fashion. That is, when shown an entire array of objects, an observer first organizes the elements into larger patterns. The Gestalt principles adequately describe which overall groupings will result, although they do not explain the means by which the observer achieves such organization. The observer is first aware of the emergent properties of the organized wholes but not of the characteristics of the component parts. However, if the task demands that the observer respond on the basis of the subparts, the subject can begin to break down the organized wholes for further analysis of the components. The more elements there are, the longer this analysis takes. Such a global-to-local approach is, of course, quite different from a strictly local-to-global approach in which the component elements are thoroughly analyzed and identified before they are organized into larger patterns.

Experiments by Navon (1977) confirm the global influence of organization on recognition of the component elements. Navon's basic method was to set the overall organization, or *global properties,* of a stimulus array into competition with the properties of the individual elements, the *local properties.* In order to understand his experiments, we must first consider a very simplified version of his task.

The subject's task was to decide on each trial whether the name of the letter *H* or the letter *S* had been spoken by a voice heard through headphones. If the subject has no other task to carry out, he can respond correctly in about 550 milliseconds. However, suppose on some trials the subject is shown a letter while hearing a letter name. If the visual stimulus is the same letter as the one named, the subject is still quite fast in responding correctly to the auditory task. However, if the visual stimulus conflicts with the auditory stimulus, the response latency for identifying the auditory target increases some 100 milliseconds. In addition to presenting consistent and conflicting visual stimuli, we can also present a neutral visual stimulus, such as O. A neutral visual stimulus raises the auditory identification latency by only about 50 milliseconds. Clearly the neutral visual stimulus conflicts with the auditory stimulus because it has different visual features than the named letter, but the name of the neutral stimulus is not the name of the incorrect response in the auditory task.

Navon noted that there are two ways to define the degree of consistency between the visual stimulus and the auditory stimulus. Under one definition, consistency depends on whether the overall configuration of the visual stimulus is H- like, S- like or O- like. However, if we construct a visual stimulus such that the overall organization of the elements is H- like or S- like, but the component elements are letters themselves, then we could tell whether the consistency of the individual elements also affects the auditory latencies.

Navon's nine experimental visual stimuli are shown in Figure 4.5a. Across each row we see patterns that share global consistency, that is, the overall configurations of the patterns within a row are identical although their components differ. Thus, if the name of the letter *H* were pronounced in the auditory task, the characters in the first row would be globally consistent, the characters in the second row would be globally neutral, and the stimuli in the third row would be globally conflicting. Similarly, each column in Figure 4.5a defines one level of local consistency. The stimuli in the first column are all locally consistent with the auditory stimulus *H*, those in the second column locally neutral with respect to *H*, and those in the third column locally conflict with *H*.

If we repeat the experiment with visual stimuli of the type shown in Figure 4.5a, we can determine whether the global or the local characteristics, or both, affect the amount of difficulty the subject has in responding to the auditory task. The results, shown in Figure 4.5b, indicate that globally defined consistency has a profound effect on the auditory response latencies, but that auditory latencies were unaffected by changes in the local consistency level. That is, the subjects seem to be immediately aware of only the global characteristics of a visual stimulus and not of the individual components. This is very strong evidence for the global-to-local hypothesis.

Of course, we may wonder if the reason the global properties were so much more influential than the local properties is peculiar to the nature of the task. Perhaps we would get evidence for local-to-global processing if the task itself required that more attention be paid to the local properties of the visual stimuli. In a second experiment Navon compared the effects of global and local characteristics in two tasks designed to emphasize either the global or local properties of the stimulus. Only visual stimulus were used, and the subject's task was to decide as quickly as possible whether an H or an S had been presented. In the global-directed condition, the subject was to decide whether the overall configuration of the elements was an H or an S, regard- less of the individual component elements. The stimuli in this task were those from the top and bottom rows of Figure 4.5a. In the local-directed condition, the subject was to decide the identity of the component elements of the larger configuration. The six possible stimuli were the ones in the first and third columns of Figure 4.5a.

Figure 4.5c shows the reaction times for the two tasks as a function of the relationship between the overall configuration and the component elements. Here, *consistent* means that the global form and the component elements were the same, and *conflicting* refers to an overall configuration of an H composed of S's, or vice versa. Inspection of Figure 4.5c shows two important results. First, global-directed responding is much faster than local-directed

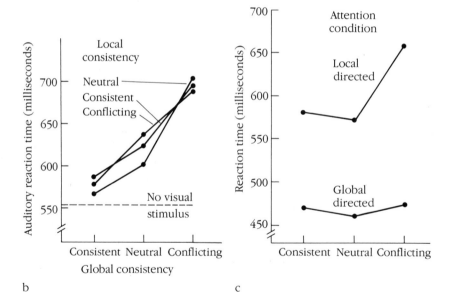

```
H     H      O     O      S     S
H     H      O     O      S     S
H     H      O     O      S     S
HHHHH        OOOOOO       SSSSS
H     H      O     O      S     S
H     H      O     O      S     S
H     H      O     O      S     S


HHHHH        OOOOOO       SSSSS
H     H      O     O      S     S
H     H      O     O      S     S
H     H      O     O      S     S
H     H      O     O      S     S
H     H      O     O      S     S
HHHHH        OOOOOO       SSSSS


 HHHH        OOOO          SSSS
H     H     O    O        S    S
H           O             S
 HHHH        OOOO          SSSS
    H           O             S
HHHH        OOOOO         SSSS
```

a

Figure 4.5 (a) Examples of the stimuli used to show that global characteristics are processed faster than local characteristics. (b) and (c): Navon's data. [From Navon, 1977.]

responding, regardless of consistency. This finding suggests that global features are detected faster, or earlier, than local features.

Second, although consistency shows no influence on the speed of global-directed responses, it has an obvious effect on local-directed response times. In particular, when the overall configuration of the stimulus conflicts with the individual components, reaction times greatly increase. It appears then that the subject first notices the overall configuration. If a response can be made on the basis of those features, the local features need not be processed, and therefore do not affect response times. However, when the global features are not sufficient to complete the local-directed task, the individual elements are then processed. Thus local-directed responses are slower overall, and if the previously identified global character conflicts with the individual letters, the analysis of the individual letters takes longer still.

The ability of a global configuration to interfere with processing of local figures clearly does not apply to all stimulus situations. Common sense suggests that prior processing of global features is not inevitable, especially if the global arrangement is so large that parts of it fall on less sensitive parts of the retina or it cannot be viewed in a single fixation. Kinchla and Wolf (1979) show that Navon's results are partly dependent on the limited size of his stimuli. While Navon's large letters were no larger than 5.5° of visual angle, Kinchla and Wolf used similar stimuli of several sizes, ranging from 4.8° to 22.1° of visual angle. They report that it is easiest to identify the global character when it is 8° or less and approximately five times the size of the component letters. When the global character is greater than 8°, the local letters are actually easier to respond to than the global one. Kinchla and Wolf therefore suggest that processing is neither always global-to-local nor local-to-global; rather, "forms having an optimal size in the visual field are processed first" (p. 228). Forms composed of spatial frequency bands to which the visual system is most sensitive are identified most quickly.

The reaction time results we have discussed so far suggest that the parts of a stimulus are processed in an order determined by the stimulus' structure. Navon's experiment, in particular, suggests that we first process information about the features of the overall configuration and then proceed to an analysis of the smaller parts. Of course, the subparts themselves, namely the small letters, have features as their subparts. This type of analysis is formalized by Palmer (1977), who suggests that visual form is represented and analyzed hierarchically starting with the overall configuration down through intermediate elements to the basic features of the individual elements. At each level of the hierarchy, Gestalt principles can be used to determine how the lower-level units have been formed into more organized wholes at that level.

To support the assumptions that underlie this analysis, Palmer did two kinds of experiments using simple line figures of the type shown at the left of each row in Figure 4.6. For the figure in the top row, as an example, at the lowest level of organization we have a collection of six simple line segments at different orientations. However, these segments appear to organize themselves into a few major subparts, such as the upside-down squared U and the three-lined zig-zag on top of it. Here principles such as figural goodness, symmetry, and proximity seem to create the organization. At the highest level of organization, these subparts compose a unified line drawing. Of course, not all combinations of line segments produce equally good intermediate subparts. Some, like the second figure in the first row (labeled H for high

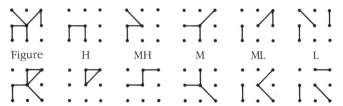

Figure 4.6 Stimuli used to show that good subparts can be spotted more quickly in whole figures than poor subparts. [From Palmer, 1977.]

figural goodness), are good subparts and are well organized within themselves. These are often familiar and nameable shapes. Others, such as the one labeled L (for low figural goodness) are poorly organized subparts, and would probably never be analyzed as an organized subpart of the figure.

Palmer used line drawings of the type shown in Figure 4.6 and constructed subparts of them, ranging from high figural goodness (H) to low figural goodness (L) as shown across each row of the figure. Ratings by a group of subjects confirmed the ranking of the organizational goodness of these various subparts. The figures and their subparts were then used in a verification task in which subjects were shown one of the complete line figures and then shown a test pattern of line segments. The task was to decide whether the entire test pattern had appeared in the original figure.

Palmer's hierarchical representation and analysis scheme posits that on seeing the original figure, the subject first analyzes the total form, then breaks it down into its good subparts, and then further breaks and then these subparts down into their component line segments. Since the subject has to remember the complete form for later comparison with the test pattern, the subject must represent each level of this hierarchy in memory. When the test pattern appears, the subject first attempts to compare it to the representation at the highest level of the hierarchy. Since there is no match at this level, the subject then compares the test pattern to each of the good subparts represented at the next level of the hierarchy. If the test pattern is a good subpart, a match is soon found, and the verification response is made quickly.

However, if the test pattern is a poor subpart of the entire figure, a match is not found at the subpart level of the hierarchy, and the test pattern is then compared line by line to the individual elements at the lowest level of the representational hierarchy. Thus any match found at this level will take a relatively long time. The hierarchical model therefore predicts that verification times decrease as a function of the test patterns' goodness as a subpart of the test set. That is, the better a test pattern is as a subpart of the whole figure, the more likely a match can be made at a higher level of the hierarchy and the faster the response times. The experimental data confirm these predictions entirely.

Summary

The experiments discussed in this section illustrate some important principles, while leaving other issues unresolved. The organization of a stimulus certainly affects how that stimulus is processed. We presented several examples in which global properties emerge immediately from a stimulus configuration and determine how easily the local components can be processed. Global-to-local processing seems particularly important for information that is to be stored in memory (Palmer, 1977) as it provides an efficient means of organizing the information. However, to say that global properties are noticed first begs the question of how the visual system picks out global properties *before* it processes the entire stimulus. To date, the only partial answer to this question is one suggested by Kinchla and Wolf (1979), that global properties are immediately detected by the processing of the low-frequency components of the stimulus array.

A second unanswered question is how global-to-local processing relates to the more general issue of *top-down processing.* A top-down process is one in which higher, more abstract levels of analysis influence the operation of low-level operations such as feature detection. In Chapter 3, for example, we discussed the object-superiority effect (Weisstein and Harris, 1974), the finding that the knowledge that an object is present (a top-level process) influences the way in which individual line segments are detected. If perception were merely a matter of combining line segments into higher-order objects in a *bottom-up* fashion, such a result would not have been obtained. In the present chapter we have seen that global arrangements of objects may interfere with or facilitate the identification of local objects, but we have no firm evidence that global considerations actually change the lower-level processes by, for example, limiting the choices available during pattern recognition. Perceptual psychologists are yet unable to explain how a subject's prior knowledge works downward to affect low-level visual processes.

DIMENSIONAL STRUCTURE AND ATTENTION

To fully understand the role of organization in visual information processing, we must consider how the component attributes of a single stimulus influence its processing. Although many stimuli appear as organized aggregates of smaller forms, many multiattribute stimuli do not have obvious subparts; for example, consider a simple form such as a completely red square. Although it has edges, it has neither line segments nor any other subparts. However, it has such attributes as size, shape, and color. In this section we examine how attributes such as these are processed and combined to form the percept of a single, whole stimulus.

Integral and Separable Dimensions

Color, size, and form are examples of a particular type of attribute called a *dimension*. A dimension is an attribute of a set of stimuli that meets the following criterion: Each of the stimuli in the set must possess one and only one value of that attribute. For example, consider a set of colored forms. Size is a dimension of that set because each form has one and only one particular size. Different stimuli in the set may have different sizes, but a given stimulus has only one size (different sizes are mutually exclusive). Similarly, stimuli vary along the dimension of color as each one has exactly one of many different possible colors. Experimenters can construct a series of stimuli that vary along only one of many component dimensions (such as red squares of different sizes) in order to observe how such variation affects perceptual processing.

In discussing the role of stimulus dimensions in visual processing, we find it useful to graph sets of stimuli that differ along one or more dimensions. Figure 4.7a depicts a graph of a set of four rectangular stimuli that vary along the dimensions of height and width. Each of the four stimuli is represented as a single point in a plane described by axes that correspond to the height and width dimensions, as shown in the small inset in the figure. The actual stimuli are depicted in the larger figure. Notice that rectangles A and B are equally wide and thus have the same value on the width dimension of the graph. Similarly, rectangles C and D share a common, but larger value on the width dimension. For the dimension of height, the two short rectangles, A and D, have the same height, while B and C share a common, larger height.

Everyday experience confirms that the dimensions of height and width are combined in the processing system in some manner to produce an overall impression of a rectangle. But how are the dimensions combined? Are we first aware of the overall, global rectangle, and only later do we analyze it into its component dimensions? Or, do we first analyze the dimensions separately and then construe the overall stimulus? Finally, how does the analysis of one of the dimensions influence analysis of the other? Is it possible to selectively attend to one or the other dimension?

The answers to these questions depend on which dimensional combinations are being considered. Garner (1974) distinguishes several types of dimensional combinations or structures, but the two that concern us most are those dimensional combinations that are integral and those that are separable. Dimensions are said to be *integral* if it is impossible to specify the value of one dimension without simultaneously specifying the value of the other dimension. Dimensions that are integral cannot exist without one another; for example, the height and width of rectangles are an integral dimensional combination, since it is impossible to draw a rectangle of a particular width without also making it some particular height. Another integral combination of dimensions is the hue (color) and the brightness of a colored form.

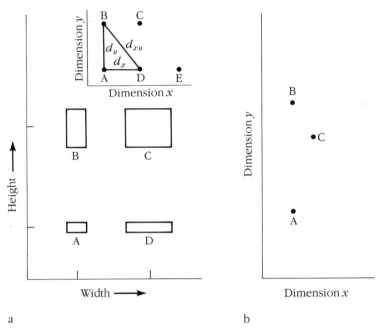

a   b

Figure 4.7 Graphical representation of (a) stimuli that vary along two dimensions, and (b) the type of stimulus triad used in the restricted classification task.

Dimensional combinations that are *separable* can exist independently of one another. Take, for example, this set of circular stimuli:

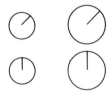

These stimuli vary along the dimensions of the size of the circle and the angle of the interior radius. These two dimensions are separable because it is possible to draw a circle of some specified size without having any interior radius present at all. Conversely, it is possible to make a set of line stimuli that vary with respect to the angle of tilt without drawing a circle around any of them. Many other pairs of dimensions are separable as well, including some, as we will see, that do not intuitively seem separable.

Although we define integrality and separability of stimulus dimensions in terms of the characteristics of the stimulus, Garner contends that the two types of combinations are processed in very different fashions. Integral stimuli are initially processed as single, whole, unanalyzed stimuli. Although we can see dimensional variations for such stimuli, we first process or apprehend integral stimuli as wholes and only later analyze them into their component dimensions. Stimuli having separable dimensions, however, are immediately seen as having independent dimensions. In this case the dimensions are apparent first, and do not result from the decomposition of the whole stimulus. If indeed the dimensional characteristics of the stimulus necessitate certain kinds of visual processing, then the two types of stimuli should yield very different patterns of results in certain experimental situations. Let us examine three types of experiments, all of which support Garner's analysis. These are (1) dissimilarity ratings, (2) restricted classification, and (3) speeded sorting.

Dissimilarity Ratings

One of the simplest ways to determine how dimensional structure influences a subject's processing of a set of stimuli, is to pose a dissimilarity rating task. The subject is shown all possible pairs of stimuli within the set being studied, and is asked to rate, say from 1 to 10, how different the two members of each pair appear to be. For example, two stimuli that appear very much alike are given low dissimilarity ratings, such as 1 or 2, while stimuli that appear very different are rated 8 or 9. Clearly, the dimensional structure of the stimuli will influence the subject's ratings, but we wish to know how information from two dimensions is combined to yield an overall assessment of differentness.

To understand how dimensional information might be combined, let us refer to Figure 4.7a and consider how dissimilarity ratings for the stimulus pairs (A,D), (A,B), and (B,D) might be generated. If subjects are asked to rate the dissimilarity between stimuli A and D, which share a common dimension along the x-axis (width), the rating will be a function of the distance between A and D along that axis. In the inset of Figure 4.7a this distance is denoted by d_x. Similarly, stimuli A and B differ only along the dimension depicted on the y-axis (height), and the dissimilarity rating should be a function of d_y. Finally, a dissimilarity rating for stimuli B and D should be a function of d_{xy}. The Pythagorean Theorem allows us to compute d_{xy} as a function of d_x and d_y:

$$d_{xy} = \sqrt{d_x^2 + d_y^2} \qquad (4.1)$$

If the distance between two points that differ on more than one dimension can be computed from unidimensional distances using equation 4.1, the distances are said to be described by a *Euclidean metric*. If perceived dissimilarities between stimuli are a function of the "psychological distance" between them, then dissimilarity ratings could also be governed by a Euclidean metric.

The Euclidean metric does accurately describe the dissimilarity ratings obtained with integral combinations of dimensions. Krantz and Tversky (1975) show that dissimilarity ratings between pairs of rectangles that differ in both height and width can be computed by using equation 4.1 to combine the dissimilarity ratings obtained from pairs that differ on only one dimension. Similar results are obtained for other integral combinations of dimensions; for example, Handel and Imai (1972) show that the saturation and brightness of a color are perceived integrally. In their dissimilarity rating experiment the x-dimension was the brightness of a colored form, and the mean dissimilarity rating for pairs of the type (A,D) was 5.7. The y-dimension was the saturation of the color, and the mean dissimilarity rating for (A,B) pairs also 5.7. Using equation 4.1 to compute the dissimilarity rating for (B,D) pairs according to a Euclidean metric, we would predict $\sqrt{[(5.7)^2 + (5.7)^2]} = 8.1$. This prediction is very close to the observed dissimilarity rating of 8.5 for the (B,D) pairs.

An alternative way of combining information from two dimensions is to sum the two factors. For example, if we wanted to determine the dissimilarity between B and D, we might first compute their difference along the x-axis, d_x, then compute their difference along the y-axis, d_y, and add the two distances. This additive method yields the formula:

$$d_{xy} = d_x + d_y \qquad (4.2)$$

Equation 4.2 is the characteristic way of computing distances between two points for situations that adhere to the *city-block metric*. The city-block metric takes its name from the way one must travel from one point to another in a big city. Although the shortest distance between point B and point D is a straight line, the presence of city buildings makes it impossible to walk diagonally through a city block. The only way to make the corner-to-corner trip is to walk along one street (i.e., traverse the distance along the x-axis), and then turn and walk to the destination along a perpendicular street (i.e., traverse the distance along the y-axis).

The city-block metric accurately describes the dissimilarity data obtained for separable pairs of dimensions. Burns et al. (1978), for example, had subjects give dissimilarity ratings for circles that varied in size and angle of radius. (A,D) ratings averaged 4.35 for the size dimension, and (A,B) ratings averaged 4.45 for the angle dimension. The observed rating of 7.8 for (B,D) pairs is much closer to the prediction of a city-block metric (8.8) than that of the Euclidean metric (6.3).

Shepard (1964) obtained dissimilarity ratings that are more clearly indicative of separability and a city-block metric for size and angle of radius. He compared ratings for two types of stimulus pairs. In one type of pair, for example, stimuli A and C, the two members differed on both the circle size and the angle dimensions. For the other type of pair, for example A and E in the inset of Figure 4.7a, the stimuli differed along only one dimension, but the difference along that dimension was twice that of the type (A,C) pair. If the dimensional dissimilarities were combined according to a Euclidean metric, C would be rated as more similar to A than would E. However, by the city-block metric, C and E are equally different from A. Shepard's data confirm that E and C are rated as equally dissimilar from A, thus confirming the city-block metric for this set of dimensions.

When we recall the definitions of integral and separable dimensions, we are not surprised to observe these differences in the metrics that describe dissimilarity ratings. To the extent that two dimensions are separable, differences between stimuli must be based on differences in the two dimensions independently. However, the straight-line, Euclidean distance between stimuli having an integral structure reflects the interdependence of the component dimensions.

Restricted Classification

A second processing task in which integral and separable dimensions yield qualitatively different patterns of data is the restricted classification task. The subject is shown three stimuli from a set that varies along two dimensions, and is asked to divide the triad into two classes. An illustration of the type of triad used in such an experiment is shown in Figure 4.7b. Each triad is composed of two stimuli, denoted by points A and B, that share value on one of the dimensions. If height and width are the two dimensions, then A and B might be rectangles of the same width. The third member of the triad, C, differs from A and B on both dimensions. However, C is chosen so that its direct-line distance from B is less than that from A.

How does the interaction of dimensional information during processing affect the subjects' groupings for such triads? If the dimensions are separable, as are size of circle and angle of radius, then the dimensional structure of the stimulus becomes immediately apparent, and the equivalence of A and B on one of the dimensions is obvious. Therefore subjects are most likely to put stimuli A and B together into one group, and leave stimulus C by itself. This type of grouping is called a *dimensional classification* because it is based on the fact that two of the stimuli are identical on one dimension.

However, if the dimensional nature of the stimuli is not immediately apparent to the subject, stimuli B and C will appear more similar to one another overall than either A and B or A and C. Thus if the separate dimensions are not important to the subject, he is likely to group B and C together, since they are very close, though not identical, on both dimensions; and A will be in a separate class. This grouping is called a *similarity classification* because the final classification is based on the overall similarity, or closeness, of the stimuli rather than on individual dimensions.

Obviously, the type of classification method used for triads depends on whether the stimulus structure is integral or separable. With separable dimensions the component dimensions are immediately apparent, and the majority of classifications should follow the dimensional pattern. Burns et al. (1978) report that for the separable dimensions of circle size and angle of radius 78 percent of the triads were classified dimensionally. Height and width of rectangles, however, are integral dimensions, and their dimensional structure is not immediately apparent. Thus it is not surprising that subjects made a similarity classification on 90 percent of the triads composed of these two dimensions (Shepp, Burns, and McDonough, 1980).

Speeded Sorting and Reaction Time

A third task that distinguishes between different types of dimensional combinations is one in which subjects must make rapid classification decisions about the stimuli based on one or the other of the component dimensions. One way to estimate the amount of time necessary to process information about each dimension is to use a card sorting task. In the easiest version of this task, the subject is given a shuffled deck of 32 cards to sort into two piles along one of the dimensions, while the other irrelevant, dimension is held constant. For example, if the stimulus set contained rectangles varying in height and width, we could give the subject a deck that contained 16 short, narrow rectangles (type A in Figure 4.7a) and 16 short, wide rectangles (type D). We could then measure the total amount of time it takes the subject to sort the narrow stimuli into one pile and the wide ones into another. Since all the stimuli are short in height, we would not expect the height dimension to differentially affect processing of the narrow and the wide stimuli.

We could also make up card decks containing only B and C stimuli—the height would still be constant (but at a different level) and the sort would again be based on width. Two analogous decks, one containing A and B stimuli and the other containing C and D stimuli, could be used to measure the subject's ability to discriminate along the height dimension when width is held constant. The speeds with which these sorts are made is indicative of how quickly the subject can process information from one dimension when the other dimension is not varied and cannot enter into each sorting decision. Such sorts serve as the *control sorts* for the experiment.

We can then assess the effect of variation along a second dimension by using two other types of sorting decks. In a *correlated sort,* variation in the irrelevant dimension is correlated with variation in the dimension along which the sort is made. A sample correlated sort deck for the rectangle stimuli would have 16 short, narrow stimuli (type A) and 16 tall, wide stimuli (type C). No matter whether the subject sorted according to height or width, the irrelevant dimensions would covary with the relevant one; a change in width accompanies a change in height and vice versa. Another correlated sort deck could contain type B and type D stimuli.

The second type of bidimensional variation occurs in an *orthogonal sort* deck. The subject is instructed to sort the cards according to one of the dimensions, and the second, irrelevant dimension is allowed to vary randomly. The deck is therefore composed of equal numbers of A, B, C, and D stimulus types. For this sort, it is impossible to predict which level of the relevant dimension will be present based on the level of the irrelevant dimension.

We can easily predict the behavior of integral and separable dimensions under each of these sorting conditions because the speed of the orthogonal and correlated sorts, relative to a control sort, will depend on how easily the subject can pay attention to the relevant dimensions. The sorting time will show, therefore, the extent to which selective attention is possible for integral and separable dimensions. We have already seen that the individual dimensions in the separable case are readily apparent to the subjects. Subjects have little difficulty in attending to one dimension while disregarding the other. They would easily ignore the random variation in the irrelevant dimension for an orthogonal sort, and the orthogonal sorts should take no longer than the control sorts. In the correlated condition, the irrelevant dimension reinforces information from the relevant. However, this extra information should not particularly help the subject because it is routinely separated and is likely to be ignored. Therefore correlated sorts for separable dimensions should also take the same amount of time as control sorts.

Our expectations change when we consider integral dimensions. In this case, the integral nature of the two dimensions—the fact that they cannot be immediately decomposed into individual dimensions—precludes the subject from easily ignoring information from the irrelevant dimension. In the correlated condition, the irrelevant information merely serves to reinforce, or help, the processing of the relevant information. Thus we would expect the correlated sort to be faster than the control sort. In the orthogonal condition, the fact that the subject cannot filter out the random information from the irrelevant dimension will hurt performance. That is, the subject must decompose the integral stimulus into its component dimensions before sorting the stimulus into the correct pile. Orthogonal sort times should therefore be slower than control sort times.

Sorting data on separable dimensions were obtained by Garner and Felfoldy (1970) using the circle size and the angle stimuli. As predicted, the sorting times for the three conditions were nearly uniform: 17.3, 16.5, and 17.3 seconds for the control, correlated, and orthogonal conditions respectively. (The slight improvement in the correlated condition was not statistically significant.) Felfoldy (1974) obtained the other pattern of results for the dimensions of height and width of rectangles using a slightly different procedure. Instead of giving the subjects a deck of cards to sort, Felfoldy displayed the stimuli one at a time and measured the subject's reaction time to correctly classify each stimulus into one of two categories based on one of the dimensions. Thus each trial was essentially the same as the sorting of an individual card in the sorting task. Felfoldy found that the mean classification time for a stimulus in a series that varied along only one dimension (the control condition) was 404.6 milliseconds. The means for the correlated and orthogonal series were 388.5 and 448.2 milliseconds. The data show both the facilitation for correlated series and the inhibition for orthogonal series that are expected for integral dimensional structures.

The Integral-Separable Continuum

As we have seen, integral and separable stimulus structures yield quite different patterns of results in three processing tasks. These results are summarized in Table 4.1. Integral stimulus structure produces dissimilarity ratings between pairs of stimuli that are best described by a Euclidean metric. In a graphical representation, the differences between the members of a pair can be represented by the straight-line distance between them in two-dimensional space. These straight-line distances also explain why integral stimuli produce similarity classification in the restricted classification task. In order for the subject to decide which two stimuli should be grouped together to the exclusion of a third, the subject merely has to decide which two are closest overall. Finally, stimuli with integral stimulus structure show facilitation with correlated dimensional variation and inhibition with orthogonal dimensional variation in sorting. All these results are expected since integral stimuli are those in which the individual dimensions are not immediately apprehended or perceived. They are thus processed in a manner determined jointly by the two dimensions and immediate selective attention to just one dimension is not possible.

Stimuli having separable stimulus structure show a different pattern of results. Such combinations produce dissimilarity ratings that conform to city-block distance computations, show dimensional groupings in the restricted classification task, and show neither facilitation with correlated variation nor inhibition with orthogonal variation in the speeded sorting task. Clearly the

Table 4.1 Summary of the effects of integral and separable dimensional structure in several processing tasks.

Visual Processing Task	Integral Structure	Separable Structure
Dissimilarity rating	Euclidean metric	City-block metric
Restricted classification	Similarity classifications	Dimensional classifications
Speeded sorting		
Correlated variation	Facilitation	No change
Orthogonal variation	Inhibition	No change

individual dimensions in a separable combination can be perceived immediately, and responses can easily be made on the basis of either dimension alone.

Integral and separable dimensions, however, are not the only possible characterizations of dimensional combinations. Some dimensional combinations behave like integral dimensions in some tasks while showing separable characteristics in others. A case in point are the dimensions of size and brightness. We can construct a set of gray, square stimuli that differ in their size and in the brightness of the shade of gray. We would intuitively expect these dimensions to behave integrally—after all, it is impossible to specify the brightness of a square without also giving it some particular size, and vice versa. The data, however, indicate otherwise. Both Burns et al. (1978) and Handel and Imai (1972) show that dissimilarity ratings for size and brightness stimuli are well described by a city-block metric.

In particular, Handel and Imai's data show that the average rating given for variation along the brightness dimension alone (d_x) and along the size dimension alone (d_y) are both 5.0. Stimuli that vary along both dimensions are rated at 9.7 (d_{xy}), a value that is very close to the city-block value of 10.0. The scaling data thus imply that these dimensions are perceived separably. This conclusion is further supported by Burns et al.'s (1978) restricted classification data, which show that 90 percent of the size and brightness triads are classified dimensionally. The sorting data, however, are ambiguous. Gottwald and Garner (1972) show that classification times are not inhibited when size and brightness are varied orthogonally, a result that favors separable structure. However, Biederman and Checkosky (1970) show that these dimensions do facilitate the correlated sort, a result favoring an integral structure.

These experiments suggest the inadequacy of a priori or logical reasoning in determining whether a pair of dimensions is integral or separable. In making this determination, we must rely less on logic than on the effect that the dimensional structure has on human information processing behavior. Regrettably, experimental data do not always yield an unambiguous answer, as in the case of size and brightness. This case led Garner (1974) to suggest that integrality and separability are merely endpoints of a continuuum along which pairs of dimensions may fall. Thus dimensional combinations need not be completely integral nor completely separable, but may be more or less one or the other.

Furthermore, some combinations may not fall on the integral-separable continuum at all. Garner (1976) calls one possible alternative *asymmetric separable*. Such a situation arises when one of a pair of dimensions that is otherwise separable is more salient and is easier for the subject to process. For example, consider the dimensions of circle size and angle of radius when the variation in circle size is large and noticeable, while the differences in angle among the stimuli are small and difficult to detect. Such stimuli would still yield city-block dissimilarity ratings and would yield dimensional restricted classifications.

However, some obvious anomalies would show up in the sorting task. In the control condition, the subject would find it easier to sort along the salient dimension than along the less obvious one. Second, the orthogonal sorting condition would exhibit asymmetrical inhibition. Since the subject would first notice circle size on each stimulus card, he could sort according to size with relatively little effect of orthogonal variation in the angle of radius. However, orthogonal variation in the salient dimension of circle size would slow the sorting times along the angle dimension. Finally, the sorting times in the correlated condition would be somewhat facilitated insofar as correlated variation of the salient size dimension would reinforce the less noticeable variations in angle, but not vice versa.

Attention to Configural Properties of Subparts

The work of Garner, and the experiments that followed from it, serve to emphasize the role of stimulus structure even for stimuli that have no obvious subparts. Garner provides a framework within which to analyze both the interactions between dimensions composing a stimulus and the problem of selective attention. There are, however, some resemblances between this analysis and the global-to-local analyses of stimuli with subparts. The most important commonality is that when viewing integrated wholes that comprise either subparts or individual dimensions we first focus our attention on the whole and only later direct it selectively to one subpart or dimension.

This similarity between Garner's approach to stimulus structure and some of the top-down approaches to stimulus configurations (for example, Palmer's) allows some of the tasks Garner used to support his analysis to be applied to the study of organized arrays of features or individual elements. Pomerantz and Garner (1973) used the card sorting task to examine the operation of selective attention to stimuli composed of right and left parentheses. The stimuli used in this experiment were the following:

$$\begin{array}{cc} ((&)(\\ \text{B} & \text{C} \\[6pt] () &)) \\ \text{A} & \text{D} \end{array}$$

Notice that each of these stimuli is composed of two elements, but that the variation among the four stimuli can be described bidimensionally. That is, stimuli A and B share a common left element, while C and D share a common, but different, left element. Similarly, B and C have the same right element, as do A and D. Since either parenthesis could exist without the other, we might expect these stimuli to have separable structure. However, comparisons between the sorting times for the control, correlated and orthogonal conditions disconfirm our expectation. Control and correlated sorts for these stimuli were nearly the same, 14.42 and 14.44 seconds per deck respectively. However, the orthogonal sort took much longer (16.99 seconds). Thus these stimuli do not exhibit facilitation for correlated element variation, and observers cannot easily attend to one element while filtering out the other.

Garner (1976) classifies dimensional structures that give this pattern of sorting results as *configural* stimuli. Perceptions of configural stimuli depend much less on the values of the individual dimensions than on the features that emerge from the arrangement as a whole. In the case of the parenthesis stimuli used by Pomerantz and Garner, subjects may be more likely to notice an emergent feature such as the distance between the individual elements rather than whether each one faces right or left. Noticing such emergent features does not make the correlated sort particularly easy, since when the deck is composed of stimuli B and D, the emergent feature of interelement distance remains constant and useless to classification. The orthogonal condition is difficult, however, because there are three interelement distances in this set of stimuli, and they do not perfectly predict classification.

Configural stimuli have also been studied using the rating and classification tasks. Lockhead and King (1977) show that configural stimuli are more easily grouped by similarity than by dimensional criteria. This result follows from the fact that emergent features of the configuration are more important than dimensional values. Moreover, the classification is based on Euclidean distances insofar as those distances reflect the emergent features of the configuration. Finally, Monahan and Lockhead's (1977) data indicate that dissimilarity ratings are also based on the configural features and are not necessarily described by any combination of distances along the original component dimensions.

The Gestalt principles enable us to make a good guess as to why pairs of parentheses, which would logically seem to be separable elements, are processed in a nonindependent way. Their physical closeness allows the Gestalt proximity principle to operate. Pomerantz and Schwaitzberg (1975) confirm this speculation by showing that the configural pattern of sorting results is obtained only when the elements are close enough to be grouped by proximity. Their subjects sorted several decks under the control, correlated, and orthogonal sort conditions. In some decks the two parenthesis elements were close to each other, while in other decks the two elements were farther apart. When the elements were close to each other the orthogonal sorts were more difficult than the control and correlated sorts, as found by Pomerantz and Garner. However, the orthogonal sorts became easier and easier as the distance between elements increased. The physical arrangement of the distant spacings probably made it easier to disregard the irrelevant and potentially interfering element.

SUMMARY

In this chapter we examined the ways in which component parts of a stimulus are combined into wholes. We also examined the effects various arrangements and combinations of components have on visual processing. In the earlier sections of the chapter, we saw that when individual elements or subparts can be organized into larger wholes, processing proceeds in a global-to-local fashion. Gestalt principles, such as those of proximity, closure, and similarity, describe the types of arrangements of elements that are used to organize these into wholes. In particular, the experiments by Navon and Palmer suggest that processing of global characteristics are compelling and that the presence of global features delays processing of more local properties.

In the last section of the chapter, we observed that many of these same processing principles may govern the perception of stimuli composed of dimensions rather than subparts. The component dimensions interact such that selective attention to individual dimensions is difficult in processing an integral structure, while easy in processing a separable structure.

Both organized, multipart arrays and combinational dimensional structures present some situations in which the properties of the stimulus itself force an organization onto both the overall configuration of the stimulus and visual processing of it. We were able to specify and predict the nature of such organization and its processing effects. Equally important, our discussion provided us with some idea of when individual elements and dimensions are not organized into larger structures. In this case, too, we were able to hypothesize how individual components and dimensions are processed.

SUGGESTED READING

Two collections of articles provide a more detailed discussion of many of the issues raised in this chapter: Kubovy and Pomerantz (1981) and Beardslee and Wertheimer (1958). The latter is recommended for readers interested in Gestalt psychology; the chapter "Principles of perceptual organization," by Wertheimer, is particularly helpful.

Perceiving Several Patterns at Once

We have seen that recognizing even the simplest type of pattern often requires complex processing operations. These operations involve the extraction of visual features, the organization of small visual components into whole objects, and the interactions among different parts or aspects of a single object. Although even simple pattern recognition requires all these processes, it obviously occurs very quickly and quite effortlessly. Pattern recognition is all the more amazing when we consider that we usually do it when there are many things to see and recognize at once. Yet we are still fast and accurate in our identifications of almost everything we see.

In this chapter we consider what happens in the first few fractions of a second after several patterns come into a person's view. We are interested in identifying the initial perceptual processes, discovering how so much visual information can be remembered, and discerning how recognition of any one object affects the recognition of the other objects in view. Many of the experiments that psychologists perform to study these questions use letters or digits as the individual objects in a stimulus. Therefore, many of our examples concern the identification of stimuli composed of several individual characters. Even this relatively small set of possible stimuli reveals a great deal about how people perceive large arrays of individual items.

ICONIC STORE

To begin to understand how people recognize several objects at once, let us examine an experiment done by Sperling (1960). Because Sperling wanted to know about the perceptual processes, rather than the memory processes, that people use to recognize patterns, he presented his stimuli using a *tachistoscope,* a device capable of displaying a stimulus for only a few milliseconds. That is, the array of items that the subject must identify is lit up and visible for only a few thousandths of a second. Using such short presentation intervals, Sperling planned to observe the results of his subjects' initial, fast, perceptual processing of the stimuli. Any nonperceptual processing that occurred later would not take place during so short a presentation and would therefore not influence the subjects' ability to report the stimulus elements.

Sperling was not the first researcher to study the perception of multi-element arrays using tachistoscopic presentations. Several psychologists interested in reading and perceptual phenomena performed similar experiments (see Erdman and Dodge, 1898; Cattell, 1885; Huey, 1908), and Sperling found the same results as earlier investigators. If the briefly presented stimulus array contained three or four letters, subjects could generally report all of them even if they were present for only 50 milliseconds. However, as the number of letters in the array was increased to 5, 6, 8, 9, 10, or even 12, subjects did not report any more of them correctly. No matter how many letters were presented to the subject, the average number reported correctly was only 4.3 letters. Taken at face value, this result suggests that there is a limit to the number of individual items we can recognize at once, and that this number is roughly four or five. This apparent limit on immediate perceptual recognition is called the *span of apprehension* (Woodworth and Schlosberg, 1954).

Everyday experience tells us that we often recognize more than four objects at once. For example, on entering someone's living room we immediately distinguish the chairs, the television, the couch, and the potted plants. If we could not do this quickly, we would have to take a great deal of time to assess the scene in order to avoid approaching and sitting down on a rhododendron. The puzzle presented by the span of apprehension is more understandable if we observe, as Sperling did, that even though we ask subjects to fully report "everything they see" from a brief exposure, they can really only report the things they remember. In fact, Sperling's subjects complained that they felt that they had seen much more than they were able to report, but that they couldn't remember everything they had seen. Apparently the tachistoscopic procedure is not entirely effective in eliminating the influence of such processes as memory, which occur after the initial perceptual pattern recognition.

The Partial-Report Procedure

Since Sperling wanted to know exactly how much visual information the subjects possessed immediately after the stimulus presentation, and not how much they could remember several seconds later, he developed the *partial-*

report procedure. The stimuli were arrays of letters arranged in rows. On many of the trials the letters were in three rows like this:

T D R
S R N
F Z R

The stimulus array was displayed for 50 milliseconds, and a dark field of view was shown after the letters were removed. Immediately after the letters were taken away, the subjects heard one of three tones. If the tone was high in pitch, the subject was supposed to report the top row. If the tone was low, the subject reported the bottom row, and if the tone was of medium pitch, the subject reported the middle row.

When the cueing tone was played immediately after the letters were taken away, subjects could report almost every letter in the row that had been signaled. This means that the subjects did see all the letters in the cued row. And since they did not know in advance which of the three rows they would have to report, we can infer that the subjects could also see all the letters in the other two rows as well. Therefore, immediately after the stimulus presentation, the subjects perceived virtually everything presented.

Even though it appears that almost all the stimulus elements are available to a subject at the end of the presentation interval, considerably less information is available if report is cued 150 milliseconds later. When the tone is thus delayed, subjects correctly report only about 2.4 letters from a row, which means that they have only about 7.2 of the 9 letters available. If the tone is delayed 500 milliseconds, report drops to about 2 letters per row, or a total of 6 from the whole display. With a 1-second delay, the subject has available no more letters with a cue tone than with ordinary full report.

This pattern of results suggests that when we present several items simultaneously and briefly, all the items are registered on the retina, and most information about them is initially available to the subject. In fact, subjects in these experiments report that the stimuli appear to persist for a fraction of a second after they are removed from the field of view. However, the visual information seems to decay rather rapidly, so that virtually no visual information remains even 1 second later. Sperling (1963) calls this persistence of visual information the "visual information store," a term synonymous with a more common name, the *iconic store* (from the Greek word *icon,* meaning "image").

Sperling reasons that because of the extremely short life of visual information in the iconic store, the subject's problem in a tachistoscopic report task is to read information from the iconic store and encode it into a more permanent form that can be remembered in short-term memory. The results from the full-report procedure suggest that the subject has time to encode only four or five items before the icon completely decays. However, if we cue the subject with a tone while the iconic image still exists, attention can be directed to the cued row, and the subject can recognize and read out almost the entire image before it disappears. The longer the cue is delayed, the worse is the iconic image of the cued row, and the less the icon helps the subject in responding. If the cue is delayed until after the iconic image completely disappears, the subject does no better than when asked to read out all the letters in the full-report procedure.

Masking in the Iconic Store

Sperling's experiment establishes the existence of a very short-term visual memory system that is capable of maintaining stimulus information for up to half a second or so. This system poses a problem for experiments of perceptual processing that use tachistoscopic methods because we cannot know just how long a subject has stimulus information available for pattern recognition processing. Certainly stimulus information is present as long as the stimulus itself is in view, but some or all of the information may remain in the iconic store longer. However, information in the iconic store can be influenced by visual masking. Using either backward masking or metacontrast—a special form of backward masking in which the target and mask do not overlap spatially—we can destroy the iconic image of a visual stimulus and thereby control the exact amount of time a stimulus is available for recognition.

Averbach and Sperling (1960) demonstrate one way in which information in the iconic store can be removed. In a variation of a partial-report experiment, they used a stimulus presentation condition in which the subject saw a bright, white field just before and just after the stimulus letters. The light pre- and postexposure fields served as masks to the stimulus letters (see Chapter 3). When the partial report tone occurred immediately after the stimulus, report accuracy was much worse with the light fields than with the dark pre- and postexposure fields. Moreover, when the tone was delayed by as little as half a second, report accuracy sank to the level of the span of apprehension. Clearly the two bright fields served to degrade the iconic image of the stimulus letters.

The fact that information in the iconic store can be erased or degraded permits us to accurately determine the duration of the iconic store. Averbach and Coriell (1961) asked subjects to report letters from a tachistoscopically presented array. Eight letters were arranged in two rows and were shown for 50 milliseconds. There were two conditions in the experiment. In one condition a bar marker appeared to cue the subject to report the letter that had appeared in one of the stimulus positions. The bar appeared above the critical location if the designated letter had been in the top row, below the location if the letter had been in the bottom row. The marker appeared anywhere from 100 milliseconds before to 500 milliseconds after the stimulus. In the other condition, the location to be reported by the subject was cued by a circle that ringed the cued location. Therefore each display had only one of the two possible cues shown here:

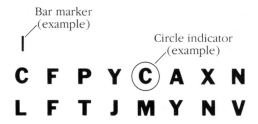

Figure 5.1 shows the percentage of letters an average subject reported correctly for the two cue conditions for different delays. For the bar marker, the results are very similar to Sperling's: Accuracy is quite high at short cue delays, but drops off quickly as the icon decays. By about 200 milliseconds performance seems to have leveled off at about 30 percent accuracy. Since the stimulus arrays contained 16 letters, the span of apprehension was about 4.8 letters, which is very similar to Sperling's estimate.

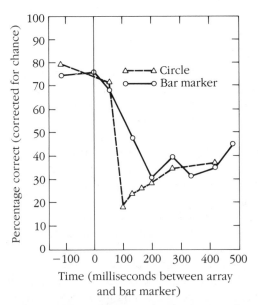

Figure 5.1 Data from the experiment by Averback and Coriell (1961) show a partial-report effect with a bar marker and a metacontrast effect with a circle marker. [Copyright 1961, American Telephone and Telegraph Company. Reprinted with permission.]

A very different result is obtained with the circle marker, though. At the 0-millisecond delay the circle marker is integrated into the display, and the designated letter appears to the subject to have been presented with a circle around it. Report accuracy is very high. When the circle marker is delayed by 200 milliseconds or more, it acts just like the bar marker: Report decreases to the span of apprehension level because the icon has faded away. However, at intermediate delays, when we would expect the subject to have some information available about the stimulus in the iconic store, performance with the circle marker is terrible. This is another example of a metacontrast in which the circle effectively erases all the visual information about the stimulus (see Chapter 3). To the subject it appears that the original stimulus position was presented as a blank space surrounded by a circle. Only after the icon has completely decayed, at 200 milliseconds, does the presence of the circle marker no longer have a masking effect, and report performance approximates the span of apprehension.

Reading Items from the Iconic Store

When several letters are presented simultaneously for a subject to recognize and read out of the iconic store, he must perform a pattern recognition process on each one. In some sense, then, he must mentally "scan" the array, but he cannot actually move his eyes across the array because the presentation time is much too short. We can determine how long it takes to read out each successive letter in the array and the order in which an array of letters is processed.

One way to determine how fast each letter in an array is scanned is to vary the amount of time between the stimulus and a succeeding masking field. Sperling (1963) did this by briefly presenting a row of two to six letters followed by a visual noise mask. Subjects needed 40 milliseconds to report the first letter correctly. After that, for each additional 10 milliseconds that passed before the mask, the subjects were able to report one additional letter correctly. This result suggests a scanning rate of about 10 milliseconds per letter. Of course had the arrays been much larger than six letters, the span of apprehension would have been seriously exceeded for most subjects. Then the number of letters correctly reported would not have increased no matter how much time elapsed before the mask was presented.

If a subject has only a limited amount of time to read out letters from iconic store before a mask appears, which letter will be processed first? Which will be processed next? There are several ways to extract features and perform pattern recognition of several items at once. One way is to start with the left-most item, process it until it is recognized, then proceed to the second letter, and so forth. This is an example of the *serial processing* strategy discussed in Chapter 3, but here entire letters, rather than features, are processed. The visual processing system might also recognize items serially, but have no set order in which to proceed. In this case, the fourth letter, for

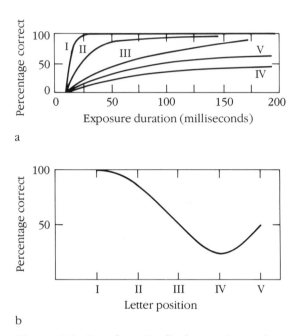

Figure 5.2 Data from Sperling's experiment show (a) how report accuracy for each of the five letter positions changes with exposure duration and (b) how accuracy varies across array positions at a 100-millisecond exposure. The first letter position is denoted by I, the second by II, and so on. [From Sperling, 1967.]

example, could be recognized first, followed by the second, then the fifth, and so forth. Or the system might perform pattern recognition on all the items at once by extracting features from all the letters simultaneously and processing all the letters at once. This strategy is, of course, *parallel processing* because equivalent, or parallel, operations are executed for all the items at the same time.

Later in this chapter we discuss ways to determine whether the visual information processing system operates serially or in parallel, and we evaluate some suggestions various psychologists offer about how parallel and serial systems might work. For now, however, we can use the tachistoscopic procedure to obtain a rough idea of the order in which letters are read out of iconic store. Figure 5.2a presents the percentage of letters correctly reported as a function of duration of exposure for arrays of five letters. The data are from one of Sperling's experiments and are represented by letter position. We see that even for very short exposure durations, accuracy on the first position is quite high and is virtually perfect once the stimulus is presented for 25 milliseconds or more. Report for the letter in position two is somewhat worse at short presentation durations but increases to almost

100 percent as exposure increases. The other three positions are never reported as well as the first two at any duration.

Notice in Figure 5.2a that letters in position five are reported better than letters in position four at every duration. This result suggests that scanning of items in the iconic store is not strictly left-to-right even though people normally read that way. Although every subject has his or her own preferred scanning order, the result shown in Figure 5.2a is quite typical of many subjects. That is, at any given exposure duration the accuracy of report across positions in the stimulus is a U-shaped function in which accuracy improves slightly on the last letter instead of declining steadily from left-to-right. This type of serial-position function is illustrated in Figure 5.2b.

Characteristics of the Iconic Store

We have observed that the iconic store is a very short-term visual memory capable of holding information for 200–500 milliseconds after the physical stimulus is removed from view. It also appears that even though the iconic image fades rapidly, it does initially contain information about virtually all the letters that appeared in the stimulus. Another important aspect of the iconic store is the nature of the information it contains. Many experiments show that the information in the iconic store is very similar in form to the actual physical stimulus and is *precategorical*. By precategorical we mean that the subject does not yet know the names of the characters present, and the subject cannot make decisions about the information in the icon on any basis other than physical characteristics.

One experiment that shows the precategorical nature of the iconic store was done by von Wright (1972). The method was like Sperling's except that the stimulus arrays contained two lines with four characters in each line. Of the eight characters displayed, four were letters and four were digits. Also, half the characters were written in black ink, and half in red ink. Partial report was always cued by one of two tones. In one of the partial-report conditions, the location condition, one tone signaled the subject to report the top line, and the other tone signaled report of the bottom line. In the color partial-report condition, one tone was used as a signal to report the red characters and the other tone signaled the black characters. Finally, in the category condition one tone was used to cue report for the letters and the other for the digits.

The accuracy of the subjects in each of these three partial-report conditions was compared to their accuracy in a full report. Remember that whenever information from the iconic store is used, partial report will be better than full report. Von Wright found that partial report was better than full report for the location and color conditions, but not for the category condition. This result implies that physical information about the letters, such as their position and their color, was present in the iconic store, but that information about their classification as a letter or digit was not present. Therefore, information in the iconic store must be precategorical.

Locus of the Iconic Store

The precategorical, sensory qualities of the iconic store suggest a similarity to other kinds of visual afterimages we commonly experience. For example, if we fatigue the retinal receptors responsible for detecting a certain color by staring at a colored object for a long time, we experience an afterimage of the complementary color if we look at a white piece of paper or shut our eyes. Or, if we are looking at a flashbulb when it goes off we continue to see a bright spot in front of our eyes for a long time. The iconic image is more like the flashbulb afterimage, because in both we continue to see the stimulus even after it goes away. One obvious difference between these two types of afterimages is that the iconic image is much shorter.

The analogy between an iconic image and a flashbulb afterimage suggests that both might be caused by the same sort of processing in the visual nervous system. In fact, both appear to be effects caused by neurons continuing to respond even after the actual stimulus disappears. To complete our description of the iconic store we need to know its location, that is, which neurons continue to respond for a few milliseconds after a stimulus vanishes.

One possibility is that receptor cells in the retina continue to pass impulses on to other parts of the visual information processing system after the stimulus vanishes. If the icon were caused by the firing of retinal cells, the icon store would have a *peripheral locus,* one peripheral to or outside the brain and the central nervous system. The other possibility is that the iconic image is caused by continued firing of cells in the visual cortex of the brain. If this were true the icon would have a *central locus.* Many experiments have been done to determine whether the icon is central or peripheral, but the answer is not yet clear. However, let us examine some of these experiments to see how psychologists try to discover the answer.

Turvey (1973) conducted a series of experiments that concern the central-peripheral question. To understand the logic of Turvey's experiments, recall the arrangement of the visual nervous system discussed in Chapter 2: Any stimulus appearing to the right of a central fixation point is transmitted to the left visual cortex, and any stimulus appearing to the left of center is transmitted to the right visual cortex. In Turvey's experiments the target stimulus was always a single letter that was shown for 4 milliseconds. It was followed by a blank *interstimulus interval* (ISI) of variable length and then by a masking field of visual noise containing many randomly placed dots. The random noise appeared for 1, 2, 3, 4, 5, 6, 8, 10, or 50 milliseconds. Turvey sought to determine how long the blank period between the target and the noise had to be in order for the iconic image of the letter to be good enough for the subject to identify the letter. He called this amount of time the *critical ISI* and measured it by gradually increasing the ISI in 2-millisecond steps from 0 to the interval at which subjects correctly identified the target in four consecutive trials. Turvey assumed that in cases where the mask erased the iconic persistence, the critical ISI would be well above 0. If, however, the noise did not mask the iconic image the subject would be able to identify the target even at very short ISI intervals, and the critical ISI would be close to 0.

Turvey carefully placed the target and the noise within the visual field of the subject in order to determine whether the mask's effect was a central or peripheral one. In one condition, the target and the noise mask were presented to the same part of the same eye, one after another. This presentation is called *monoptic* because both the target and the mask are shown to one eye. In the other condition, the *dichoptic* condition, the target was presented to one half of one eye by placing it far to the side of the subject's field of view. The mask in the dichoptic condition was presented to the other eye in such a way that the information was transmitted to the same side of the visual cortex as the target.

Thus if the icon is peripheral a monoptic presentation of target and mask would cause the mask to fall almost immediately on the retinal receptor cells that produce the iconic image, and the image would be destroyed. The subject then could identify the target correctly only if the ISI were lengthy. In the dichoptic presentation, the mask does not fall on the retinal receptor neurons and no critical ISI is necessary for subjects to identify the target. However, if the iconic store is central, then both the monoptically and the dichoptically presented masks will have an equal masking effect because both will affect the cortex, in which the iconic image is preserved. If the icon has a central locus, the critical ISI should be large for both monoptic and dichoptic presentations.

Figure 5.3 summarizes the results of Turvey's experiment with the random noise mask: Only the monoptic presentation of target and mask yielded large critical ISIs. This result would argue for a peripheral locus for the iconic store. However, Turvey did another similar experiment in which the masking field was a pattern mask instead of random noise. A *pattern mask* consists of randomly arranged, overlapping line segments and parts of letters. The results of this second experiment show that both monoptic and dichoptic presentations of the pattern mask cause significant masking effects. It seems that the locus of the iconic store depends on the type of mask used.

Several recent experiments attempted to determine the role of retinal receptors in producing the iconic image. Sakitt (1975) provides evidence that the icon results from activity of the rods. She did a partial-report experiment with a subject who was a *rod monochromat,* that is, a person who is completely color-blind because the cones do not function properly. Also, a rod monochromat cannot see in very bright light because the person's sole retinal receptor system, the rods, reaches a functional limit at very high light intensity. The subject in Sakitt's experiment was adapted to a very bright field and was then shown a tachistoscopic presentation of a letter array printed in a white even brighter than the background against which it appeared. Since the subject's rod system was incapable of detecting brightnesses greater than the background field, she could not see the letter array. However, if she closed her eyes after the stimulus flash, an iconic image of the letters

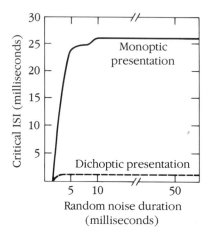

Figure 5.3 When Turvey used a random noise mask, monoptic presentation caused masking and a large rise in the critical interstimulus interval (ISI) needed to see the stimulus. Dichoptic presentation produced no masking. [From Turvey, 1973. Copyright 1973 by the American Psychological Association. Reprinted by permission of the publisher and the author.]

appeared briefly. Sakitt argued that the iconic image of the letters was present in the rod system of this subject, but that the subject could not see it with her eyes open because the rod system cannot differentially signal its presence when saturated by the brightness of the background. On the basis of these data Sakitt argues that the icon is caused by activity of the rods.

Adelson (1978) argues that the role of the rods is to increase the subjective duration of a visual stimulus, but that information in the cone system is responsible for the partial-report advantage. Adelson showed this by presenting letters of one color against a background field of a different color. Sometimes the two colors were ones that could be distinguished only by the cone system, sometimes only by the rod system, and sometimes by either system. When the eyes were adapted to the dark and only the cones could respond to the colors of the stimulus, partial report was just as good as when both the rods and the cones were involved. This result shows that some of the icon is in the cones as well as in the rods. To show that the role of the rods is to make the stimulus seem to appear for a longer period of time, Adelson had subjects adjust two auditory clicks to correspond to the apparent beginning and end of the stimulus. Subjects estimated the duration as longer when the stimuli could be detected by both the rods and cones than when by the cones alone.

The research on the locus of the iconic store is obviously inconclusive. We can say that whenever a stimulus falls on the retina the rods help make it seem as though the stimulus were present for longer than it actually was. The cones also contain information that aids the pattern recognition process and yields a partial-report effect. In fact, Adelson suggests that many of the effects that psychologists commonly attribute to the iconic store arise because the cones continue to send information to more central parts of the visual system after the stimulus disappears. This reasoning may explain why Turvey was able to find a central component to the iconic store. This central component to the icon, the component that can be masked by a pattern mask, plays an important role in the rest of this chapter because most of the experiments we discuss used pattern masks.

PROCESSING STIMULI IN THE ICONIC STORE
The Detection Method

The full-report and the partial-report methods used by Sperling to study the iconic store are just two of many methods devised to figure out how people recognize several stimuli at once. Although the partial-report method gives us useful data on the actual perception of stimuli because it reduces the role of memory, Estes (Estes and Taylor, 1964; Estes, 1972) developed a procedure called the *detection method* that completely eliminates the need for the subject to remember any of the stimulus letters.

In the detection method the subject is assigned two target letters at the beginning of the experiment. On each trial an array of letters is shown tachistoscopically, usually followed by a mask, and the subject must decide which of the two target letters appeared in the display. Each stimulus array contains one or the other of the critical letters but never both. For example, suppose the targets are B and F, and the stimulus display consists of the following:

$$
\begin{array}{cccc}
S & P & N & K \\
D & T & V & L \\
W & R & F & M \\
H & G & X & C \\
\end{array}
$$

The subject would indicate that the display contained an F. The response can be made by having the subject say which of the two targets occurred or by having the subject press one of two response buttons that correspond to the two target letters. The button-pressing response gives both accuracy data and the amount of time, or *latency,* it takes the subject to process the array and make a choice.

Notice that the detection procedure does not place the same types of demands on the subject as the full-report and the partial-report procedures do. Both the report tasks require the subject to have completed the pattern recognition process for every element reported. The subject must extract enough features from each stimulus letter to distinguish it from the other 25 letters of the alphabet. In a detection experiment, though, each letter in the stimulus must only be analyzed well enough to distinguish it from the two targets. In the case the stimulus W, for example, the subject need only see the diagonal line on the left to known that the stimulus is not a B or an F. The scanning process then eliminates the W as a possible target and proceeds to process another stimulus letter. Usually only a few feature tests are needed to distinguish a stimulus letter from a target. Therefore, although the subject may not have enough feature information to correctly identify any of the background letters in an array, he can make a correct detection. Results from the detection procedure do not reflect complete pattern recognition; rather, they reflect the processes that operate on information in the iconic store that might lead to pattern recognition.

Detection Experiment Results

Many of the results from detection experiments are similar to those obtained in full- or partial-report experiments. One of these similar results is known as the *array length effect*. Remember that on a full-report task subjects were 100 percent correct in their report for arrays of one or two letters, but that for larger arrays the number of letters correctly reported leveled off at the span of apprehension. Since the number of letters correct remained the same as the array lengthened, the percentage correct declined steadily. Quite simply, the array length effect is this decrease in perceptual performance as the number of elements in the stimulus array increases.

Estes and Taylor (1964, 1965) demonstrate that the array length effect occurs in the detection task as well. In one experiment they showed arrays of 8, 12, or 16 letters, and the percentages of correct detections were .78, .72, and .67 respectively. Estes and Wessel (1966) show that detection latencies increase as display sizes increase. On trials in which subjects correctly detected the critical letter, the latencies were 1220, 1253, and 1337 milliseconds for display sizes of 8, 12, and 16 characters. If these differences in response times seem small, remember that they measure the time needed to carry out processes that seem effortless and automatic in everyday life. During 100 milliseconds a great deal of processing takes place in the visual system.

The array length effect is common in perceptual experiments, but its presence and strength vary with two other important factors: confusability and retinal location. The confusability of letter stimuli that share many features is particularly important to performance in the detection task. If the distractors and the background letters are similar, subjects must make more feature tests on each background letter to distinguish it from the target letters. As expected, arrays containing letters that are confusable with the target letters cause many more detection errors (Estes, 1972). Also response latencies are larger for confusable arrays than for nonconfusable arrays (Estes, 1972).

However, the array length effect seems to occur only when the target letters and the background characters have some features in common. Estes (1972) shows that if the distractor elements are not letters but are matrices of dots, then subjects are very good at detecting which critical letter is present no matter how many background elements are displayed in the array. Furthermore, the decision latency is the same no matter how many of these unconfusable elements are presented.

The second factor that influences the array length effect is the place on the retina where the stimulus characters fall. The retinal receptors are not evenly distributed; rather the density of receptor units is highest near the fovea and decreases with distance from the fovea. As the number of characters in the array stimulus increases, more elements fall on the part of the retina that has relatively few receptors. Therefore, it is difficult to tell whether the array length effect is caused by the length of the array or by the retinal location of some of the stimulus characters. However, Estes (1972) found that detection of targets that fall on the outer portion of the retina is more difficult when the nearby background items are confusable with the targets than when they are not.

A final result obtained in detection experiments is that performance sometimes improves if the display includes more than one instance of the target letter. The number of duplicate, or redundant, critical elements affects both the probability of detection and the decision latency for confusable arrays but not for nonconfusable arrays. For example, Estes' (1972) data show that for confusable arrays the percentage of correct detections increases as the number of redundant critical elements in a display increases from one to four. Also decision latency decreases across the same range. For nonconfusable stimulus arrays detection rates are uniformly high and latencies are uniformly low no matter how many duplicate targets appeared.

It is easy to understand why Estes obtained these results. If a stimulus array contains dot matrices everywhere except where the target letter appears, the subject easily spots the target whether one, two, three, or four of them are present. However, if the background characters are all letters, it is much harder to find the target letter. If there are several target letters in the array the subject generally need scan through fewer background characters before coming upon one of the targets. The more duplicate target letters, the faster one of them will be found, and the more likely that one will be detected before the display fades from the iconic store.

Serial Versus Parallel Processing

Having seen which characteristics of an array of letters influence the ease of processing, we turn our consideration to how individual characters interact when several of them are being processed. Both the array length effect and the effects of confusability in the detection experiments suggest that the perceptual processing of individual characters is not completely independent; that is, recognition of one letter can be influenced by the letter's context.

One question about how individual elements interact is whether pattern recognition takes place serially or in parallel. The data from Sperling's experiment, shown in Figure 5.2a, are ambiguous on this question. A strictly serial process would require subjects to identify one letter with 100 percent accuracy before they proceed to the next one. However Figure 5.2a shows that subjects are sometimes able to report the letter in position two although inaccurate in their identification of the letter in position one. This result suggests that the recognition system is not completely serial. However, recognition performance in this experiment is not completely parallel either. A strict parallel system would treat every letter position equally and concurrently, which would produce the same recognition curve for each of the five positions. In the face of these ambiguous data, let us review the results of other experiments that tell us more about whether letters are recognized serially or in parallel.

Eriksen and Spencer's (1969) experiment suggests that items in the iconic store are not processed serially. The subject's task was to determine whether the target A appeared in an array comprising the background stimuli T and U. Each stimulus array contained 1, 3, 5, or 9 letters, and the array was presented one letter at a time for 2 milliseconds each. The subject fixated the center of the stimulus field, and the letters appeared around the circumference of an imaginary circle centered on the fixation point. Thus all the letters were equidistant from the fovea, and retinal position was eliminated as a possible influence on detection performance. In addition to varying the size of the stimulus array, Eriksen and Spencer also varied the time interval between each letter. The presentation interval was either 5, 15, or 30 milliseconds. The ability of the subjects to detect the target decreased as the number of items in the array increased, but the rate of presentation of the letters had no effect on performance. Had subjects been processing the letters in a strictly serial fashion, they should have done better as the presentation interval increased.

Shiffrin and Gardner (1972) made a more direct test of serial and parallel processing. Examples of the stimulus displays used are shown in Figure 5.4a. Shiffrin and Gardner used a detection task with T and F as targets. Four characters were shown on each trial and the array formed a square around the fixation point so that each letter fell at the same distance from the fovea. Two factors were varied in this experiment. On half the trials the background characters were the nonconfusable letter O, while on the other trials the background positions were filled by a character that was a visual hybrid of T and F. As Figure 5.4a shows, this hybrid was highly confusable with the two targets. The second factor that was varied was the presentation of the arrays. Figure 5.4b shows, on the simultaneous trials the four-character array was presented simultaneously, with a dot masking pattern appearing both before and after each array. On the sequential trials, the four-character array was presented one character at a time in a regular circular order. Masks again preceded and followed the set of four displays of the array.

Shiffrin and Gardner obtained one expected result and one unexpected one. As expected, the ability of the subjects to detect which target letter was present was significantly worse in the confusable arrays. We expect this result on the basis of Estes' experiment and on the basis of confusion matrix data for individual letters. However, Shiffrin and Gardner surprisingly found no difference between the simultaneous and the sequential presentation con-

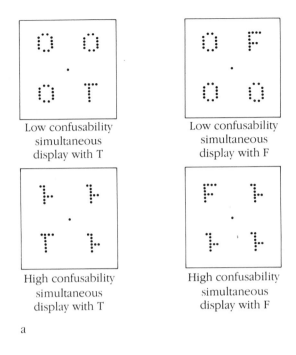

Low confusability
simultaneous
display with T

Low confusability
simultaneous
display with F

High confusability
simultaneous
display with T

High confusability
simultaneous
display with F

a

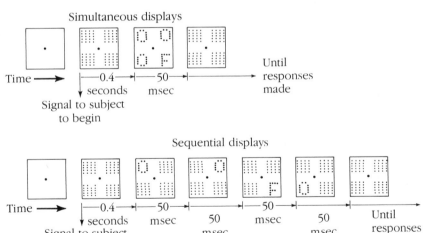

b

Figure 5.4 Shiffrin and Gardner's experimental procedure for determining whether scanning the iconic store occurs serially or in parallel: (a) sample stimulus displays; (b) simultaneous and sequential presentation conditions. In both conditions, the first display is the central fixation point, and the second and last displays are dot masking patterns. [From Shiffrin and Gardner, 1972. Copyright 1972 by the American Psychological Association. Reprinted by permission of the publisher and the author.]

ditions. Had serial processing been used, subjects would have performed better on the sequential condition because each character was present for 50 milliseconds in that condition, whereas the simultaneous condition allowed 50 milliseconds to process all four characters, or an average of only 12.5 milliseconds to process each.

Another example of parallel processing is offered by Shiffrin, McKay, and Shaffer (1976). They report that subjects could monitor 49 positions in a stimulus array for the presence or absence of a dot even when the stimulus duration was less than 50 milliseconds. Subjects could also monitor nine locations successfully when the stimuli were letters, and could report the letter that appeared in any of those locations with a display duration on the order of 20 milliseconds. This later result could be obtained from a serial processor only if less than 3 milliseconds were alloted to each letter in the array. Again the more likely conclusion is that such processing is parallel.

Although the results of the experiments seem to provide quite convincing evidence that iconic processing occurs in parallel, it is often difficult to distinguish parallel and serial processes. Townsend (1971, 1974) points out that serial and parallel systems may often yield the same set of results because for every parallel system that can process several characters in a certain amount of time, there is an equivalent serial system that could process the same number of characters in the same amount of time. Townsend shows that one cannot tell whether a set of experimentally obtained data comes from a serial or a parallel process unless one performs some very complicated data analysis. Such analytic methods are beyond the scope of this book. For our purposes the data suggest that read-out from the iconic store can be done by parallel processing. In the next section we examine the most successful models of how the iconic store is encoded, and these models make use of parallel processing.

MODELS OF VISUAL ENCODING

The data we have just discussed offer a relatively clear understanding of how information in the iconic store is processed, although psychologists do not yet agree on a single best theory of how all the necessary processes take place. The difficulty is that very different models often lead to nearly identical predictions about what should happen in any particular experiment. Also, models that differ from one another in several ways all seem equally reasonable. For instance, some models assume that the visual information processing system is limited in the amount of information that can be extracted from the iconic store or in the rate at which it can be processed. Other models assume that these processes are practically unlimited. Too, some attribute most of the experimental effects to feature detection and the distribution of receptor cells across the retina, others to the way that information is interpreted later on. Finally, some models assume that individual characters in the iconic store interact with each other during encoding, while others do not assume that. In this section we examine three models in detail and compare them using the three characteristics just discussed.

The Limited Capacity Model

Rumelhart (1970) made one of the first systemic attempts to specify how information is read out of the iconic store. Building on Sperling's results, Rumelhart assumes that the visual information from a multielement stimulus display is registered in the iconic store. As long as the stimulus is present the iconic image contains all the stimulus information. When the stimulus is turned off, the information about each position begins to decay in a fashion described by the partial-report curves of Sperling. The subject's problem is to extract enough visual information about each of the display locations to identify them before all the information decays. The subject thus must quickly extract the visual features of each of the characters. Because the feature extraction must be done so hurriedly, Rumelhart's model is sometimes referred to as the "rat race model."

According to Rumelhart, the feature extraction is not a strictly parallel process. At any one time, only one feature is extracted from the entire display, although it may be extracted from any of the letter positions. Thus, the first feature may be extracted from the third letter, the next feature from the first letter, and so forth. Clearly if only one letter is present, all the features will be extracted from it. If two letters are present, half the features identified from the whole stimulus will generally be from the first letter, and the other half from the second letter. As a rule, the more letters presented, the fewer the number of features that can be extracted from any one letter.

As each feature for a given position is identified, the information is passed along to a process that determines which letter is present in that position. This interpretation process is very similar to the pandemonium model (Chapter 3) in that each feature extracted increments a counter associated with a particular letter category. A criterion number of features is needed to make a positive identification of a letter, and whenever that criterion is met, the letter in a particular position is identified and reported. The criterion may vary depending on the conditions in the experiment. If all the letters look very much alike, the criterion value would be very high because a large number of features would be necessary to distinguish a letter from several that closely resemble it. However, if the letters in the experiment are not very confusable, only a few features are needed to distinguish them, and the feature criterion value will be low.

A final aspect of Rumelhart's model is the role of attention. It is assumed that subjects are most likely to extract features from those letter positions to which they are paying the most attention. For a linear array of characters, the most attention would probably be paid to the left-most character. More features would be extracted from this position, and the character would be identified correctly more often than characters in other positions. However, attention can be shifted by changing the experimental conditions. For instance, we might instruct a subject to start scanning from the right or to pay particular attention to the letter in the middle. The subject would then be most likely to extract features from the right-most or the middle letter and would identify these letters most accurately.

Rumelhart's model can account for many of the experimental results obtained by Sperling and Estes. The array length effect is explained by the proposition that as the number of letters in the stimulus increases, fewer features can be extracted from each one; therefore, the criterion number of features for identifying each letter is less likely to be met and thus correct reports for any given letter are few. The confusbility effects obtained by Estes are explained by adjustments in the feature criterion value, as we noted earlier. The superiority of partial report is explained by the attention shift caused by a poststimulus cue given before the stimulus has decayed from the iconic store. The cue causes the subject to shift attention to the designated letter or letters, and thus more features are extracted from these positions and report accuracy is much greater. Of course, if the cue comes too long after the stimulus, most of the useful information is gone and an attention shift does not help identification.

Although Rumelhart's model accounts for all these results, other experimental findings challenge this approach. First, Shiffrin and Gardner's results for simultaneous and sequential displays present a problem. The limited capacity for feature extraction in Rumelhart's model would certainly predict performance in the sequential presentation condition to surpass performance in the sequential presentation condition to surpass performance in the simultaneous condition because the sequential condition allows more time for extracting features from each of the letter positions and thus more letters would be likely to exceed criterion and be identified.

Second, Rumelhart's model would also predict that array length should affect detection performance for both confusable and unconfusable arrays. However, Estes obtained the array length effect only for confusable displays. Finally, Rumelhart's model would predict that in Eriksen and Spencer's experiment detection accuracy would improve with increases in the interval between successive letters for reasons similar to those used to derive the prediction for Shiffrin and Gardner's experiment. But the predicted result was not obtained in the experiment. Altogether, it does not appear that Rumelhart's model is entirely accurate. We return to it later to compare it with other models of iconic processing.

The Independent Channels Confusion Model

One of the major problems with Rumelhart's limited capacity model is that sequential feature extraction unrealistically limits processing. An alternative assumption is that each letter in an array is processed simultaneously with, and completely independently of, the others. This approach is taken by Gardner (1973) in his independent channels confusion (ICC) model.

The assumptions of the ICC model are simple. Features from each letter are extracted and interpreted by a separate processing mechanism, or channel, that operates independently of the mechanisms for the other letters. The number of channels available for recognizing letters always exceeds the number of letters in the stimulus unless the resolving power of the eye is exceeded. Thus, the ICC model assumes an unlimited processing capacity that is affected only by the duration of the stimulus.

Once the features are extracted from each letter position, each channel makes a best guess as to the identity of the letter in that position. These best guesses are called *endstates,* and they will be accurate if enough featural information is extracted from each position to effect a correct match with the memory representation of a letter. The number of features needed for a match depends on which letters can possibly occur in the experiment.

In the detection task there are three endstates for the position containing the critical letter, and three types of endstates for the other positions. For example, let us assume that the detection task has the targets B and F and that the display contains an F. The three endstates for the target position are: (1) the target position is correctly identified as an F; (2) the target position is incorrectly identified as a B; (3) the target position is incorrectly identified as some nontarget character. Similarly, the nontarget positions may be identified as an F or a B (both of which are wrong identifications), or some nontarget character.

The most important element of the ICC model is its decision rule. How will a subject respond in the detection task under various combinations of these endstates? Very simply, if the endstate for one or more positions yields a single target letter, and none of the other endstates dictates the other target, the subject will respond with the indicated target letter. Otherwise the subject will guess at random between the two target letters. Thus the subject will respond correctly if he correctly identifies the target location and does not erroneously judge any other position to contain the other possible target. The subject will also be correct if he wrongly judges one of the background letter positions to contain a target *and* wrongly judges the target position to contain a nontarget. In this second case the subject's response is correct, although entirely accidental. Similarly, the subject will be incorrect if he judges the target location to contain the incorrect target and none of the background positions to contain the correct target. The subject will also be wrong if he misidentifies the target letter as a background character and misidentifies one of the background positions as the incorrect target. Finally, if there is conflicting evidence from several positions, the subject makes a random guess between the two targets.

Most of the experimental results from the partial-report and detection masks are easily explained by Gardner's model. First, it easily explains why

Shiffrin and Gardner (1972) obtained equally good detection performance with simultaneous and sequential displays. Since the ICC model assumes that four simultaneous letters are processed just as quickly and accurately as each of four sequential letters, the model predicts no difference in accuracy between the conditions. Moreover, the model does not expect an increase in the time between successive letters to improve detection performance if the presentation time for each letter is long enough to produce nonconflicting endstates.

Finally, the effects of confusability and array size are accommodated by this model. For nonconfusable arrays, the correct endstates are easily reached for each position regardless of the size of the array. Therefore, the number of letters in the stimulus is not expected to significantly affect detection accuracy. However, a confusable array will lead to many wrong endstates because the pattern recognition mechanism cannot easily extract enough features to distinguish between confusable letters. The more confusable letters there are in the stimulus, the more likely that one of the background positions will be misidentified. Of course, when a background position is misidentified the chances of an incorrect response increase.

The ICC model resembles the pandemonium model. Their assumptions about feature extraction are identical except that the ICC model posits that featural analysis occurs for several letters at once. The main distinguishing feature between the two models is the decision rule that tells the subject what response to make once all the decision demons have decided which letters are present. The ICC model is less like Rumelhart's limited capacity model, however. Feature extraction is virtually unlimited in the former, while it is limited in the latter. Also, predictions regarding performance in the simultaneous and sequential conditions of a detection differ because the ICC model posits a decision rule that operates well after feature extraction. Thus, Rumelhart's model and Gardner's model represent two relatively extreme views of how information is read out of the iconic store.

The Interactive Channels Model

A third model of array recognition is able to predict both accuracy and response latencies in a variety of experiments. The interactive channels model, proposed by Estes (1972), ascribes to feature extraction a capacity that lies somewhere between Rumelhart's limited approach and Gardner's unlimited approach. Estes assumes that all letters can be recognized in parallel and that the processing system can extract features from all the letter positions at once. The features from each stimulus position are matched to memory representations of individual letters. However, the subject's ability to extract features is not unlimited. Recall that the greatest number of feature detectors lie near the fovea of the eye and that the density of detectors decreases with distance from the fovea. The interactive channels model assumes that a feature can be extracted only if there is a nearby, available feature detector. Moreover, any one feature detector can process only one letter in the array; a detector that is busy recognizing one letter is not available to help in the processing of a nearby letter.

The presence of a target letter in a detection experiment can be discerned in two ways. If the target falls on a region of the retina that has many feature detectors, all its features will be recognized and it will be recognized without error. In this case, it does not matter whether neighboring letters require detectors for the same features as the target nor does it matter how many letters are in the display. Estes calls this type of detection a *primary response*. These primary responses are completely accurate and can be made very quickly.

Under many circumstances, however, a brief display does not give the subject enough time or allow him sufficient detector resources to make a primary detection. However, the subject may still respond correctly. If the subject does not have enough feature information to positively identify a target, he will make a decision based on whatever featural information has been extracted from each stimulus position. These partial descriptions may not be entirely accurate, but the subject can scan the set of partial descriptions and try to match each one to the target letters. If a match is found the scan stops, and the subject responds. If no match is found the subject takes a guess at the end of the scan. Both the results of the matching process and the guessing can be either correct or incorrect. In either case, the response latencies are much longer than the times for primary responses. Detections made as the result of this scanning and decision process are called *secondary responses*. Secondary responses often lead to errors and always to slow response latencies.

By positing that different display conditions lead to different frequencies of primary responses, the interactive channels model can account for experimental results. First, remember that detection accuracy increases and response latencies decrease when the number of duplicate targets in an array is increased. The model predicts this result because the more target letters present, the greater the chances a target will fall on the fovea. Of course, the chances for a primary response also increase. Therefore, accuracy improves because there are more error-free primary responses, and latencies diminish because these responses are fast.

The model also explains why confusable arrays lead to slower and less accurate performance than nonconfusable arrays. In a confusable array the target letter is competing with nearby, similar letters for the same feature detectors. Thus the target is unlikely to be completely processed or detected with a primary response. If the target is detected at all, detection will probably result from a secondary response. Thus the number of errors will be quite high and the latencies will be long. However, in a nonconfusable array the target does not compete with the background letters for feature detectors. Detections are likely to result from primary responses and will be both fast and accurate.

The effects of array length can also be explained by this model. In a confusable array the more letters in the display, the more likely that the background letters compete with the target for detectors because many of the letters fall far enough from the fovea that there are not enough detectors to recognize every letter. Each additional letter in the array occupies scarce receptors at the periphery of the retina, and thus more secondary responses occur. Of course, the number of errors will then increase and the decision latencies will also increase with larger confusable arrays. In a nonconfusable array, the background letters and target do not compete for the same feature detectors no matter how many elements the array contains. Therefore most detections result from primary responses for all array sizes. Errors are few and their number does not vary with array size. Latencies are short and also do not vary with array size.

The interactive channels model predicts the sequential-serial presentation result, and interletter interval result, and the partial-report effect in much the same way as Gardner's independent channels confusion model. Performance on the simultaneous presentation condition in Shiffrin and Gardner's experiment is expected to equal that on the sequential condition because the four stimulus elements do not tax the feature detector system under either condition. In Eriksen and Spencer's experiment the sequential presentation of the letters allows the letters to be processed individually without competing for feature detectors. Therefore, many primary detections are made regardless of the period of time that elapses between the letters. Finally, partial-report superiority is attributed to the influence of limited short-term memory on the full report. It is therefore not a perceptual effect that concerns this model.

Summary

We can summarize and compare these models by referring to the criteria introduced earlier. While the limited capacity, the independent channels confusion, and the interactive channels models all assume that recognition of multielement stimuli takes place through feature extraction, they differ in their estimates of the capacity of the feature extraction process. Rumelhart posits the process to be limited to one feature at a time; Gardner assumes the process can handle unlimited numbers of letters; and Estes holds that the process is limited only by the distribution of detector units across the visual field.

These models also differ in their assumptions about whether letters can be processed independently. Of the three, only Estes' interactive channels model suggests that the processing of one letter influences the processing of other letters. Finally, the models propose different explanations of the decision process. All three models assume that an attempt is made to individually identify each letter by matching extracted features to representations of the letters in memory. In the limited capacity model an identification or a detection is made whenever the appropriate letter exceeds a criterion value. This process is a very passive one, since the system is assumed to wait for something to happen. In the interactive channels model some letters are identified as features mount up (primary responses), and some letters are identified by a special, active decision process (secondary responses). In the independent channels confusion model all letters are identified by an active decision process working on a set of tentative identifications from partial sets of features.

These three models all account for many experimental findings. However, the independent channels confusion model and the interactive channels model perform somewhat better by being able to explain the results of experiments that show parallel processing. As we noted at the beginning of this section, although the several models make very different assumptions about how processing occurs, all may be able to account for the same body of data.

ATTENTION AND SCANNING

We earlier referred briefly to attention, noting that some characters in an array are processed more accurately than others and that the ability to identify stimultaneous stimuli depends on how attention is divided among them. Attention is obviously related to serial and parallel processing, and experimental results show that subjects can pay attention to more than one object at a time. In our discussion of various theories, only Rumelhart's limited capacity model contained assumptions about how letter recognition might depend on attention. However, since his limited capacity model is inadequate in other respects, other attentional models are needed.

The principal issue regarding attention is illustrated by the serial-position curve in Figure 5.2b. Recall that Sperling said that letters could be read out of the iconic store at the rate of about one every 10 milliseconds up to the number in the span of apprehension. However, this serial-position curve in the figure shows that unequal attention is given to different positions in the same stimulus. The curve suggests that a great deal of attention is paid to the letters near the beginning and that more attention is paid to the last position than to the preceding one. In this section we examine scanning in the iconic store and consider how attention is allocated across elements in a display. We begin by investigating the factors that influence both the shape of the serial-position curve and the distribution of attention.

Experiments in Scanning

The shape of the serial-position curve for tachistoscopic report and detection depends on several factors besides the order of the stimuli in the array. One obvious factor is the position of the entire array on the retina of the eye. Wolford and Hollingsworth (1974b) presented subjects with nine-letter arrays for full report. Subjects were instructed to fixate the center of the stimulus field before the letters appeared. After a 200-millisecond presentation of the array, subjects reported the letters from left to right. Wolford and Hollingsworth varied the location of the strings. Some of the strings started far to the left of fixation so that all the letters appeared to the left of the fixation point. Others started just to the left of the fixation point, and the first few letters appeared near the fovea with several extending to the right of center. Still other stimuli began to the right of the fixation point and extended far into the periphery of the right visual field. Thus many of the displays fell largely on less sensitive portions of the retina.

Wolford and Hollingsworth's data are shown in Figure 5.5. Each curve in Figure 5.5a represents accuracy for strings starting at each of several places on the retina. Notice that no matter where the latter string starts, subjects are most accurate at reporting the letters near the fixation point because those letters fall on the very sensitive fovea. Accuracy drops off dramatically a few positions away from fixation.

The data are replotted in Figure 5.5b. In this graph each of the curves is a serial position curve for a different distance from the fixation point. The curve denoted by $r = 0$, for example, is for report of letters that fall at the fixation point. The curve denoted by $r = 1$ is for report of letters that fall one position to the right or left of fixation, and so forth. Notice that for all the retinal locations the left-to-right report procedure in this experiment yields a U-shaped curve. Subjects still seem to pay more attention to early items and the last item in a string even if the letters fall far from the fovea.

Wolford and Hollingsworth's data show that with left-to-right report the left-most letter of a string is reported best no matter where it falls on the retina. One way to reverse this effect is to ask subjects to report the letters from right-to-left. Estes and Wolford (1972) investigated the effect of report order by plotting serial-position curves for full report under both left-to-right and right-to-left scanning instructions. This experiment also varied the retinal position of the stimulus relative to the point of fixation.

Estes and Wolford also obtained U-shaped position curves. When subjects were asked to report the letters from left to right, the greatest accuracy was for the left-most one or two letters. Performance dropped off greatly for letters in the middle of the string, and the right one or two items were slightly better reported than the items in the middle. When report was made in a right-to-left order, accuracy was greatest for the one or two letters on the very right, with slightly better accuracy for items on the left than in the middle. These results suggest that order of report is the principle determinant of the serial-position curve, although it may have its effect by determining the order in which the elements are originally identified.

A third determinant of the serial-position curve is whether gaps appear in the stimulus letter string. Both Estes and Wolford (1971) and Wolford and Hollingsworth (1974a) show that in a full-report task the presence of a gap improves report accuracy for letters appearing on either side of it. For

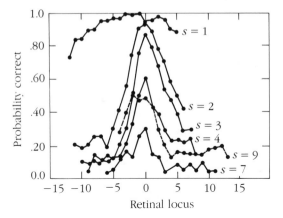

a

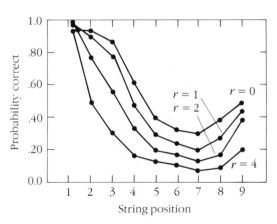

b

Figure 5.5 (a) Report accuracy in the experiment by Wolford and Hollingsworth is better near the point of fixation than at positions farther from the fovea. (b) When the data are plotted as a function of string position, all retinal locations show a U-shaped curve. [From Wolford and Hollingsworth, 1974b.]

example, suppose report accuracy for each position is measured for the following two letter strings:

DLNFHJTWR   (a)
DL   HJTWR   (b)

For string (a) we get the common serial position curve. For string (b) we can look at report performance particularly for the L and the H. These letters are both adjacent to a large space in (b) but not in (a). Accuracy of report is about 20 percent better for these two letters in situation (b) than in situation (a). However, the degree of improvement for these two letters depends on the direction of report. If report is from left to right, L will benefit more from the gap than will H. However, if report is from right to left, H will benefit more. It therefore appears that a gap following a letter helps its recognition more than a gap preceding it. Shaw (1969) shows that this same effect can also be obtained in an Estes-type detection task.

There are three possible explanations of why a gap might help to improve perceptual processing of a string of letters. First, letters in a string might tend to mask one another. Adjacent letters interfering with one another would explain at least part of the serial position curve. Under this explanation, letters at the ends of the stimulus, which have adjacent characters on only one side, would be subject to less masking and would be reported better. A gap in the stimulus string would help recognition of the two letters on either side of the gap because those letters would also have masking from only one side.

A second explanation is that the gap reduces competition for feature detectors, as is suggested by the interactive channels model. If this is the case, then the presence of a gap should be of more help when there is a shortage of available feature detectors, such as in processing stimuli near the periphery of the visual field. We would expect a gap near the periphery to help performance more than a gap near the center of the visual field. Wolford and Hollingsworth (1974a), however, show that a gap near the periphery actually produces less benefit than a gap centrally located. Moreover, both Shaw· (1969) and Harris, Shaw, and Bates (1979) show that the gap effect is exhibited when the gap is replaced by a black bar. This result argues against the lateral interference explanation because a black bar next to a letter should interfere with letter processing rather than facilitate it.

The positive effects of a black bar, however, are not strong evidence against a visual interference explanation for the serial position and gap effects because the bar does not contain fine contours that might interfere with letter processing. Also several visual benefits of gaps other than their failure to compete for feature detectors might facilitate processing, as we will see when we consider Wolford's perturbation model.

The third explanation of serial-position and gap effects is an attentional one. An attentional theory would argue that the end letters in a stimulus string are reported better because more attention can be paid to them. The first letter is processed before any others enter the system, and processing on the last letter is accurate because no further scanning diverts attention from its processing. The gap allows extra attention to be paid to the letters on either side of it; that is, a gap creates two substrings, and the letters on either side of the gap are the last and first items of the substrings. Before discussing how such a system could work, however, we will describe the perturbation model.

The Perturbation Model

The perturbation model is suggested by Wolford (1975) to account for report accuracy data for a full-report procedure. Several aspects of this model are similar to models we have already discussed. For example, Wolford says that letter processing requires the extraction of featural information. Extraction is carried out in a parallel and independent fashion, and ease of feature extraction depends on physical characteristics of the stimulus such as size, brightness, and retinal position. One additional assumption about featural extraction is that spaces are treated in the same manner as other characters. Featural information about their width and location must be coded.

Once visual information is extracted from the stimulus letters and spaces, each character must be identified. The individual characters are scanned in serial order, though the subject can control the order. In order to identify a character the subject must first separate the character to be recognized from the spaces around it. Then the group of features for that character is identified. The rule for deciding which letter is present depends on the task. For a full-report task, the subject identifies a letter if the feature group contains all the features for that letter and no others. For a detection task the subject may decide the target is present if one or two critical features are present in the feature group. Therefore the response time for identifying each individual letter depends on the task. Tasks that require the matching of only a few features require less time per letter than do tasks that require the matching of many or all the features for each letter.

The perturbation model gets its name from a further set of assumptions that describe how letters in a stimulus can be confused with one another. Other models assume that features extracted from the characters and spaces in a stimulus are maintained in their spatial order. However, the perturbation model says that changes, or perturbations, occur in the ordering of the visual features. The likelihood that a perturbation will occur is greater for letters in the periphery than in the fovea, and perturbation is more likely if the spaces between letters are small. In such cases subjects are uncertain about which letter position generated a particular feature, and their identifications of letters may be based on featural information obtained from nearby letters.

Wolford puts these assumptions into a quantitative form that allows him to express the probabilities of features extracted or perturbed as a function of retinal locus, surrounding spaces, and the like. Wolford used this quantitative model to design a computer simulation of how humans perform the full-report task. The simulation generates performance curves that are nearly indistinguishable from those in Figure 5.5a. He also performed a simulation that duplicates performance on stimuli with gaps.

The success of Wolford's perturbation model in predicting how human subjects will perform in a full-report task is good, though indirect, evidence in support of his perturbation assumptions. We can intuitively understand why these assumptions work. Human performance, according to Figure 5.5a, is worst for letters near the periphery. According to the perturbation model this is the location at which the fewest features are extracted and the most perturbations occur. Therefore errors should be common. Also, if perturbations are less likely when wide spaces occur between letters, then gaps should minimize perturbations for the letters on either side of them. This reasoning predicts the gap effects seen in experimental data. Finally, letters at each end of a stimulus string will be relatively less prone to perturbations because of the infinitely large spaces on either side of them. All in all, the perturbation model provides a good explanation of scanning results in full report.

The Overlapping Processes Model

An alternative explanation of scanning results in feature processing relies on attentional mechanisms. Shaw's overlapping processes model (Harris, Shaw, and Bates 1979; Shaw 1978) is designed to explain both accuracy and reaction time results for detection experiments in which subjects must search for target letters in displays with and without gaps.

Shaw argues that detection in a linear array is accomplished by the execution of several stages. A scanning mechanism is assumed to pass feature bundles to a subsequent encoding, or recognition process. The encoding stage decides which letter is present and passes the result to a comparator. At this stage, the recognized character is compared to each of the letters designated as possible targets. If a match is found, the whole process stops and a "yes" response is made. If no match is found, succeeding identified characters are passed on to the comparator until one matches or until the whole stimulus is processed. If the whole stimulus is processed without a match, a "no" response is made.

The model is called "overlapping" because the processing of several characters can overlap in time at each of the stages. To understand this overlap, consider the operation of the encoding stage. A strictly serial encoder would finish recognizing each letter before beginning the next one. It would allocate all its attention to just one letter at a time. A completely parallel encoder, however, would recognize all the stimulus letters at the same time. It would divide its attention among every letter in the stimulus. An overlapping encoder, in contrast, can work on several letters, but not all, at one time. When the scanner passes the first feature group to the encoding stage, all the resources of the encoding process are used to process this item. A little later the scanner passes on the second feature group. Of course, if the first letter is not yet completely recognized, the encoding stage will have to work on two letters at once and will have to divide its attention. The result is that processing of the first letter is now slower than it was before.

As more letters are scanned and passed to the encoding stage, several of the letters, but not all, must be processed by the encoder at once. Some letters will be closer to being fully recognized than others. Also, the more letters there are, the less attention is paid to any one of them. Therefore, it will take longer to recognize the first letter when other letters follow it than when it is presented alone. Eventually, of course, encoding of the first letter will be completed and this information will proceed to the comparator.

Figure 5.6 illustrates this model. Each bar represents the amount of time required to encode a single letter. The bottom bar represents the first letter, and processing on it starts when the stimulus is presented. Following the findings of Sperling (1963), a new item is begun every 10 milliseconds. Subsequent items take longer to process because they are encoded while the system is working on several other items. Therefore they are represented by bars that are longer than the bars for the beginning items. Finally, because more attention can be paid to letters that have nothing following them, the bars representing processing time for the last two items are shorter than that for the third item from the end.

The right ends of each of the bars in Figure 5.6 indicate the time at which each letter is fully encoded. In a detection task the information is passed on to the subsequent comparison and decision stages, but in a report task, these times represent the times at which the letters become available for report. Notice that these times almost exactly mimic the U-shaped accuracy curves for a serial-report task. The overlapping processes model accounts for the serial-report curve by positing that letters encoded the fastest are reported the best. Needless to say, the order of the bars would be reversed if right-to-left scanning instructions were given to the subject.

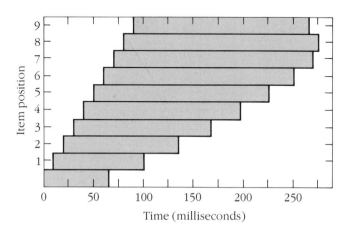

Figure 5.6 Schematic representation of Shaw's overlapping processes model shows that processing for each letter in a display begins at a different time and the rate of processing is determined by the number of other letters being processed at the same time. Each horizontal bar corresponds to the amount of encoding time required for each letter in the stimulus. [From Harris, Shaw, and Bates, 1979.]

The model also accounts for the effect of gaps on processing. Whenever a gap occurs, the scanner need not pass along any new character for encoding. During this break, relatively more attention than usual can be paid to the preceding item, which will be encoded faster and better. When the scanner then passes along the item following the gap, processing of this item is facilitated because the gap permitted earlier items to have been completed sooner than usual.

In total, then, the overlapping processes model seems to provide a very good account of the experimental data. It explains both reaction times and accuracy data for the serial-position curve, for the effects of different report orders, and for the effects of gaps. The model as we have described it, however, is not as clear in its explanation of differences in performance on letters in the periphery compared to the fovea of the retina. This variable is assumed to influence how attention during encoding is allocated. When several items are being encoded simultaneously, relatively more attention is assumed to be allocated to those letters whose features are clear. In short, more attention is paid to items from the fovea. In this way, more centrally located letters are processed more quickly and more accurately than letters from the periphery.

This model is based on a very different approach to that of the perturbation model, yet produces similar and equally adequate predictions. At present there is no satisfactory set of data that differentiates between the two approaches and we must await more evidence in order to decide which, if either, is correct.

The Category Effect

Before we discuss one other attentional model of visual processing, we must examine another set of experimental data. These data describe a phenomenon called the letter-digit phenomenon, or *category effect*. Briefly stated, the category effect states that the ease with which a subject can detect or recognize a letter or digit depends on what category the other items in the display fall into. It is easier to recognize a letter if the background items are digits than if they are letters. Similarly, it is easier to recognize a digit if the background items are letters than if they are other digits.

Jonides and Gleitman's (1972) experiment illustrates this effect using a detection task in which the subject had to search for a target character specified at the beginning of each trial. For half the subjects the target letter was always an A, a Z, or an O. For the other half the target digit was always a 2, a 4, or a 0. On some trials the target was contained in the briefly displayed stimulus array, and on other trials no target was present. Two other variables were used: the display size, which was either two, four, or six characters, and the category of the stimulus characters. Some displays contained characters of the same category as the target; others, characters of the other category.

Jonides and Gleitman measured the reaction times for detecting the targets in each of these conditions. When the target was embedded in an array of characters from the same category as the target, decision times increased with the size of the display. In contrast, when the target was in an array of characters from the other category, the decision times did not increase with increases in display size. Moreover, the detection times for between-category detections were faster than those for within-category detections. This effect was obtained even for the targets O and 0. Even though these two characters are similar, subjects told to search for the letter O detected it faster when the background contained digits; subjects told to search for the digit 0 detected it faster against a letter background than a digit background.

These results have some important implications for any stage model of perceptual recognition. Most conventional models of recognition from iconic store assume that information is gathered from low levels of processing before it is gathered from higher levels of processing. First comes featural information, then information about what character is present, and finally, determination of the character as a letter or a digit. This classic bottom-up processing assumes that naming the character necessarily precedes recognizing it as a letter or a digit.

The category effect implies the opposite, however. Reaction times for rejecting a background item of a different category are uniformly faster than times to identify and fully recognize a character from the same category. Moreover, the rejection of characters from the different category can be done in parallel since array size exhibited no effect on these decisions. Recognition of within-category items occurs interactively or in serial because of the array length effect for these displays. Moreover, the effects of within- and between-category latencies cannot be explained by the possibility that characters in one category are simply easier to recognize than characters in the other. The result is obtained no matter which category serves as the background as long as the other category provides the target. The implication of the category effect is therefore that a subject may recognize which category, letters or digits, a character is from before fully identifying the character itself. This implication exemplifies classic top-down processing.

How might we explain the category effect? Gleitman and Jonides (1976) suggest the *partial processing hypothesis*. They reason that between-category searches are easy because either fewer features are analyzed to make the between-category distinction or the features that distinguish the categories are somehow easier to detect. One implication of the partial processing hypothesis is that the background characters are less fully processed in the between-category condition than in the within-category condition. Gleitman and Jonides (1976) confirmed this implication in two ways. In one category effect experiment they used between- and within-category conditions. Sixteen unique arrays of characters were used in each condition, and each subject saw each stimulus array many times over the course of the experiment. When Gleitman and Jonides tested their subjects' memory for the 16 stimuli, the subjects in the between-category condition were very poor at recognizing the arrays they had seen, and the subjects in the within-category condition did much better. This result suggests that the within-category subjects more fully processed the stimuli.

In a second experiment Gleitman and Jonides supported the partial processing hypothesis by using a "catch trial" procedure. The method and logic of this experiment are as follows. If a subject in the between-category condition is only partially processing the stimulus array, then his task is to detect the presence of *any* letter or *any* digit, depending on which category the specified target comes from. Therefore, if the target for a particular between-category trial is a 2, then the subject need only find *any* digit in the array. Thus the subject in the between-category condition is likely to respond to any digit, rather than only to the 2.

The experiment consisted of a detection task for either a within- or a between-category condition. Subjects completed 192 trials, and on trial 193 a catch trial was presented. On this trial the subject was given the name of a target character, just as on all the previous trials. However, the display did not contain the target; rather, it contained another character from the same category. The subjects in the within-category condition were fully processing the characters in the display and therefore correctly decided that the target was not present. However, subjects in the between-category condition were partially processing the display and most made a false detection response to the incorrect category member.

Two potential difficulties confront the partial processing hypothesis. First, as noted earlier, the category effect can be obtained for the targets O and 0. Since search time thus depends on how the target is specified to the subject and on the nature of the background letters, the category effect does not result entirely from physical characteristics of the stimulus and background items. Instead it seems also to be a function of the instructions given to the subjects.

In this sense, the presence of the category effect depends on what we tell and lead the subjects to think is important. For example, Gleitman and Jonides (1978) show that the category effect depends on the subjects' forming a "mental set" for the target. In this experiment subjects were to search the displays for either one of two target characters. When both characters were from the same category, the standard category effect occurred when between- and within-category searches were compared. However, when one of the targets was a letter and the other a digit, latencies were the same no matter which of the two actually appeared in the display and no matter which category the background letters were from. Under these conditions, the subjects could no longer "pay attention" to the critical features that allow a category-based decision to be made about each background letter.

The second potential difficulty for the partial processing hypothesis is that it assumes that some visual features reliably distinguish letters from digits. If letters were always written in black ink and digits in red ink, such a feature, in this case ink color, would be easy to specify. However, such simple features as line segments and curves in various orientations appear in both digits and letters. Which one or two features would a subject look for to discover if a character were a digit or a letter? One possibility is the "direction" of a character: Characters such as M or 8 are symmetrical to a vertical median, while the digits 2, 3, 4, 7 and 9 for example, are generally agreed to face left. The only letter that faces left is J, while many letters, such as B, C, D, E, F, G, K, L, P, R, and S, appear to face the right; and only two digits, 5 and 6, face right. Although the direction a character faces is not a completely reliable indicator of its category, it is an example of the type of feature that could be used in partial processing.

Shiffrin and Schneider's Attentional Model

We have reviewed a number of experiments that use the detection or search procedure to discover how humans encode visual information from the iconic store. Some of these experiments, notably those in which we observed an array length effect, provide evidence of serial or interactive processing. Others, such as Shiffrin and Gardner's experiment and the category effect experiments, offer clear evidence of processing in parallel. Shiffrin and Schneider (Shiffrin and Schneider, 1977; Schneider and Shiffrin, 1977) suggest an attentional model to explain these varied results. Let us examine some additional data they collected to provide a basis for their model and then discuss the model itself.

Shiffrin and Schneider sought to determine which characteristics of detection experiments lead to limitations on attention that prevent the use of completely parallel and independent processes. The identification of these characteristics would enable them to predict when processing would be limited and when it would be unlimited. Their second goal was to determine, in both a qualitative and a quantitative way, how those task characteristics influence detection.

Schneider and Shiffrin (1977) chose a task that allowed them to vary several experimental conditions that they thought would influence processing. They selected the *multiple-frame detection task,* which combines elements of the visual search task used by Neisser (1963) with the detection procedures discussed in this chapter. As shown in Figure 5.7, the subject saw a rapid sequence of 20 frames on each trial. Each frame consisted of four positions, and each position had a digit, a letter, or a dot matrix. At the beginning of each trial, the subject was given a memory set of target items and was to search for the presence of any one of these items in the array sequence. Only one of the target items appeared on any trial, and it could appear in any frame except the first three or the last two. Whenever the subject detected a target he pressed a button to indicate this. If the subject

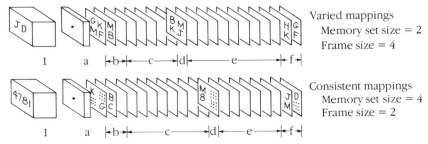

Varied mappings
Memory set size = 2
Frame size = 4

Consistent mappings
Memory set size = 4
Frame size = 2

Figure 5.7 The two detection conditions in Schneider and Shiffrin's experiments: the varied mapping condition and the consistent mapping condition. On each trial the sequence of events was: (1) presentation of the memory set; (a) a fixation point; (b) three dummy frames that never contain the target; (c) distractor frames; (d) frame containing the target; (e) more distractor frames; (f) dummy frames that never contain the target. [From Schneider and Shiffrin, 1977. Copyright 1977 by the American Psychological Association. Reprinted by permission of the publisher and the author.]

did not detect a target by the end of the sequence of frames he pushed a different button to signal no target. Half the trials contained targets and half did not.

Several characteristics of the experimental task were varied. The first was the duration of each frame, which varied from 40 to 800 milliseconds depending on particular combinations of the other experimental variables. The second variable was the size of the memory set of targets. On some trials the subject searched for a single target, and on other trials for any one of four target characters. Finally, frames contained either one, two, or four characters; any unused frame positions were filled with dot matrices.

The choice of these particular variables was based on the following rationale. Frame time is important because the ability of the subjects to fully encode the items depends on the amount of time they are given. The frame size manipulation was included to determine the extent to which the number of positions in an array influences parallel versus serial encoding. Finally, the number of possible targets was varied because it affects the comparison process needed to detect a target. Although it might be possible for a subject to compare in parallel a single target item to each of several spatial positions, this variable allowed the experimenters to determine whether several targets can also be compared in parallel.

The final variable in this experiment was the relationship between the characters in the distractor set and the characters in the memory set. A set of five items was chosen as possible distractors, and the nontarget characters were drawn from this set without duplication for each frame. In the *consistent mapping* condition the distractors were from one category (e.g., letters) and the memory set targets were from another category (e.g., digits). Thus the memory set items were never used as distractor items, and the distractor items were never used as memory set items. In the *varied mapping* condition, the distractors and targets were all letters or all digits. Memory set items on one trial could be distractor items on another trial and vice versa.

Figure 5.8 shows the results of this experiment, both the percentage of times the subjects correctly detected the presence of the target (hits) and the percentage of times the subjects indicated a detection when no target was shown (false alarms). Considering the varied mapping condition first, we see that all the variables have effects on the number of hits . Increasing the frame time clearly increases subjects' performance in detecting targets when they were present. Next, performance is decidedly worse for a large memory set than for a set of only one. Finally, the frame size significantly affects detection performance: Increasing the array length decreases the subjects' ability to detect the targets. Note that the effects of frame size and frame time are very similar to the results discussed earlier for the detection procedure in which all the targets and distractors are letters.

The consistent mapping condition yields a very different set of results. The only variable that seems to affect processing is frame time. The number of hits increases and the number of false alarms decreases when subjects are given more time to process each frame. However, neither frame size nor memory set size have any appreciable effect on the results. Apparently with consistent mapping subjects can simultaneously match in parallel several memory set items to all elements of a frame.

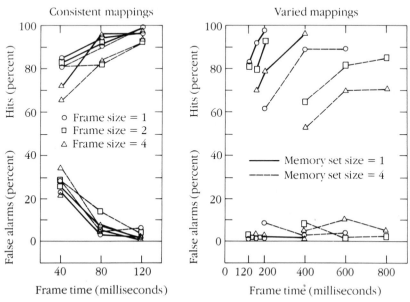

Figure 5.8 Results of Shiffrin and Schneider's experiments. Subjects in the varied mapping condition showed the effects of frame time, frame size, and memory set size. In the consistent mapping condition performance was affected only by frame time. [From Schneider and Shiffrin, 1977. Copyright 1977 by the American Psychological Association. Reprinted by permission of the publisher and the author.]

The very obvious differences between the varied mapping and the consistent mapping conditions suggest that a different type of processing occurs in each condition. Shiffrin and Schneider suggest that the varied mapping condition shows a *controlled search*. In controlled search each member of the memory set is compared individually and serially with each character of each frame until a match is found. In a standard detection or category effect experiment, a negative response will be made after all items in the display have been scanned. In the multiple-frame task, scanning of a new frame will begin even if scanning of the previous one is not yet completed. Time is needed to make each comparison, to retrieve another memory set item, and to switch attention from one frame to the next frame. For this type of processing the number of comparisons needed to detect a target increases with both memory set size and frame size; accuracy therefore is an inverse function of these two factors, as we observed in the data. Increased frame time should increase the likelihood of a subject detecting a target before the next frame appeared. Therefore the controlled search accounts for the results of the varied mapping condition.

In contrast to this controlled search process, subjects in the consistent mapping condition use *automatic detection*. In automatic detection an attentional process directs the scanning process to relevant locations or characters in the display. The attentional shift could result from partial processing of the kind suggested by Gleitman and Jonides. Thus the target items tend to "pop out" of the display, and the subject can dispense with a controlled search of irrelevant positions. Such an automatic process operates in parallel on all memory and frame items, and the effects of frame size and memory set size are eliminated. Automatic detection does not require attentional control by the subject.

Shiffrin and Schneider argue that automatic processes develop after a great deal of experience with particular sets of target and distractor items. In the case of the category effect, for example, adult subjects have developed an automatic method of distinguishing letters from digits after years of practice using controlled search. Visual representations of digits have so strongly built up associations with the digit category that only a very few features are sufficient to trigger a direct association between the features of any particular digit and the category itself. This automatic process allows subjects to categorize digits before they can identify them. An analogous argument applies to the visual features of letters and the category of letters.

The distinction between automatic and controlled processing drawn by Shiffrin and Schneider is based on perceptual learning, that is, the associations between a visual character and a category are learned through a great deal of practice using controlled search. If Shiffrin and Schneider's argument is correct, one ought to be able to "teach" a subject to automatically process artificial categories of visual stimuli. A detection procedure with characters that conform to arbitrarily defined categories would show a pattern of controlled processing at first. However, with enough practice, these two categories of characters should show automatic processing.

Schneider and Shiffrin tested this argument with an experiment in which consonants were arbitrarily divided into categories for use in a detection task. For example, one category might be the set G, M, F, and P, while the other category would consist of C, N, H, and D. Schneider and Shiffrin found that as long as the two categories were always consistently defined, subjects could learn the visual characteristics of the categories. After extensive training of thousands of trials with the categories, the subjects were able to carry out automatic detection with them under a consistent mapping condition.

To summarize, the manner in which items are scanned in the iconic store seems to depend on the type of attentional control needed to perform the task. When well-learned distinctions between classes of characters can be used, such as that between letters and digits, subjects can use automatic processes that require little or no attentional control, and such processing can occur in a parallel fashion. However, when distinctions between characters are not well learned, controlled search is necessary. Controlled search demands the attention of the subject, and occurs in a serial manner.

SUMMARY

In this chapter we explored how people recognize several visual stimuli presented at once. In doing so we focused on perceptual processes that occur half a second or so after a stimulus is shown. We first saw that information is stored in a temporary visual memory called the iconic store. The iconic store lasts only 250–300 milliseconds but is capable of registering nearly all the individual items presented. Information in the iconic store is susceptible to masking at both the peripheral and central levels, and iconic information at the central level is tremendously important for the subsequent recognition of the stimuli.

Then we considered how information is read out, or encoded, from the iconic store. Evidence from the detection procedure indicates that these processes depend on the confusability and number of items in the display, but that individual items are often processed in parallel. Three models of encoding—Rumelhart's limited capacity model, Gardner's independent channels confusion model, and Estes' interactive channels model—all account for much of the experimental data; the latter two a bit more adequately than the first. Interestingly enough, all three models are able to account for many of the same results even though they differ in their assumptions about processing capacity and the nature of the interactions between individual elements.

In the last section we examined attention and its effect on scanning multielement displays. Retinal position, direction of report, and the presence of gaps between adjacent elements all effect how subjects scan the contents of the iconic store in making their reports. Wolford's perturbation model accounts for the scanning results by positing an attentionally directed scanning process coupled with assumptions about the visual characteristics of the display. Shaw's overlapping processes model, however, relies strictly on attentional mechanisms to account for the same body of data just as effectively.

Finally, we examined Shiffrin and Schneider's attentional model in relation to results of detection experiments and to the category effect. The category effect refers to subjects' apparent ability to classify a character as a letter or a digit more easily than to fully identify it. Evidence suggests that subjects need only partially process a character in order to decide whether it is a letter or a digit, and that this partial processing allows an automatic detection response. An automatic process requires no attention on the part of the subject, operates in parallel, and is learned through experience in classifying the visual stimuli. When no automatic process exists for differentiating classes of stimuli, a controlled, serial process operates instead. In this way attention plays an important role in determining which stimuli are processed and how quickly they are processed.

SUGGESTED READING

A discussion of the research on iconic store is offered by Holding (1975) and by Coltheart (1975) in reply to Holding. For more information on the processing theories discussed in this chapter, the reader should consult the articles cited. Treisman and Gelade (1980) present an interesting synthesis of the organizational theories discussed in Chapter 4 in relation to the attentional and scanning issues discussed in this chapter.

_____ Chapter 6 _____

Word Recognition

In the previous chapter we examined letter processing as an example of how people process simple forms under limited viewing conditions. Experimental results such as the array length effect, confusability effects, and uncertainty about letter positions seem intuitively right when we consider that only a limited set of operations is necessary to process simple letters. However, most people spend more time reading words than identifying arrays of unrelated letters, and there are obvious differences between the two situations. For instance, we rarely experience difficulty in preventing letter features from becoming spatially perturbed. Also, for most people, visual confusions between letters in a word are minimal, and longer words such as *crocodile* are not necessarily more difficult to read than shorter words such as *crocus*.

In this chapter we examine several experimental results that indicate that reading letters in words is quite different from reading unrelated arrays of letters. We also discuss a variety of explanations for these differences. Because words are both visual patterns and conveyors of linguistic meaning, some experiments and theories concern general properties of the human visual information processing system, while others are based on properties of the English language. We begin by describing two experimental phenomena that illustrate the special properties of word processing.

EXPERIMENTAL FINDINGS
The Word Apprehension Effect

One of the most common results of tachistoscopic report experiments with letter strings is that subjects can report letters from a briefly exposed stimulus much more easily if those letters form a word than if they do not. This superiority for words, or *word apprehension effect,* was first reported nearly a century ago by Cattel (1885–1886). Cattel showed his subjects letter displays for 10 milliseconds and asked them to report as many letters as possible. At this short presentation interval subjects reported only four or five individual letters correctly if random letter strings were shown, but they reported three or four entire words if the display consisted of several actual words. Many other investigators have obtained this same result.

However, Cattel's full-report procedure does not permit us to conclude that his subjects actually saw the letters in the words more accurately. Perhaps their superior report for words resulted from better memory for them or from more accurate guessing. To understand the limitations of the full-report procedure, suppose that subjects actually see the letters in words and in random letter strings equally clearly. Therefore the subjects should be able to identify the letters in each type of stimulus with equal precision. However, in the full-report task the subject must not only identify each letter but also must remember the letters long enough to report them. Memory research shows that it is easier to remember a number of items for a few seconds if those items can be formed into a meaningful unit, or "chunk," such as a syllable or word (Miller, 1956). When reporting letters from a tachistoscopic display, subjects can easily chunk letters in a word but usually not letters in a random array. Therefore words are remembered more efficiently than random letters, and subjects may be able to report letters in words better because they simply remember them better.

Similarly, it is possible that the word apprehension effect might be caused by guessing rather than more perceptual factors. Suppose, again, that the letters in words and random strings are equally well perceived. However, not all the letters in either type of stimulus are necessarily identified with complete accuracy. What letter will the subject report in cases when the sensory information is not sufficient for a definite identification of a particular letter? Goldiamond and Hawkins (1958) show that even in the complete absence of visual information, subjects are biased in favor of guessing letters that form words. Given such a bias, subjects in a full-report task are more likely to guess correctly by chance when the stimulus is a word than when it is not. It is not clear whether such informed guessing is sufficient to account for the large differences in accuracy commonly found between words and random strings of letters. However, another type of tachistoscopic task allows us to discover whether the word apprehension effect is obtained when both sophisticated guessing and memory factors are ruled out.

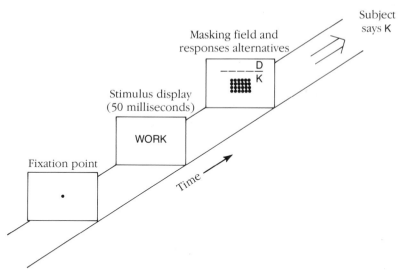

Figure 6.1 Subjects in Reicher's experiment fixated on a small black dot and then saw a briefly exposed four-letter string. The masking field that followed the stimulus showed two letters. The subject had to decide which had appeared in the designated position in the stimulus. [After Reicher, 1969.]

The decisive experiment on the word apprehension effect was originally carried out by Reicher (1969), and it has since been replicated by many others using the same type of method (e.g., Spoehr and Smith, 1975; Thompson and Massaro, 1973; Wheeler, 1970). Figure 6.1 shows the sequence of events for a trial in Reicher's experiment. Subjects first saw a briefly exposed four-letter string that was either a word, such as WORK, or a random rearrangement of such a string, such as ORWK, that was unpronounceable. After the brief exposure of the stimulus string, the subject saw a visual noise mask that covered the area where the stimulus had appeared. Also on the masking field were two, single-letter alternatives positioned such that one was above and one below one of four dashes in the corner of the masking field. Each dash represented one of the letter positions in the stimulus. Rather than reporting all the stimulus letters, the subject merely had to decide which of the two alternative letters had appeared in the cued position in the stimulus. On half the trials the correct alternative appeared above the dashes, and on the other half it appeared below.

The choice of alternatives for each position served to control the effect of guessing: Both the correct and incorrect alternative for the word stimuli formed a word when combined with the other three letters from the stimulus. In the example in Figure 6.1, notice that K, the correct alternative, and D, the incorrect alternative, both form words when added to the string

WOR—. Similarly, both alternatives for the random strings formed random strings when combined with the other three letters in the stimulus. Therefore, chance guessing alone would yield correct answers on about 50 percent of the trials in both conditions, and subjects could not guess more accurately on the words than on the random strings.

The influence of short-term memory is eliminated in this experiment in two ways. In half the experimental sessions, subjects were given the alternatives before the stimulus appeared (the pre-cue condition), while in the other sessions they received the alternatives after the stimulus presentation (no pre-cue). In the pre-cue condition subjects need not process the uncued positions; they do not have to remember the stimulus at all. Even without the pre-cue, memory demands are minimized because the subject has to report only one letter position. The other letters can be forgotten when the alternative choices appear immediately after the stimulus disappears.

Even with the memory and the guessing variables controlled, Reicher obtained a substantial word apprehension effect in both the pre-cue and the no pre-cue conditions. When the stimulus duration was set just above threshold, the average rate of errors in the pre-cue condition was .30 for random letter strings and only .17 for word strings. The corresponding values for the no pre-cue condition were .43 and .26. Superior accuracy in reporting letters from words must be caused by some processing mechanism that allows letters in words to be identified more readily than letters in random letter strings.

Approximation to English

One interesting aspect of the word apprehension effect is that superior report accuracy is not limited to words alone. Nonword letter strings are not all alike; they differ with respect to how "wordlike" they are. Some nonword strings, such as KEND, look very much like English words since they are easy to pronounce and follow all the spelling rules of English. Other nonword strings, such as NKDE, are not at all wordlike and cannot be pronounced. Nonword letter strings vary along a continuum of regularity from those that are very similar to real words to those that are completely irregular. The more regular a nonword is, the better the letters in it are reported in a tachistoscopic task.

An experiment that shows this correlation between report accuracy and regularity was carried out by Miller, Bruner, and Postman (1954). The stimuli in this experiment contained eight letters, and varied along a regularity continuum defined by approximation to English word structure. Zero-order approximations to English were chosen by randomly sampling letters from the alphabet such that each letter had an equal chance of occurring in a stimulus item (e.g., GFUJXZAQ). First-order approximations were constructed by sampling individual letters such that the probability of a letter being picked was proportional to its frequency in printed English (e.g.,

RSEMPOIN). Second-order approximations (e.g., ACOSUNST) were constructed such that letter pairs occurred in the stimuli with the same relative frequency with which they occur in English. Fourth-order approximations (e.g., PREVERAL) sampled four-letter sequences with probability equal to their probability in English. When stimuli of these four types were presented tachistoscopically, the greater the approximation to English, the better the subjects could report the letters.

The results we have considered so far suggest that very regular nonword letter strings are perceived like real English words. In fact, Baron and Thurston (1973) show that report accuracy in a tachistoscopic task is indistinguishable for real words and very regular nonwords. Thus the word apprehension effect must be caused by some processing mechanism that does not depend on whether the stimulus string is an actual English word. Rather, words and regular nonwords share some properties that allow perceptual processing to proceed easily for both. Later in this chapter we consider what kind of structure might be shared by these two types of stimuli, and we look at some mechanisms that would take advantage of such structure.

The Word-Letter Phenomenon

Reicher's (1969) experiment, which we discussed in the previous section, is important not only because it ruled out memory and guessing explanations of the word apprehension effect but also because it was the first experiment to show the unexpected finding that has come to be called the word-letter phenomenon. In addition to including four-letter words and random strings in his experiment, Reicher included a condition in which the stimulus was a single letter. Each single-letter trial was matched to a word and a nonword trial in the following way. Every time a word such as WORK was presented, there was a nonword trial such as ORWK, and a single-letter trial where the stimulus was simply K. The alternatives for each of these three trial types were $— — — \frac{D}{K}$. Of course, Reicher also included equal numbers of trials testing the other three letter positions in each word.

The array length effect, which we discussed in Chapter 5, would suggest that because the single-letter stimuli contain only one element, they should be more accurately reported than either of the other two stimulus types. However, Reicher found that subjects made just as many errors on the single-letter stimuli as they did on the nonwords in both the pre-cue and the no pre-cue conditions. Many fewer errors were made on the words. This counterintuitive finding, that it is easier to process a letter in the context of a word than one presented alone, is called the *word-letter phenomenon*. Many explanations have been offered to account for the word-letter phenomenon, and a consideration of several of these will highlight the special characteristics of word processing.

Wheeler (1970) was the first to suggest some causes of the word-letter phenomenon, and his experiment allowed several aspects of Reicher's original procedure to be ruled out as possible explanations. Wheeler considered three hypotheses: the interference hypothesis, the response bias hypothesis, and the word frequency hypothesis. In conjecturing the *interference hypothesis* Wheeler noted that Reicher's alternatives appeared at the same time as the mask. Some of Reicher's subjects reported difficulty in recognizing the stimuli when they also had to identify the alternative letters immediately after the stimuli disappeared. We would expect the amount of interference to be greatest for stimuli that were most physically similar to the alternatives. Such selective interference could occur if recognition of the alternatives interfered with the process of locating memory representations of the stimuli during pattern recognition. Thus recognition of the single-letter alternatives might have interfered more with the recognition of the single-letter stimuli than with the recognition of the words. Wheeler decided to test this explanation by introducing a delay between the onset of the mask and the appearance of the alternative letters.

The *response bias hypothesis* follows from the observation that Reicher did not equate the frequency of occurrence in English of the stimuli and the words formed by the incorrect alternative letters in the word condition. When guessing, subjects tend to guess letters that form words that occur frequently in English (Goldiamond and Hawkins, 1958). Therefore Reicher's subjects might have guessed incorrectly when the incorrect alternatives formed a higher-frequency word than the stimulus word itself. Wheeler corrected for this by presenting both the base word (e.g., WORM) and its alternative form (e.g., WORD) as stimuli in the word condition, and tested both with the same alternatives. If subjects do poorly on WORM because it is a low-frequency word, then they will do much better on WORD because it is a higher-frequency word, and the two effects will cancel out.

The third possible explanation of the word-letter phenomenon, the *word frequency hypothesis,* is based on the common finding that words that appear in printed English more frequently are easier to recognize than low-frequency words (Pierce, 1963). In the present experiment, suppose that both words and single letters are processed by subjects as if they were words. Since single letters are usually not words in English, subjects could have done better in recognizing words because they occur as words more frequently in English. Wheeler therefore included the single-letter words I and A as stimuli to see if they functioned differently from other single-letter stimuli by virtue of their status as words.

Wheeler's results show that the word-letter phenomenon occurs even with delays as long as 2 seconds between the stimulus and the alternatives. This finding rules out the interference hypothesis. Next, Wheeler eliminated the response bias hypothesis because the word-letter phenomenon appeared in all conditions of the experiment even though word frequency was controlled as described earlier. Finally, report accuracy for the letters I and A was 14 percent better when they were embedded in four-letter words than when they appeared alone. Thus Wheeler also dismissed the word frequency hypothesis.

Since the word-letter phenomenon is robust, and it cannot be attributed to obvious procedural causes, we must look for properties of the stimuli themselves that might lead to differences in processing. One such property was observed by Mezrich (1973) when he attempted to replicate the word-letter phenomenon. In his preliminary work, Mezrich's subjects reported that they were not choosing the correct alternative letter in the same way for the word and single-letter stimuli. Subjects attempted to remember single-letter stimuli as bundles of visual features that could be matched to the visual features of the alternatives. Words, however, were processed as verbal wholes. Subjects apparently named the words silently to themselves and then picked the alternative consistent with the word they had named. Of course, if a visual mask is presented immediately after the stimulus it is very difficult for subjects to maintain the physical feature bundles for single letters. The word-letter phenomenon could result from the inability of subjects to remember the features of single letters long enough to pick the correct alternative. Mezrich's data show that if subjects are left to their own devices, report for letters in words is better than for letters alone, just as Reicher and Wheeler showed. However, if subjects are forced to pronounce all the stimuli aloud before choosing between two alternatives for one of the positions, report accuracy on single-letter stimuli increases substantially and is even better than accuracy on words.

Mezrich's experiment shows that one possible cause of the word-letter phenomenon is an inefficient visual processing strategy adopted by subjects for the single-letter stimuli. Additional support for this position is offered by Johnston and McClelland (1973), who compared tachistoscopic report accuracy for single letters and four-letter words. Their data show a substantial word-letter phenomenon when a mask immediately followed the stimulus. However, single letters were actually reported better than words when the poststimulus field was plain white. In this second situation, subjects who adopted a visual feature matching strategy for the single letters did not have to contend with interference from a pattern mask. However, these results cannot help us understand why subjects can so easily treat words as verbal wholes.

REDUNDANCY AND WORD RECOGNITION
Spatial Frequency Redundancy

One of the major reasons that words and regular nonwords are easily treated as wholes is that they possess the property of *redundancy*. By redundancy we mean that the letters in words are somewhat, though not completely, predictable. That is, if we know which letters are present in a few of the letter positions, we can make better-than-chance guesses about the rest of the letters. There are at least two ways in which the letters in words are redundant. First, there is *spatial frequency* or *positional redundancy* (not to be confused with the type of spatial frequency discussed in Chapter 2). Some letters are more likely than others to occur in certain spatial positions in an English word. For example, many more words begin with T than with K. If you were to randomly guess a letter in a stimulus string you would be correct on only 1 of every 26 guesses. But if you were to guess the first letter of an English word, you could use your knowledge of spatial frequency to guess T more often than K, and you would be correct on more than 1 of every 26 guesses.

Mason (1975) shows that spatial frequency redundancy helps good readers process strings of letters. Her experimental task was one in which subjects had to search through a single, six-letter string for a predesignated target letter. Three types of letter strings were used. One set of strings were words (W), and these items all had very high spatial frequency redundancy. Mason computed redundancy using norms collected by Mayzner and Tresselt (1965) that give the frequency with which letters occur in each position of words in English. The second type of letter string consisted of nonword rearrangements of the letters from each word item, and these nonwords had high spatial frequency redundancy (NW-H). The third set of letter strings were rearrangements of word items that formed nonwords with low spatial frequency redundancy (NW-L). On half the trials the target letter appeared in the background string, and the subject was to press the yes response key. Thus, a subject might be asked to search for the letter *s* in either the word seldom (W), the nonword somled (NW-H), or the nonword sdelmo (NW-L). On catch trials the target letter did not appear in the stimulus, and the subject was to press the no key.

The important data from Mason's experiment are the decision times for the catch trials. In these trials the subject had to read the entire string before making a response. Mason's good readers were able to take advantage of spatial frequency redundancy, and they responded to both the words (W) and the nonword high-redundancy (NW-H) items faster than to the low-redundancy nonwords (NW-L). Mason notes that regular nonwords and English words share the property of high spatial frequency redundancy, which may help explain why both types of letter strings are recognized quickly and accurately.

Sequential Redundancy

The second type of redundancy is called *sequential redundancy*, which refers to the fact that some letters are much more likely to follow other letters in written English. Several examples will make this clearer. Suppose you know that the first letter of a word stimulus is M and you wish to predict what the next letter will be. If you guess at random you have 1 chance in 26 of being correct. However, in English words only certain letters follow an initial M: A, E, I, N, O, U, and Y. If you limit your prediction to one of these letters your chances of being correct go up to 1 in 7. Similarly, if you know that the last two letters of a three-letter word are —CT, the only choice for the first position is A. In this case sequential redundancy allows you to perfectly predict the missing letter.

Sequential redundancy has also been shown to be an important factor in recognizing letter strings, and several studies show that it may well account for the word-letter phenomenon. We know, for example, that Reicher's and Wheeler's procedure for selecting alternatives did not adequately eliminate the effects of redundancy in the processing of words. Two experiments by Thompson and Massaro (1973) show why this is so. In their first experiment Thompson and Massaro followed Wheeler's procedure in presenting four-letter words and single-letter stimuli tachistoscopically. They also used single-letter alternatives on the poststimulus masking field. On some of the trials the alternatives were visually similar to the correct alternative, while on other trials the alternatives were visually distinct. For example, if the first position of the stimulus word REAL was cued, the alternatives in the similar condition were $\frac{R}{P}$——— , while in the distinct condition they were $\frac{R}{M}$———.

Thompson and Massaro found a statistically significant 9 percent accuracy advantage for letters in words, a finding which replicates the word-letter phenomenon. However, they found no effect of visual similarity of alternatives. This result is surprising because we would expect that if the subject had only partial information about the cued letter on some trials, he would have more difficulty picking the correct alternative when the two alternatives were very similar. With distinct alternatives, even partial information about the cued letter would allow the subject to distinguish the correct letter from the incorrect distinct alternative. Since subjects were equally able to choose the correct alternative in the similar and distinct conditions, Thompson and Massaro conclude that subjects have completely identified each stimulus letter before the alternatives appear. Thus, if equally predictable alternatives appear after the stimulus they come too late to eliminate the effects of sequential redundancy in recognizing words.

The only way to eliminate the effects of sequential redundancy in word recognition is to have the subject know the alternatives while the stimulus is being processed. Thompson and Massaro carried out a second experiment in which the subjects had to decide on every trial which of the letters P, R, C, or G occurred. This is basically a detection task with four target letters. On half the trials one of these letters appeared in the middle position of the three-letter string A—E, a context in which all four alternatives form a word. On the other trials, one of the four letters was presented alone. Since the subjects knew the alternatives during the stimulus presentation on every trial, words no longer had a sequential redundancy advantage over single letters. Under these conditions the word-letter phenomenon was reversed, and single letters were reported with 11 percent better accuracy than words. However, accuracy on words was still better than on nonwords. In addition, on error trials subjects were significantly more likely to respond with a visually similar alternative letter than with a visually distinct alternative.

Positional Uncertainty

Thompson and Massaro's results are among several that show that the word-letter phenomenon can be eliminated if a detection procedure is used and the subject knows the possible alternatives at the time he is processing the stimulus array. Similar results in Estes' laboratory (Bjork and Estes, 1971; Estes, Bjork, and Skaar, 1974) led him to propose a theoretical account of word recognition that clearly specifies the role of redundancy in producing superior report accuracy on words (Estes, 1975a, 1975b). The rationale for the model comes from the experimental results discussed thus far in this chapter and from the results of an additional experiment Estes (1975a) carried out. The stimuli for this experiment are shown in Table 6.1. In this experiment subjects were shown a randomly ordered sequence of word, random nonword, and single-letter stimuli for 50 milliseconds each. A row of dollar signs was used as both a preexposure and a postexposure pattern mask. The stimuli in the single-letter condition contained number signs in the nonstimulus positions occupied by letters in the other stimulus types. The three types of stimuli were matched in the same way Reicher matched his stimuli, and subjects were cued to report the letter from one of the positions after the stimulus presentation. No alternative letters were presented for the cued locations, and subjects could pick any letter of the alphabet they wanted.

However, on one-quarter of the trials, designated as "L-R" trials, the cued stimulus letter had been either an L or an R. On word trials either an L or an R would have produced a word (e.g., CO—D), and on nonword trials either letter would have produced a nonword (e.g., OD—C). Thus, for the L-R trials the same stimulus constraints held as in Reicher's and Wheeler's experiments. Estes found that both the word apprehension effect and the word-letter phenomenon appeared on the L-R trials. The accuracy scores for the three types of stimuli are shown in Table 6.1.

To determine how redundancy exerts contextual effects, Estes examined the types of errors made by subjects on these L-R trials. First he compared errors on word and single-letter trials. Subjects made L/R confusions (incorrectly reported L for R or vice versa) on only 1 percent of the single-letter trials and on only 2 percent of the word trials; this difference between the two conditions was insignificant. Omission errors, in which subjects failed to report the cued letter, occurred on 17 percent of the single-letter trials and on only 5 percent of the word trials; this difference is significant. Finally, subjects made intrusion errors (responded with something other than L or

Table 6.1 Subjects in Estes' (1975b) experiment saw briefly exposed single letters, words, or nonwords. Rows of dollar signs were used as masks, and number signs were used to fill empty positions for single-letter stimuli. When asked to identify the critical letter L or R, subjects did better on the words than the nonwords.

Condition	Display	Percentage Correct
Single letter	$ $ $ $ # # L # $ $ $ $	59
Word	$ $ $ $ C O L D $ $ $ $	69
Nonword	$ $ $ $ O D L C $ $ $ $	63

R) on 23 percent of the single-letter trials and on 18 percent of the word trials, an insignificant difference. Clearly, most of the difference in report accuracy between words and single letters results from the inability of subjects to respond at all on many of the single-letter trials.

A similar comparison was made for the types of errors made on word and nonword trials. Subjects made equal numbers of L/R confusions, omission errors, and other intrusion errors for the two types of stimuli, but many more transposition errors were made with the nonword stimuli; transposition errors are those in which a subject responded to a cue with a letter from another position in the stimulus.

What processes could account for this pattern of errors and for both the word apprehension effect and the word-letter phenomenon? Estes claims that the main reason that subjects make mistakes in experiments like this is that they experience *positional uncertainty* about the visual cues; that is, subjects are not always able to keep track of which letter positions are generating the visual features being extracted from each letter. Therefore, subjects may not be able to respond with a letter that is consistent with the features extracted from the cued position. Instead, they may make responses that are consistent with information from nearby letter positions. The role of word context is to help the subject organize and retain positional information.

The claim that visual features are subject to positional uncertainty is based on some experimental results. For instance, in Chapter 5 we saw how feature perturbation explains errors that occur when subjects are asked to recognize arrays of unrelated letters. Also, Bjork and Estes (1971) show that subjects are likely to make errors of one or more positions if they are asked to give the location of a prespecified target letter after a brief stimulus is shown.

Information about position is very important in explaining the word-letter phenomenon. Obviously positional uncertainty is not a problem for single-letter stimuli. For these the subject sometimes has enough information to correctly identify the letter. Other times he has only enough information to make a guess from a set of likely letters that are consistent with the partial featural information from the stimulus. In such cases, an intrusion error occurs when an incorrect letter response is chosen. However, on a significant proportion of the trials, the visual information is insufficient to even generate a guess. Since the subject has no other source of information for help, he makes no response and commits an omission error.

On word trials information about both the position of the cued letter and the identities of the other letters help the subject make a guess when he has only a limited amount of featural information about the cued letter. Omission errors are therefore much less likely to occur on word trials. The subject is more accurate on word trials because knowledge about redundancies in English help generate correct responses on trials when only partial information is obtained from the stimulus.

The word apprehension effect is a direct result of the effects of positional uncertainty. For both words and nonwords, information is extracted from several letter positions at once, and positional information can easily become confused. Consider what happens with words and nonwords if there is not enough information from the cued position to identify the letter there. For a nonword the subject's positional uncertainty would often generate a response of a letter that had occurred near the cued letter. Such responses would contain many transposition errors, just as Estes' data show. With words, however, redundancy provides additional information about which letter positions should be used to generate the response. In this case the responses would be based on the correct letter position more often, and transposition errors would be less frequent. Words would also be recognized more accurately.

Since words help recognition of their component letters by maintaining positional information, Estes states that words will be better recognized only if the other letters are present when the cued letter is being processed. To verify this conjecture, he ran a slightly different version of his previous experiment. Single letters, nonwords, and words were again shown tachistoscopically. The cued letter was presented in the usual fashion, but the other stimulus letters in the word and nonword conditions were presented 200 milliseconds after the stimulus. For example, in the word condition the subject would see the sequence:

```
$  $  $  $    (preexposure field)
#  #  L  #    (stimulus field)
#  #  #  #    (200-millisecond delay)
F  O  #  D    (poststimulus context field)
```

In the nonword condition the analogous stimulus sequence would be:

```
$  $  $  $
#  #  L  #
#  #  #  #
D  F  #  O
```

For single letters the following sequence would appear:

```
$  $  $  $
#  #  L  #
$  $  #  $
```

Since the word context could not contribute positional information through its redundant properties for a letter that had been recognized long before the context appeared, both the word apprehension effect and the word-letter phenomenon disappeared. Responses for single letters were 68 percent correct, for words 66 percent correct, and for nonwords 65 percent correct. These results provide strong evidence that redundancy in English helps readers keep letters in their proper places. In summary, Estes' notion of positional uncertainty provides a convenient framework within which to understand the word superiority effect and the word-letter phenomenon. It also explains the types of errors subjects make on word, nonword, and single-letter stimuli.

HIGHER-ORDER UNITS

A Hierarchical Model

So far we have discussed several stages, or levels, of perceptual processing in word recognition. The lowest level is the extraction of visual features from each of the characters presented in the stimulus. At the next higher level individual features can be combined to form letters. The discovery that redundancy, especially sequential redundancy, influences word recognition allows us to posit another level of processing. At this level the predictability of English spelling allows individual letters to be combined into multiletter units. These units can be treated as wholes for some purposes during word recognition. We refer to such multiletter groups as *higher-order units,* and in this section we examine different types of letter groups that seem to function as higher-order units in word recognition. Among these higher-order units are consonant clusters, syllables, and entire words.

Figure 6.2 shows a hierarchical system of feature detectors, letter detectors, and higher-order units. Featural information is first extracted from each letter position in the stimulus. The features are then combined to allow recognition of individual letters. Letters may be combined into spelling clusters or syllables, and the higher-order units themselves can even be combined into words. Of course, letters do not always have to be formed into higher-order units before words are recognized. The figure shows that letters may also be combined directly into words.

Estes suggests that a system of the type illustrated in Figure 6.2 is responsible for the redundancy and positional uncertainty effects he obtained in his experiments. Figure 6.2 includes some additions to Estes' original version, as we discuss later in this chapter; however, we can use the figure to follow Estes' argument. He says that word recognition is accomplished by a hierarchical system in which information is filtered through a succession of levels of detectors. If a match is not found at a given level, the identification process stops and a response is made based on the current state of processed information from the lower level(s). If there is a match, the identification process will continue to higher levels.

Notice that words contain higher-level processing units but that single letters and nonwords do not. Thus words can be matched at higher levels in the hierarchy, and these higher-level matches can help organize positional information about the letters. Also, if a word context is presented before or with a cued letter, the context can activate detectors for classes of letters or letter groups. These detectors can help the subject make good guesses when the visual information is poor.

This model shows how contextual redundancy can help word recognition by activating detectors for higher-order units. Now we can show that spelling clusters, syllables, and whole words are reasonable candidates for redundant higher-order units. For each of these three units we present evidence that the unit influences performance in word recognition, and we then explain why a word recognition model incorporating that unit would work.

Spelling Patterns

Everyday experience in reading shows that some letter sequences are allowable in English and some are not. Permissible spellings in English are governed by *orthographic rules. Graphemes* are letters, and the word *orthography* refers to the written, as opposed to the spoken, form of a language. Every language has its own set of orthographic rules, which are merely generalizations about what letters can occur in certain positions in correctly

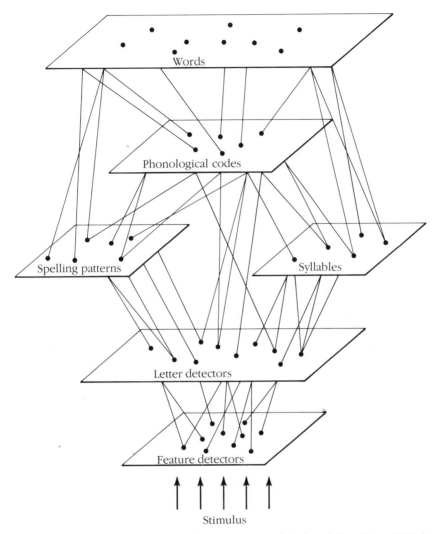

Figure 6.2 In the hierarchical word recognition model adapted from Estes (1975a), visual information can be identified at five levels, ranging from low-level features to entire words.

spelled words in the language. It is very difficult to write down a complete set of such rules for English because there are generally exceptions to even the broadest of rules.

All languages also have *phonological rules*. A *phoneme* is an individual speech sound, and phonological rules state what sounds are found together in the language. English is an *alphabetic* language, which means that the letters used in its orthography are related to the phonemes used in pronouncing written words. Although most languages are alphabetic, in a few, such as Chinese, each word is represented by a distinct, and often complex, symbol. The parts of such symbols usually do not give any clues as to how the word is pronounced, so that the relationship between the orthography and the phonology of the language is arbitrary.

However, in an alphabetic language, such as English, many orthographic rules are related to phonological rules. That is, certain letters never appear together in spelling because their corresponding sounds cannot be pronounced together. For example, the cluster GK never occurs in the spelling of an English word because the "guh" and "kuh" sounds cannot be said together without an intermediate vowel sound, such as "uh." A slightly different type of orthographic rule is illustrated by the group LT. The orthographic rules of English do not allow it to appear at the beginning of a word, but they do allow it to appear in the middle or at the end of a word (e.g., felt). Although English phonology does not have a pronunciation for LT at the beginning of words, it does have a pronunciation for a medial or final LT.

Grapheme-phoneme correspondence rules tell us how a written word is pronounced. The observation that orthographic rules in English are related to phonological rules led Gibson (1965) to suggest that an important higher-order unit in the recognition of words is the *spelling pattern*. A spelling pattern is a group of letters "in a given environment which has an invariant pronunciation according to the rules of English" (p. 1071). To understand this definition, let us consider an example. Gibson analyzes the regular nonword GLURCK into three spelling patterns: GL/UR/CK. UR is a spelling pattern because when these two letters appear together between clusters of consonants in words, the pronunciation is always "er." Similarly an initial GL is a spelling pattern, pronounced "gluh," as is a final CK pronounced "kuh."

By transposing the initial and final consonant pairs of GLURCK to yield CKURGL , one destroys the structure of the spelling patterns. The medial UR is still a spelling pattern because it still appears between two consonant clusters. But the initial CK and the final GL are no longer spelling patterns because neither an initial CK nor a final GL have pronunciations. Whereas the regular nonword GLURK contains three spelling patterns, GL/UR/CK, the irregular nonword CKURGL contains five, C/K/UR/G/L.

Gibson et al. (1962) measured full-report accuracy for both the regular and irregular types of nonwords in a tachistoscopic task. Subjects saw the stimuli in a random order at a 50-millisecond exposure and recorded what they saw for each stimulus. Then the stimuli were presented again at 100, 150, and finally 250 milliseconds, with the subject recording each stimulus at each duration. At each of the exposure durations subjects reported the regular items more accurately than the irregular items.

It is easy to interpret this result within the framework of the hierarchical model in Figure 6.2. When a regular item has good spelling pattern structure, subjects can make identifications at a relatively high level of processing, at the level of spelling patterns. Information from this level of recognition helps disambiguate positional information and leads to accurate responses. Recognition of the irregular items, however, takes place mainly at the level of individual letters. There is little higher-order information to help keep distinct the positions for each feature, and more errors are made. Furthermore, the presence of spelling patterns provides a type of redundancy that aids subjects in making guesses when they do not have enough visual information to completely recognize a letter.

Spelling patterns are not just another way of describing redundancy. True, GL is a spelling pattern in GLURCK and GL has high spatial frequency redundancy at the beginning of six-letter words, whereas GL in CKURGL is not a spelling pattern and GL has low frequency redundancy at the ends of words. However, Massaro, Venezky, and Taylor (1979) compared the effects of orthographic regularity (i.e., presence of spelling patterns) with the effects of spatial frequency redundancy to show that spatial frequency redundancy does not fully explain why spelling patterns help word recognition.

The experimenters generated four types of nonword stimuli by rearranging the letters from six-letter English words. For example, the word modern was used to generate two nonword stimuli, remond and rmnoed with high spatial frequency redundancy; that is, the sum of the spatial frequencies of the six letters is quite large. Notice, however, that while remond is orthographically regular, rmnoed is highly irregular and violates several orthographic rules, among them that English words do not have an initial rm. The word modern was also used to generate two nonwords with low spatial frequency redundancy, endrom and rdenmo. Again, the first of these is regular and the second irregular.

Subjects were given a short presentation of the stimulus word, then a pattern mask and a single target letter. The subject's task was to decide whether the target letter had appeared in the stimulus. On half the trials the target had appeared, and on the other half it had not. Since the subjects' decision depended on how well they had recognized the stimulus, the dependent measure was the accuracy of the responses. Accuracy on the strings with high spatial frequency redundancy was 5 percent better than accuracy on the strings with low redundancy. In addition, performance on the regular strings was 4 percent more accurate than on the irregular strings. Both differences were statistically significant. The conclusion is that the regularity aided by the presence of spelling patterns facilitates recognition of letter strings.

Syllables

A second type of higher-order unit that seems to play a role in word recognition is the syllable, which is both an orthographic and a phonological unit. In writing, a syllable consists of a vowel and its associated consonants. In speech, the syllable is the minimal spoken unit within which all the constraints of pronunciation can be specified. For example, we cannot pronounce the letter a in a word until we know what, if any, consonants surround it. As an example, consider the different pronunciations of a in the words hay, ham, hall and ha.

Several experiments used a naming latency task to show that the syllable is a unit of word recognition. Eriksen, Pollack, and Montague (1970) found that subjects took 20–30 milliseconds longer to begin to pronounce a three-syllable word than to pronounce a one-syllable word. It is generally assumed that in order for the subject to say a word aloud, he or she must first recognize the word. This recognition time must then be reflected in the interval between the appearance of the stimulus and the start of the response. If pronunciation cannot begin until all units in the stimulus are recognized, then three-syllable words should take longer to recognize because they contain more syllabic units.

Unfortunately, such naming tasks as that used by Eriksen, Pollack, and Montague confuse several factors. First, subjects may be able to recognize monosyllabic and polysyllabic stimuli equally quickly, but in the naming task they pronounce the stimulus silently to themselves before saying it aloud. Thus the observed differences in naming latency could reflect this "implicit speech" time rather than the time needed to actually recognize the stimuli. Second, Eriksen, Pollack, and Montague's experiment confounds the number of syllables and number of letters of the stimuli: the three-syllable stimuli contained many more letters than the one-syllable words (e.g., cab and cabinet). Thus their results might reflect an array length effect.

Spoehr and Smith (1973) correct these problems by holding the length of the stimuli constant at five letters. Subjects were briefly shown a five-letter word of one or two syllables followed by a pattern mask. The stimuli had been selected such that for each one-syllable stimulus there was a two-syllable stimulus that had the same first letter, the same number of consonants and vowels, and the same frequency in English (e.g., PAINT and PAPER). Spoehr and Smith found that subjects recognized more letters correctly from the one- than from the two-syllable words either with a full-report response task or with single-letter alternative cues. These results indicate that it is easier for subjects to recognize words of fewer syllables, which implies that a word is not fully recognized until all its syllables are recognized. Recognition time increases with the number of syllables, and short presentation times followed by visual masks may preclude full recognition. Therefore, subjects will make more mistakes on items having more syllables.

Whole Words

A final higher-order unit that may affect word recognition is the whole word. This approach posits that feature information from each position in a stimulus string can be matched directly to memory without prior detection of individual letters, spelling patterns, or syllables. Smith (1978) details the way in which such a system would work. Like many of the models considered in Chapter 5, this model assumes that each stimulus position is analyzed for the presence of various features. As featural information is extracted from the stimulus, a multiposition matrix of information is composed. One can think of such a matrix as merely an ordered set of lists of what features are present in each serial position. The critical point of the model, however, is that these features are not matched to memory representations for individual letters. Instead, the matrix as a whole is compared to memory representations of entire words. These memory representations contain lists of features of the letters in each position. When sufficient information is gathered to match one of the word representations better than any other, recognition of the whole word takes place.

Because of the redundancies of English spelling, whole-word processing requires fewer feature comparisons to identify a word than separate processing of component letters. A complete feature list of each of a word's component letters is not needed to distinguish the word from all other words. For example, the memory representation of ACT need not have any features for the first position because no other three-letter words in English have a final CT. Similarly, only one feature is necessary to identify the second letter as C. Detection of a curvature opening to the right is sufficient because the only other possibilities for the second position—F, I, N, P, and R— all have a vertical line on the left.

Clearly, many fewer feature tests are needed to identify a whole word than to completely identify all its component letters. Therefore, the word-letter phenomenon is a natural result of this model. Similarly, the model explains that it is much easier to identify words than random strings of letters, as is the case of the word apprehension effect. However, it is difficult to see how a whole-word system, working by itself, could generate the effects of approximation to English. Given that nonwords, no matter how regular or irregular in structure, are not represented in memory, all types of nonwords should be equally difficult to recognize. One cannot dismiss this objection simply by positing memory representations for subword units such as spelling patterns because that assumption does not explain how the processing system could treat GL as a cluster in GLURCK but not in CKURGL.

Although the whole-word feature matching system cannot be the only means by which people recognize related strings of letters, it is certainly one way that word recognition could be accomplished. Whole-word matching describes a very fast, efficient way to recognize words during normal reading; reading speed would obviously decrease if all lower-level units had to be recognized first. Furthermore, since some models of whole-word matching are very successful in accounting for several aspects of the experimental data (see Rumelhart and Siple, 1974), this method must be left as an alternative in any complete account of word recognition.

SPEECH RECODING AND READING STRATEGIES

Speech Recoding

The evidence presented thus far shows that the redundant properties of English allow the formation of higher-order units of various sizes as an aid to word recognition. At least two of these units, the spelling pattern and the syllable, are the written equivalents of units used in speech. This observation suggests a possible relationship between reading and listening to English. In fact, many people report that they silently pronounce words to themselves as they read. They do not necessarily move their lips or their tongues, as when speaking, but instead form a covert, or subvocal, code for the written material that is very similar to the code used to produce speech. The process by which written words are converted to a subvocal, speech-related, phonological code is called *speech recoding*. We now consider speech recoding and how it might work during word recognition.

In order to recognize words using speech recoding, subjects must do three things. First they must group letters together into higher-order units, a process called *parsing*. Second, they must apply the grapheme-phoneme correspondence rules of English to each of the units. This procedure generates a phonological code for the stimulus. Finally, they must use that code to find a matching word in memory. This last step is crucial in reading because we can know the meaning of a word only after we have found it in memory.

Figure 6.2 shows the speech recoding process in relation to other concepts discussed in this chapter. The figure illustrates that once the higher-order units are formed they may be recoded into their corresponding phonological representations. The lines of information flow in the figure indicate that some words may be recognized directly from the visual information while others are recognized by speech recoding. In some circumstances one method is used, while in other circumstances the other is used.

The evidence that speech recoding is sometimes used to recognize words comes from several different kinds of experimental tasks. Spoehr (1978) provides evidence for such recoding in a tachistoscopic report task. This experiment is based on the observation that if recognition depends on speech recoding, then those stimuli that can be recoded the fastest will be most easily recognized, and those stimuli that require a long recoding period may not successfully be recoded during a brief, masked tachistoscopic presentation.

The time it takes to recode a word depends on the number of elements in the resulting subvocal, phonological code; the more elements in this code, the longer it should take to produce the code. The number of units in a phonological code is the number of phonemes required to pronounce the word aloud. For example, STARK has five phonemes, which correspond to the sounds of each of the five letters in the word. However, SHARK has only four phonemes because the first two letters are pronounced as the single phoneme "sh."

In order to determine whether word recognition accuracy depends on the length of the recoding process, Spoehr compared accuracy of report for five-letter items of four and five phonemes (e.g., SHARK and STARK). The two types of items were also matched for other important variables such as letter length, letter composition, and frequency of occurrence in printed English. Report accuracy was significantly lower on the five-phoneme items than on the four-phoneme items. The results therefore support the hypothesis that word recognition improves as the length of speech recoding operation is reduced.

Rubenstein, Lewis, and Rubenstein (1971) also show that word recognition may entail speech recoding. They used a *lexical-decision task,* in which subjects are shown a stimulus letter string that remains in view until the subject makes a response. The subject's task is to decide whether the string is an English word or not, and to indicate his choice by pressing one of two buttons. The dependent measure is the period of time that elapses from the stimulus' first appearance until the subject pushes a button. The faster a word is recognized, the shorter the lexical-decision time.

One of their experiments measured the lexical-decision times for different types of pronounceable nonwords. One type of nonword was homophonic with a high-frequency English word (e.g., the nonword rufe sounds like the word roof). A second type of nonword was homophonic with a low-frequency English word (e.g., brume sounds like broom), and a third type of nonword was not homophonic with any English word (e.g., slint). Rubenstein, Lewis, and Rubenstein hypothesized that if recognition occurs through the use of a subvocal speech-related code, the nonwords that are homophonic with English words should be harder to recognize. These homophonic items, which share the same phonological representation as real words, will initially be "recognized" on the basis of their phonological code. Only after the subject performs a double-check of the spelling will he realize that the stimulus is actually not a word.

Therefore the subject will make more errors on the homophonic non-words, and correct responses to these nonwords will take longer because the subject must check the spelling. As expected, the homophonic nonwords took 55 to 65 milliseconds longer to recognize than the nonhomophonic nonwords. A similar result was obtained with words. Words that have ho-mophones in English (e.g., crews/cruise or threw/through) took longer to classify as words. Again, recognition seems to involve a subvocal, phonolog-ical code that generates incorrect matches to homophonic words before the correct word is found.

Meyer, Schvaneveldt, and Ruddy (1974) also examine word recognition and speech recoding. Subjects were shown two simultaneous letter strings and were to respond yes if both strings were words, and to respond no otherwise. Some of the word pairs were both phonemically and graphemically similar; for example, the pair BRIBE/TRIBE share most of their letters (graphemic similarity) and also rhyme (phonemic similarity). Other word pairs, such as COUCH/TOUCH, were graphemically similar but phonemically dissimilar. Lexical-decision times for these two types of items were compared to times for items that had neither phonemic nor graphemic similarity, such as COUCH/TRIBE. Subjects recognized the pairs that were both phonemically and graphemically similar slightly faster than ordinary pairs, but pairs that were graphemically similar and phonemically dissimilar were recognized more slowly than ordinary pairs.

Meyer, Schvaneveldt, and Ruddy explain these results in terms of an encoding bias during the application of grapheme-phoneme correspondence rules.

Recognition of the first string is carried out using speech recoding. If that string is a word the subject begins to process the second string. However, the recoding of the second string can be influenced by the recoding of the first string if the two stimuli have many letters in common. In particular, subjects tend to apply the same grapheme-phoneme correspondence rules used for the first string to the second. If the two stimuli are phonemically similar, this tendency, or bias, accelerates processing. However, if the second string is not pronounced similarly to the first, reusing the grapheme-phoneme correspondence rules will lead to the wrong phonological code, and the process must be repeated. The graphemically similar but phonemically dissimilar pairs will therefore take longer to process.

Nonspeech Options

Alongside evidence that speech recoding is used to recognize words is evidence that speech recoding is not always used. Intuitively, we sense that subjects will not execute the extra recoding steps if they can directly match features to a word to identify it. Many experiments show that speech recoding is not necessary for word recognition, and in this section we look at a few of them.

Baron and Thurston (1973) used homophones to show that speech recoding is not used during word recognition. Subjects were shown four-letter stimuli tachistoscopically and were then shown two four-letter alternatives. They were asked to choose which of the alternatives had been presented. In one condition, the incorrect alternative was homophonous with the correct alternative; for instance, for the stimulus FOUR, the alternatives FORE and FOUR were given. Accuracy was 70.8 percent with the homophonic pairs and 69.7 percent for nonhomophones, an insignificant difference. Baron and Thurston reason that if subjects recognize the stimuli on the basis of a phonological code, they should have a great deal of difficulty in choosing the correct alternative among homophonic pairs. Since accuracy was the same for both types of pairs, subjects were basing their decision on visual information, which distinguished between the homophonic alternatives.

Kleiman (1975) also shows that speech recoding is not necessary for word recognition. Three types of tasks were used. In one task subjects had to decide whether two letter strings were graphemically similar except for their initial letter: HEARD/BEARD are the same, but GRACE/PILLOW are different. In another task, subjects had to decide whether two letter strings were phonemically identical except for their initial sound: TICKLE/PICKLE are the same, but LEMON/DEMON are different. In a third task, subjects had to decide whether two letter strings were synonymous: MOURN/GRIEVE are the same, and BRAVERY/QUANTITY are different. In the shadowing condition subjects made each of these three types of decisions while listening to, and repeating aloud, digit names that were played over headphones. During the control condition subjects made their decisions without doing the shadowing task.

It was expected that shadowing would be most detrimental to those tasks in which speech recoding played an integral role because it would compete for processing resources needed for recoding. Notice that the task that asked subjects to decide synonymity required complete recognition of both words. If recognition required speech recoding, then shadowing should greatly interfere with these decisions. Since the graphemic decisions did not require word recognition, it was expected that shadowing should interfere with this task much less. The phonemic task should be interfered with greatly because speech recoding is necessary to do this task.

Shadowing increased the average decision times for all three types of tasks. The increase with shadowing was 125 milliseconds for the graphemic task, 372 milliseconds for the phonemic task, and 120 milliseconds for the synonymy task. The fact that shadowing interfered to some extent with all the tasks indicates that subjects might have had difficulty doing two tasks at once because their attention was divided. However, shadowing interfered no more with the synonymy task than with the graphemic task, and since speech recoding is not required by the graphemic task, it must not have been required for complete word recognition either.

Task-Dependent Strategies

The evidence discussed so far shows that recoding plays a role in some tasks but not in others. It seems that speech recoding is an optional process and that word recognition can take place either with it or without it. Several experiments show that speech recoding is, in fact, just such an optional strategy, and that its use depends on the experimental conditions. Davelaar et al. (1978) present data that show that speech recoding is used unless the conditions of the experiment make recoding useless. They used Meyer, Schvaneveldt, and Ruddy's version of the lexical-decision task in which subjects saw two letter strings and had to respond yes if both were words, and no otherwise. Word stimuli were either homophone pairs (e.g., GROAN/GROWN) or nonhomophone pairs (e.g., EARN/GROWN). In one condition the nonwords were homophonic with English words (e.g., BRANE), while in another the nonwords were not (e.g., SLINT).

For nonhomophonic nonwords, a speech recoding strategy would allow the subject to make a quick decision about whether each stimulus is a word or not. The nonwords would register as nonwords because their phonological codes do not match anything in the subject's memory. However, for homophonic nonwords speech recoding will yield a phonological code that matches a word in memory, and thus recoding will not enable the subject to distinguish a homophonic nonword (BRANE) from a real word (BRAIN). In this case, then, subjects should abandon speech recoding in favor of a visual strategy that will allow them to locate words, but not nonwords, in memory.

We can tell whether speech recoding is used under these two conditions by comparing lexical-decision times for the homophonic and nonhomophonic word pairs. When speech recoding is being used, the latencies for the homophonic pairs should be different than those for the nonhomophonic pairs. As predicted, speech recoding was used when the nonwords were not homophones, resulting in a significant homophone effect for the words. When the nonwords were homophonic, speech recoding was not used and no homophone effect occurred for the words.

Hawkins et al. (1976) also show that speech recoding is an optional strategy used by subjects in appropriate circumstances. Hawkins et al. explain Baron and Thurston's (1973) failure to find that homophonic pairs are more difficult alternatives in a tachistoscopic task in the following way. Subjects realize that phonological recoding is not a useful strategy when most of the alternatives are homophones of the correct stimulus choice. Therefore they recognize the words without recoding. Hawkins et al.'s data show that when given many homophone alternative trials, subjects abandon speech recoding as a means of identifying the stimuli, and accuracy on stimuli with homophonic alternatives is the same as accuracy on stimuli with nonhomophonic pairs (66.5 percent and 67.8 percent respectively). However, if only a few of the stimulus items have homophonic alternatives, subjects continue to use speech recoding on all the stimuli. Then their accuracy on the few homophonic pairs that do appear is much worse than their accuracy on the nonhomophonic alternative pairs (58.3 percent and 78.5 percent respectively). Again, subjects appear to use speech recoding unless the experimental conditions force them to abandon it in order to perform the task successfully.

The process of speech recoding, then, fits into the word recognition process as one of several alternative routes by which visual information is matched to stored memory representations of words. Speech recoding is clearly very important in learning to read and forms the basis of the phonics method of reading instruction. However, if skilled readers always silently sounded out each word, their reading speed could never be very fast (Landauer, 1962). LaBerge and Samuels (1974) argue that there are two ways for readers to improve their speed. One is for the speech recoding step to be bypassed altogether in favor of the quicker visual matching process. The second way is for speech recoding to become an "automatic" process. While the beginning reader invests a great deal of time and attention in sounding out each letter and blending those individual sounds into the code for the whole word, for skilled readers, this process is more automatic. Recoding does not require the conscious attention of the skilled reader, and it can therefore be carried out quickly. Often recoding can be done while other processes are being carried out as well. Thus the skilled reader can use both automatic speech recoding and more direct visual processing for word recognition.

RECOGNIZING WORDS IN SENTENCES

One reason that word recognition is an important process is that it is a basic building block for natural reading. Up to this point, however, we have discussed only how words are processed when they appear alone. Processing a single word is obviously quite different from reading word after word on a printed page. Several factors make natural reading more difficult than recognizing words in isolation. For example, when our eyes come to rest at a certain point on a line, more than one word is in our field of view. Since we do not fixate on every word on a page, we must be able to process several words with each fixation. How we know where to fixate? Do we read all the words in view at the same time or do we recognize them one by one? Too, natural reading demands that we pay careful attention to the meaning of each individual word, and we must combine the meanings of words in order to understand whole sentences and paragraphs.

An examination of all these issues would require several books, and reading research is not always definitive. However, natural reading cannot be a hopelessly confusing task to perform and understand since large numbers of people are quite skilled at reading. In fact, one aspect of natural reading actually helps word recognition. Sentences in normal English prose provide contextual information for the recognition of words. Sentences help us recognize words in much the same way that surrounding letters in words provide context that aids in the recognition of individual letters.

An experiment that illustrates this phenomenon was done by Schuberth and Eimas (1977). The subject's task was to make lexical decisions about letter strings that were presented after different types of contextual information. On some trials the preceding context consisted of a 1.5-second presentation of a sentence in which the last word was omitted; for example, "The puppy chewed the _____ ." The succeeding stimulus either fit the context (e.g., BONE), or did not (e.g., HOUR). On other trials no sentence context was offered. In addition, half the stimulus items were frequent English words and half were infrequent. When the stimulus item fit the previous sentence context, lexical-decision latencies were 25 milliseconds faster than when no context was offered. When the stimulus did not fit the previous context, decision latencies were 20 milliseconds longer than when no context was presented. There was also a substantial frequency effect:

High-frequency words were responded to more quickly than low-frequency words regardless of their appropriateness to the context.

The presence of a sentence context clearly has a facilitating influence on the word recognition process. As a subject proceeds through a sentence, the grammar and the meaning of the sentence lead him to expect certain types of words in certain places. The words near the end of a sentence are quite predictable in standard English prose. For example, the sentence "The puppy chewed the ―――――― " leads us to expect a noun or perhaps an adjective to follow. Furthermore, any noun used as a direct object in this sentence must refer to a concrete thing, since puppies cannot chew on such abstract concepts as "time" or "love." Finally, the mention of a puppy prompts certain meaningful associations, things that are commonly associated with dogs. Thus in standard prose, the set of possibilities for the last word in this sentence is a relatively small subset of all English words. In a way, the sentence frame provides a type of redundancy of meaning that governs the reader's expectations and facilitates the recognition of words that fit that context.

In connected prose two types of information help generate the reader's expectancies: grammatical, or syntactic, rules and meaningful, or semantic, relations between words in the sentence. Several experiments show that the semantic relationships between individual words are effective in generating contextual facilitation in word recognition. In Becker's (1979) lexical-decision experiment the word stimuli were of either high or low frequency in English, and they were preceded by a single-word context. Four different types of context were used, corresponding to graduated amounts of relatedness between the context word and its paired target. Decision latencies for the items preceded by related contexts were 41 milliseconds faster than latencies for items preceded by unrelated contexts. Becker also found that high-frequency words were recognized 75 milliseconds faster than low-frequency words.

Theoretical explanations for the effects of context differ, and no model is entirely satisfactory at present. However, two theories illustrate two different approaches to the problem. Morton's (1969, 1970) logogen model, like several of the models discussed in this chapter, assumes that each word a subject knows is represented by a memory location, called a *logogen*. The logogen for each item contains information about its meaning, its pronounciation, and its spelling. A counter is associated with each logogen, and during the process of recognition the counter tallies the amount of input information that is consistent with the logogen. Since the logogen counter can be used either during reading or during auditory speech recognition, the logogen counter is capable of tallying all kinds of information from either modality. As each feature is extracted from a stimulus, the counters of logogens that are consistent with that feature are incremented. When one of the counters reaches a predetermined threshold value, recognition of the stimulus takes place. The logogen associated with that counter is then said to match the input.

Several additional assumptions help explain the experimental effects of context. First, it is assumed that the recognition threshold for high-frequency words is lower than the threshold for low-frequency words. Thus fewer increments will be necessary, on the average, to recognize a high-frequency word, and recognition will occur more quickly. Second, it is assumed that contextual information provides an additional source of information that can increment counters. The presence of a prior sentence or even a single-word context, serves to increment the counters of logogens that are consistent with the context. The consistent logogen counters therefore need fewer visual feature increments to reach threshold, and words that fit the context are recognized sooner than words that do not.

There are two difficulties with the logogen model, however. First, the model cannot explain how any nonword, and especially pronounceable nonwords, is ever recognized. Since logogens are associated with words in a subject's vocabulary, the only way to recognize an item is to find the logogen that matches it. It is impossible for the subject to ever find a logogen that matches a nonword that he has never seen before. Moreover, the model is also incapable of explaining why some nonwords, specifically those that are orthographically regular, are easier to recognize than others.

The logogen model is a fairly passive approach to the use of context in word recognition. That is, the memory component merely accepts input from various sources and cannot take an active role in the recognition process. In contrast, Becker (Becker and Killion, 1977; Becker, 1979) suggests the verification model, according to which visual feature descriptions of words obtained from memory are compared to, or verified against, the visual input. When a description matches, recognition occurs.

During this verification process, the subject is assumed to keep the visual representation of the word active in a short-term visual memory while he or she extracts features from it. The visual features extracted from the stimulus may not perfectly match any words the subject knows but may instead partially match several word representations. The input stimulus thus generates a *sensory set,* a set of possible words consistent with the visual input. The true visual representations of these words are retrieved from memory and are compared to the visual representation of the stimulus still residing in temporary visual memory. The first representation that matches is assumed to generate a recognition of the item. Moreover, items in the sensory set are verified in an order determined by their frequency. The higher-frequency words are verified first and are therefore recognized sooner.

When contextual information is presented prior to a word, a slightly different sequence of events occurs. The subject's expectations about what word will occur next restrict him to the relatively small set of words that fit the given context, the *semantic set.* If the context is a single word, the semantic set contains items that are related to it in meaning. If the context is a sentence, the semantic set contains items that are sensible completions for that sentence. After presentation of the stimulus and, while the sensory set is being constructed, the subject can begin to verify items in the semantic set. If a match is found among the semantic set, recognition occurs and the process stops. However, if the stimulus word is an incongruous item, it will be contained in the sensory set rather than the semantic set. The subject must then verify all the items in the semantic set before proceeding to verify the items in the sensory set. Recognition times for incongruous items in the sensory set will therefore be slower relative to times for congruous items in the semantic set.

The verification model conforms to intuitions about how contextual information can be used to restrict the set of items that must be considered in identifying a word. However, it has many of the same difficulties as the logogen model in accounting for word recognition data. For example, nonwords are assumed to be identified by virtue of a failure of the verification process to find a match between the input and an item in either the semantic or sensory sets. This assumption predicts that the lexical-decision times for all nonwords should be slower than times for any word. However, in contextual experiments response times for unpronounceable nonwords are typically the same as the times for low-frequency words (see Schuberth and Eimas, 1977). Also, differences between decision times for regular nonwords and irregular nonwords cannot be explained by the verification model.

In sum, we do not yet completely understand the interaction between visual information and complex language information during normal reading. Context is certainly a help in recognizing words, but the mechanisms by which context contributes to processing are still not well understood.

SUMMARY

In this chapter we looked at the processing of words and at the factors that affect the recognition of letters in various structured contexts. We first saw that the recognition of individual letters is facilitated by the target-letter's inclusion in a word or other structured string of letters. We then examined the types of structures that are hierarchically arranged in the visual recognition system. We saw that spelling patterns, syllables, and even whole words provide organization for the process of extracting visual information from written words. Finally, we learned that the recognition of whole words can be influenced by their context in sentences. At each of these levels the role of organization is extremely important in determining how well a word is recognized.

SUGGESTED READING

Johnston and McClelland (1980) provide an interesting and slightly different explanation of the word superiority and word-letter phenomena. West and Stanovich (1978) offer an alternative account of sentence context effects in word recognition. Finally, the individual papers presented in Tzeng and Singer (1981) provide broad coverage of many different aspects of word recognition.

## Chapter 7

Picture Processing and Memory

In everyday life our visual information processing system processes complex arrays of three-dimensional objects. We also have the ability to recognize complex scenes and objects from pictures of them. Indeed, many laboratory studies on object recognition and memory for complex scenes use stimuli that are pictures rather than three-dimensional objects. In this chapter, we examine how pictures are processed, recognized, and remembered, and how these abilities relate to analogous abilities for three-dimensional objects.

A picture is a two-dimensional surface of limited size that represents or *symbolizes* three-dimensional objects that may actually be of quite different sizes than their representations in the picture. Sigel (1978) points out that pictures may differ along a number of dimensions and still adequately fulfill their symbolic purpose. For example, pictures of an object, such as a cup, may vary with respect to how much detail is present, how spatial relationships are presented, and whether dimensional cues such as shading are present. Pictures that depict more than one object may vary in their organization of the objects, their complexity, and so on. Yet we identify the presence of a cup whether it is shown as a simple outline on a blank background or as one of many objects in a complex photograph of a kitchen.

That we can easily recognize the conceptual identity of pictures and their corresponding real objects implies that picture processing is relatively simple. Remarkably, we can recognize objects in pictures in the absence of many of the cues we normally use in processing three-dimensional entities and scenes. For example, in processing real-world scenes, we process convergence of our two eyes in fixating on objects of different depths, and information about different perspectives is generated as our head, eyes, and body move slightly. But in pictures the cues for flat surfaces and depths lie in the same plane.

In this chapter, we cannot explain all the ways in which people deal so well with the tremendous variation among pictures. Rather we will explore four specific aspects of picture processing: (1) how people scan pictures and what they look at in order to identify and make sense of the picture; (2) what organizational factors people use in identifying pictures and the objects in them; (3) the duration and capacity of picture memory; and (4) the variables that influence how well and how long pictorial information is retained. Studies of eye movements, identification and detection latencies, and recognition memory can help us understand these phenomena.

RECOGNIZING A PICTURE

Eye Movements

One way to discover how pictures are processed is to examine how people move their eyes when they look at pictures. We can monitor both voluntary and involuntary eye movements to discover which parts of the picture a subject looks at and how the eyes move between successive fixations. In discussing picture scanning, we distinguish two components of eye movements: fixations and saccades. A *fixation* is a brief period of time during which the eye is stationary and focused on a single part of the picture. Such fixations last between 200 and 500 milliseconds, and 1° to 5° of visual information is processed. Fixations are separated by quick movements, or *saccades,* during which the eye's focus is changed to a new section of the picture. According to Yarbus (1967), saccades rarely move the eye more than 15° of visual angle and are such quick movements that they occupy only about 5 percent of the total time spent scanning a picture. Saccades are so quick that they are unnoticed by the perceiver. During the movement, visual information is "blurred" across the retina, and mechanisms in the visual system act to supress the blurred information taken in during a saccade.

Several methods can be used to monitor the fixation and saccade patterns of a subject who is viewing a visual display. Most often, a narrow beam of light is reflected off the surface of the subject's eye, and photoreceptor equipment follows the deviations in that beam. That is, the beam of light reflected from a particular area of the subject's eye will be deflected proportionally whenever the eye moves. The beam may be reflected off a tiny mirror on the outside of a contact lens worn by the subject, or it may be reflected off the cornea of the subject's eye. In either case, the procedure does not interfere with the subject's normal viewing habits. By making careful alignments, experimenters can superimpose the record of the eye movements on the image of the picture being scanned. They can thus tell where and how long the subject fixates on the picture and how many fixations are made. Furthermore, the track made by the beam during saccades allows experimenters to determine the extent and duration of these movements.

Yarbus (1967) provides a thorough qualitative account of typical scanning patterns, such as that shown in Figure 7.1. Yarbus generalizes about scanning patterns, noting that a very large proportion of the fixations are made on areas that are highly informative. The record of eye movement in Figure 7.1 shows that the viewer fixated frequently on the major people in the picture, and that the fixations center on the most informative parts of these most informative objects—the faces. In scanning a picture of an animal or human face, subjects are most likely to fixate on the eyes, mouth, and nose.

Yarbus' records of eye movement also indicate which visual items do not attract many fixations. First, fixations are not necessarily drawn to either the very darkest or the very brightest regions of the picture. Second, fixations are not necessarily drawn to the regions with greatest detail. Details receive relatively few fixations unless they are informative in the sense mentioned earlier. For example, Figure 7.1 shows that subjects made very few fixations on the fine detail of the wallpaper. Indeed, comparison of scanning patterns for pictures drawn in silhouette and regular photographs or paintings shows that the fixation patterns for both are very similar. Third, contour does not seem to influence fixation patterns; that is, subjects do not appear to follow the outlines of figures as they scan. Contours are scanned only in viewing pictures such as facial profiles, in which the informative aspects lie along the contours.

Yarbus also reports that scanning patterns are affected by the subject's purpose in looking at the picture. The preceding generalizations apply to the free scanning of the picture by a subject having no particular intention to remember any details or make judgments about its contents. However, when subjects are asked to determine the approximate ages of the people shown in Figure 7.1, an even greater percentage of their fixations are directed at the faces of the human figures, since faces offer the best age cues. When subjects are asked to remember the positions of the people and objects in the picture, their eyes tend to zig-zag back and forth a great deal between pairs of objects or people. The scanning record suggests that subjects try to gauge distances by estimating the magnitude of saccadic movements. Finally, when subjects are asked to estimate the material circumstances of the people in the picture, they make many fewer fixations on the faces and many more on the objects in the room.

One of the most difficult things to understand intuitively is how a subject's purpose or plan in viewing a picture can exert such a great influence on his eye movements without requiring a great deal of cognitive effort to be expended. Research indicates that cognitive control of scanning patterns may be an automatic process so that people do not have to concentrate on moving their eyes. In fact, data collected by Cooper (1974) indicate that subjects may have very little conscious control at all. Cooper's subjects listened to short

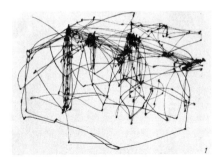

Figure 7.1 Subjects in Yarbus' experiment viewed pictures, such as that on the left, while records were made of their eye movements and fixations. The record on the right shows that subjects tend to fixate on regions of high informativeness in the picture, such as the figures' faces. [From Yarbus, 1967.]

prose stories that contained the names of several concrete objects (e.g., lion, zebra) and conceptual categories (e.g., safari, Africa). As they listened, subjects were allowed to freely view a display containing pictures of many of the objects mentioned in the story. Subjects were not aware that their eye movements were being recorded. Cooper found that when subjects heard the name of something pictured on the screen, their eyes quickly moved and fixated on the picture of the named object. They also fixated on pictures of things conceptually related to items in the stories. After the experiment, 85 percent of the subjects said that their eye movements and fixations seemed to be automatic rather than the result of any planning on their part. Apparently eye movements reflect what the brain is thinking about.

Returning to Yarbus' finding about fixations and informative regions, and recalling the discussion of information theory in Chapter 4, we ought to be able to specify more precisely the nature of this informativeness. In particular, highly informative regions are likely to be at contours and in regions that are not predicatable. Mackworth and Morandi (1967) show that such a definition of informativeness predicts fixations. They report that subjects make more fixations in regions containing contours (high information content) than in regions composed largely of unbounded textures (low information content). Moreover, more fixations are made in regions judged by a separate set of raters to have less predictable content.

Antes (1974) extends these findings by examining not only the number of fixations in regions of differing informativeness but also the duration of those fixations and the size of the saccades between fixations. On seeing a picture for the first time, subjects initially make a rather brief fixation followed by a rather lengthy saccade. Thereafter the fixations are somewhat longer and the saccades of somewhat shorter distance, but they follow a characteristic pattern. Specifically, subjects tend to move their eyes to a region of high informativeness and fixate on it briefly. They then make a series of shorter movements to the less informative areas nearby. In short, after picking out an important object or person in the picture, subjects explore the characteristics of this region before moving on. The longer saccades to a new region are not random; these movements are made only to important regions. Thus subjects must be able to obtain and process a good deal of information from the visual periphery during each fixation, information that tells them where to move their eyes next.

Both Antes (1974) and Mackworth and Morandi (1967) used post hoc measures of informativeness and predictability; that is, different parts of the stimulus picture were rated as more or less informative or predictable after the stimuli were constructed. Another way to vary informativeness is to construct the stimuli according to a particular a priori definition of informativeness. Loftus and Mackworth (1978) suggest the following definition of informativeness: "An object in a picture is informative to the extent that the object has a low a priori probability of being in the picture given the rest of the picture and the observer's past history" (p. 566). This definition is very similar to the axiom in information theory that high information content is equivalent to low predictability. Fittingly, Berlyne (1958) found that subjects given a pair of stimuli made more eye fixations on the less predictable member, such as pattern (a), than on the well-formed member, such as pattern (b).

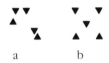

a   b

Loftus and Mackworth (1978) tested their definition of informativeness by showing subjects a series of line-drawing pictures, which they would later be asked to recognize. All the pictures showed organized scenes, but half included one object that was improbable within the framework of the overall scene. For example, a scene of a farm contained a barn, a silo, a wagon, and an octopus. Loftus and Mackworth recorded fixations on various objects in each picture and found that the improbable, informative objects were fixated more often and for longer durations than were the predictable, noninformative objects. Moreover, the informative objects were fixated sooner in the viewing period than their less informative counterparts. These results indicate that subjects were rapidly able to determine the locations of the informative objects and to direct attention toward them. As Antes suggests, subjects must be able to gain information from the periphery of each fixation in order to determine where to move their eyes next.

Processing Picture Information in a Single Glance

Studies of eye movements reveal what a person looks at when scanning a picture. Most of the viewer's information comes from fixations on a few important objects or areas in the picture. To determine what happens during each of those individual fixations, experimenters use a very short presentation duration, only 200 to 300 milliseconds, that allows subjects to make only one fixation. By measuring these subjects' ability to recall information from a picture or to identify parts of it, we can determine exactly what and how much information is obtained from a single glance. In particular, we can determine which factors facilitate or inhibit the processing.

As in other visual processing tasks, the overall content and organization of the entire picture greatly influences the processing. Several studies illustrate different aspects of this top-down aspect of picture processing. In a detection experiment performed by Biederman (1972), subjects viewed tachistoscopically presented photographs of real-world scenes and were asked to detect the presence of certain cued objects. The position of the response object was cued by an arrow that appeared on a blank field either just before or just after the stimulus picture. The subject was to identify the cued object from among a set of four pictures. The most important experimental manipulation was that half the photographs were presented in a "jumbled" form. The jumbled stimuli were constructed by cutting photographs into six rectangular sections and reassembling them in a random fashion. This jumbling destroyed many of the functional and positional relations between the component objects.

Biederman found that identification accuracy for the cued objects was significantly poorer for the jumbled pictures than for the coherent pictures. Moreover, even though the presentation of the arrow cue and the alternatives beforehand improved performance relative to receiving either or both after the stimulus, jumbled pictures were more difficult in all conditions. These results show that for complex pictures, overall organization exerts a top-down influence even when the subject knows in advance what to look for and where to look for it.

Two likely reasons that the jumbling of a picture disrupts the identification of objects within it are, first, that the spatial organization of the jumbled picture disrupts predictable expectations; and, second that the overall thematic organization of a jumbled picture does not permit the observer to make expectations about what objects will appear. In standard viewing such prior expectations help a subject detect the expected objects. Biederman, Glass, and Stacy (1973) examined these two possibilities by having subjects detect the presence of certain objects in jumbled and coherent scenes. Before each trial the subject was shown the picture of the target object for that trial. When the scene appeared, the subject was to decide as quickly as possible whether the target item had occurred. As expected, coherent scenes were processed significantly faster than their jumbled counterparts.

More importantly, however, are the comparisons of reaction times for "possible" and "improbable" negative trials. On the possible type the target object was appropriate to the scene but was not present in the scene. For example, for a picture of a city street that showed no stop signs, a possible negative trial would require the subject to detect whether a street sign was present. On the improbable type of negative trial, the target object not only did not appear in the stimulus but also was unlikely to appear in the pictured environment. For the street scene example, an improbable target would be a whale. For both the jumbled and coherent stimuli, decisions about the possible negative trials took much longer than the improbable negative trials.

In sum, the effects of jumbling in this experiment indicate that it destroys the organizational relationships between objects, while the comparison of the two types of negative trials indicates that subjects do develop expectations about what objects are likely to appear in a scene with a particular theme. When the target object is unlikely, negative decisions can be made quickly, but when the target is possible, a more careful and longer search must be made. Thus both organization and theme-induced expectations are important in picture processing.

Like picture organization, basic visual cues and visual similarity exert an influence on the identification of the objects in a picture. Palmer (1975) demonstrates that visual characteristics of individual objects and top-down scene organization influence recognition of objects in a picture. The subject was first shown a line drawing of a scene, such as a kitchen counter with various cooking utensils on it. After this contextual information was removed, the subject saw a tachistoscopic presentation of an object that was to be identified. Target items were of three types: objects that could belong in the context scene (e.g., a loaf of bread), objects that did not belong in the scene but were visually similar objects that did (e.g., a mailbox shaped like a loaf of bread), and objects that did not belong in the scene and were visually dissimilar to expected objects (e.g., a bass drum).

In another condition subjects identified objects without a prior context scene. Report accuracy was greater for objects that followed an appropriate context than those shown with no prior context. Moreover, objects that were inappropriate to the preceding context were identified less accurately than those shown with no context at all. However, the visually dissimilar objects were more easily identified than the visually similar ones. This experiment, then, illustrates both the facilitatory effects of an appropriate pictorial context and the inhibitory effects of an inappropriate context. Moreover, the results show that subjects build up some expectations about what items might occur in the context, such that they have difficulty identifying an object that appears as if it should be appropriate but, in fact, is not.

An experiment by Biederman et al. (1974) supports the contention that one effect of jumbling is to make it more difficult for the subject to determine the theme of the picture. In addition to performing cued identification of objects in jumbled and coherent scenes, subjects also carried out a task in which they had to choose the best descriptive phrase for a stimulus from a pair of possibilities. Not only did jumbling hurt the subjects' ability to identify objects, it also impaired their ability to correctly identify the theme of the picture by picking the best label for it.

Taken in total, these experiments suggest that three main aspects of a picture determine how easily processing proceeds during a single fixation: the theme or overall topic of the picture, the nature of the visual information itself, and the the spatial organization of the objects and parts of the picture. Spatial organization, however, is a very general term. Clearly, many different types of spatial relationships are disrupted when pictures are jumbled. Biederman (1977, 1981) considers the different aspects of spatial organization more closely.

Biederman (1981) observes that to comprehend a picture's content requires not only an accurate inventory of the objects present but also an understanding of the functional and spatial relations among them. Viewers must arrive at an overall representation, or *schema*, that serves to integrate all the separate aspects of the picture. Biederman explains that "the schema specifies both the items appropriate to a given scene and the physical ... relations that should hold among them" (1981, p. 215). In other words, a schema is a mental structuring of data that embodies necessary real-world constraints on the content and organization of the picture and thus contains expectations about what should appear in the picture.

Biederman lists five important types of constraint imposed by picture organization: support, interposition, probability, position, and size. The *support* constraint requires that objects be supported; for example, picture of a sofa floating in the air violates this constraint. Requirements for support are somewhat contingent on the objects depicted; for example, birds, balloons, and airplanes can float in the air without any visible means of support.

Interposition requires that the contours of an object apparently behind another not be visible. The squatting man in Figure 7.2a violates the interposition constraint because the rear right fender is visible even though the man is interposed between the car and the viewer.

The three other constraints are mainly determined by the nature of the individual objects in the picture. The *probability* constraint posits that some objects are likely and others unlikely in any particular scene. For example, a sofa in the middle of an underwater scene violates the probability constraint. The *position* constraint is violated by a picture of a car atop a skyscraper. Finally, the *size* constraint requires that objects appear in appropriate relative sizes; a telephone cannot be larger than a table, for instance. Figure 7.2b illustrates an object simultaneously violating size and position constraints.

The results of the jumbling studies cited earlier did not allow us to determine which of these five types of constraint violations were responsible for impeding subjects' performance in the jumbled conditions. Biederman's more recent studies, however, examine the individual constraints more carefully. In one experiment (Biederman, 1977), subjects were given the name of a particular object and were then presented a line-drawing scene of the type shown in Figure 7.2. The subject's task was to determine whether the

a

b

Figure 7.2 Biederman used drawings to determine what types of constraint between objects in a picture help in picture processing. (a) The gas station attendant violates the interposition constraint, and (b) the "little man" violates both size and position constraints. [From Biederman, 1977.]

cued object had appeared in the picture. The stimulus pictures varied with respect to which and how many constraints the cued object violated in the picture. Subjects made errors—failed to detect the target—on about 24 percent of the trials in which the cued object violated none of the five constraints. When the cued object violated any one of the constraints, errors were made on about 40 percent of the trials; when the object simultaneously violated two constraints the error rate was 48 percent; when the object violated probability, size, and support constraints, the error rate was more than 50 percent. It appears, then, that each individual constraint contributes to the subject's ability to use his expectations to help identify objects in a scene.

A second task showed that the number of constraints violated by a cued object affected the subject's ability to detect the presence of the violations(s). The subject was first given the name of an object and then shown a scene in which it appeared. The subject's task was to decide whether the cued object violated any constraints by indicating whether something was wrong with it. The more violations shown by the object, the faster the subjects detected that something was wrong. Biederman's results, then, suggest that jumbling a picture not only introduces general disarray but also disrupts specific and important types of constraints and relationships between objects. The greater the number of constraint violations present in a scene, the poorer the subject's ability to process the picture and identify objects in it.

ATTENTIONAL FACTORS IN PICTURE PROCESSING

The concept of attention plays an important role in the recognition and recollection of pictures. One way to study attention is to analyze eye movements, since it is unlikely that a subject can pay attention to any part of a picture that he cannot see. Two studies on visual attention examine how effectively the picture processing system can filter out irrelevant information while it is attending to some other aspect of the visual stimulus.

Can subjects selectively attend to only one organizational constraint without being influenced by others? As Biederman's (1977, 1981) experiments on constraint violation and scene organization show, subjects in a violation detection task demonstrate a certain amount of redundancy gain. That is, it is easier for them to detect that something is wrong with a picture when more than one violation occurs and when the second violation is redundant with the first. This finding suggests that subjects may be simultaneously aware of all the constraints acting on a particular object and not just one of them at a time. To confirm this hypothesis, Biederman (1981) gave subjects a violation detection task in which they were to detect the presence of a particular violation rather than the presence of just any violation. To the extent that the subject has difficulty filtering out information about irrelevant violations, detection times will be slower for cued objects having violations other than the designated one. Biederman's (1981) results confirm that selective attention to just one organizational constraint is difficult. Subjects took longer to detect a violation of probability, for example, when the cued object also violated size or support constraints. Such results show that organizational constraints are processed in an integral fashion, in much the same way as the integral stimulus dimensions discussed in Chapter 4. Correlated variation allows the subject to respond quickly because the presence of one type of violation reinforces another violation. Orthogonal variation of several violations slows detection times because the target violation cannot be easily separated from the others.

Since a scene's organization provides an overall scheme that makes the picture function as a whole, we would expect that one scene or picture can command selective attention relative to another integrated scene or picture. This conclusion is supported by a visual attention experiment done by Neisser and Becklen (1974). Two videotapes served as stimulus materials in this experiment. The first showed the hands of two persons engaged in common handgame. In this game, player A holds his hands palms up underneath the downturned hands of his opponent, player B (see Figure 7.3a). The object is for A to quickly move and turn his hands to slap the tops of B's hands before B has a chance to pull them away. We will refer to these attempts as attacking moves. The other videotape showed three players bouncing a ball to one another as shown in Figure 7.3b. The actual stimulus display showed these two tapes visually superimposed, as shown in Figure 7.3c, so that the action on each tape was discernible by the subject if careful attention was paid. Some subjects were asked to monitor the handgame and to press a button whenever an attacking move occurred. The other subjects were asked to monitor the ballgame and to press a button whenever the ball was thrown from one player to another.

In addition to observing how accurately their subjects could monitor one scene to the exclusion of the competing one, Neisser and Becklen were also interested in how much information the subjects were able to process from the unattended scene. Therefore, odd incidents were inserted into the unattended sequence. For a subject who was monitoring the handgame, the odd instances on the unmonitored ballgame were (1) a segment of a few seconds in which the ball was physically discarded but the players continued to "play" with an imaginary ball, and (2) a sequence in which the original male players were replaced by three female players. For a subject monitoring the ballgame, the odd instances in the handgame were (1) a handshake between the two handgame players, and (2) a short sequence in which the two sets of hands toss a small ball back and forth.

When subjects viewed a single tape, without the superimposition of the other sequence, performance was quite good—subjects failed to detect fewer than 1 percent of the target actions. Performance was not much worse when the unattended sequence was superimposed on the one to be monitored.

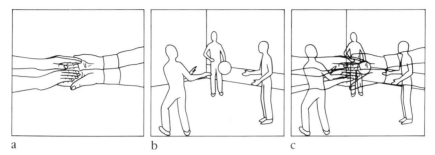

a   b   c

Figure 7.3 Neisser and Becklen superimposed a videotape of a handgame (a) and a videotape of a ballgame (b). Subjects were to monitor one of the games while watching the composite videotape (c). [From Neisser and Becklen, 1974.]

Moreover, subjects rarely noticed the odd events in the unattended sequence. In fact, only a few subjects, when questioned, were able to say that something odd had happened on the unattended sequence, and they were unable to specify what had been odd. When subjects were asked to monitor both sequences simultaneously, detection performance was quite poor; 20 to 40 percent of the target actions were missed in this situation.

The most important conclusion to be drawn from these experiments is that the overall organization of a picture has a powerful influence not only on how easily it can be processed but also on how selective attention can operate. In Biederman's studies the operation of several different types of constraint acted to integrate the visual information into an organized whole. Neisser and Becklen demonstrate that such organization can be used to segregate one sequence of pictorial information from another so that one picture can be closely processed while the other can be almost completely ignored.

MEMORY FOR PICTORIAL INFORMATION

Capacity and Duration of Picture Memory

Two of the most remarkable and noticeable aspects of visual memory are its large capacity and long duration. Everyone has experience with being able to vividly remember certain scenes from childhood, even though many years have elapsed. Moreover, although we see a huge number of different things and scenes over a lifetime, we are usually able to recognize a place as somewhere we have seen and been before. Thus memory, especially as measured by recognition, is quite good for visual material.

An equally large capacity and duration has been demonstrated for pictorial material as well. Shepard (1967) had subjects first study a set of 612 colored pictures one by one in a self-paced manner. Subjects were later tested by a series of 68 pairs of pictures. One picture in each pair was one of the original

612 stimuli, while the other was a completely new stimulus. The subject had to decide which of the two had been seen before, a task called a *forced-choice recognition test*. Subjects tested immediately after viewing the study series were nearly 97 percent correct in their choices; scores on a second test given 2 hours, 3 days, 7 days, or 120 days later were 99.7 percent, 92.0 percent, 87.0 percent, and 57.7 percent respectively. These scores show that picture memory is still excellent after as long as a week and is still above a chance level of response even after four months. Given the large number of items originally studied, this performance is quite impressive.

Haber and Standing (1969) obtained equally good performance from a group of subjects who were to remember 2560 photographs. Their subjects studied each of the original stimuli for 10 seconds in viewing sessions held over two to four days. Subjects were 90 percent correct in a forced-choice recognition test of 280 pairs given immediately after the presentation of the last of the original series. Another set of subjects was tested with test pairs in which the "old" picture had been mirror-image reversed. These subjects were 91 percent correct in recognizing the original stimuli, even though the test pictures were not physically identical to the originals. Finally, subjects asked to say whether a picture was the same as originally presented or was reversed were 85 percent correct. Pictures seem to afford a great deal of information to the observer in quite a short time, and this information is easily retained.

Determinants of Memory Performance: Viewing Time and Eye Fixations

Subjects in the memory studies cited in the preceding section were allowed to study the stimulus pictures for several seconds apiece. In this section, we consider whether subjects can extract enough information for good recognition performance when significantly less time is allowed for viewing and whether performance is a function of viewing time or a function of the number of eye fixations the subject makes during the allotted viewing time.

Potter (Potter and Levy, 1969; Potter, 1976) demonstrates that recognition memory for pictures is a positive function of exposure duration of the stimuli during initial inspection. Potter and Levy (1969) showed subjects rapid sequences of 16 color photographs. The stimuli in a series were shown for one of six durations ranging from 125 to 2000 milliseconds apiece. At the end of each sequence subjects were tested with a set of the 16 old pictures randomly mixed with a set of 16 new pictures, and they were to designate each test picture as old or new. The hit rate is the proportion of old pictures correctly identified, and it increased steadily from a low of .16 at the 125-millisecond exposure interval to a high of .93 at the 2000-millisecond interval. The false alarm rate is the proportion of new pictures incorrectly designated as old, and it was nearly 0 at all intervals. These results indicate that the longer the subject has to extract information from a picture, the more likely enough information will be obtained to lead to accurate memory. Clearly, 2 seconds is sufficient for subjects to extract enough information to be correct nearly all the time.

However, the short exposure durations during the study period may have precluded subjects from fully indentifying the stimuli or any of the objects in them. If this were the case, the low recognition scores for the short exposure durations might reflect not so much poor memory retention but subjects' failure to place anything into memory at the first viewing. In order to distinguish these two possibilities, Potter (1976) had subjects perform both a detection and a memory task. The subjects were again asked to view sequences of 16 color photographs which were presented at different exposure durations (113, 167, 250, and 333 milliseconds). Before each trial subjects in the detection group were given a target picture to detect in the following sequence. The target was specified either by showing the subject the target picture or by giving the subject a descriptive title for the target picture (e.g., a road with cars, a girl sitting in bed). When the target picture appeared they were to press a button. Subjects in the recognition group did not have to perform the detection task, but were a given a recognition test at the end of each sequence.

Performance on the detection task showed that the identification of the pictures was quite good even at the shortest exposure intervals. Overall detection accuracy was .87 for picture targets and .76 for named targets. Detection also generally improved with exposure duration, but even at the 113-millisecond exposure, detection accuracy with named targets was still above .60. Thus although the subject's ability to extract visual information and identify pictures is a function of the amount of time allowed to view the picture, 113 milliseconds is sufficient for subjects to identify a majority of pictures. Given 250 milliseconds, subjects can identify virtually all the pictures well enough to detect the target.

The recognition memory scores show much worse performance, as was expected on the basis of Potter and Levy's study. Memory performance was below .20 at 113 milliseconds and rose to slightly above .40 at 333 milliseconds. Two conclusions can be drawn from these results. First, the poor memory performance at very short exposures is not caused by subjects' inability to identify the pictures at those exposures. Clearly, subjects can identify pictures extremely well even if they are unable to remember them later. Second, apparently subjects need to extract more information or carry out more processing to remember a picture than to simply identify it well enough to distinguish it from others. Although 250 milliseconds may be enough for the initial recognition, nearly 2 seconds are needed for accurate memory.

This second conclusion has an important empirical consequence. The conclusion implies that subjects do not process the stimuli as completely in achieving high levels of detection accuracy as they do in achieving high levels of recognition accuracy. In other words, detection can be accomplished with only partial processing, a finding similar to the category effect (see Chapter 5). Potter's (1976) data confirm this finding since subjects who had performed the detection task, when later unexpectedly asked to do the recognition memory task, had much poorer memory scores than subjects who did not do the detection. The superior performance of the latter subjects presumably resulted from the fact that they did not resort to partial processing while they were viewing the original stimuli, and therefore they obtained information that was more helpful in remembering the pictures.

The length of the viewing time clearly affects how well a stimulus is recognized later, but is this effect caused by the length of time itself or by the number of eye fixations the subject makes during that time? To distinguish these two possible explanations of Potter's data, we turn to two eye fixation studies. Loftus (1972) asked subjects to perform a recognition task after viewing 180 photographs. Slides were presented in pairs for 3 seconds per pair, and subjects' eye movements were recorded. Each slide showed an assigned point value, and subjects were told they would be paid more money if they were later able to recognize the highly valued stimuli. When presented with a pair whose members had different point values, subjects tended to fixate almost entirely on the higher-valued one, while fixating on the other slide rarely or not at all.

Recognition accuracy was assessed by randomly mixing the original 180 stimuli with 180 new stimuli and having subjects identify each picture in the test series as old or new. The main finding was that the hit rate (the percentage of old stimuli recognized as old) increased with the number of fixations the subject made on the photographs during the study phase. Although the stimuli with higher point values were fixated more often and were recognized more accurately, number of fixations was the best predictor of accuracy when point value was held constant in the data analysis. Loftus also found that viewing time correlated highly with number of fixations, but did not influence memory performance independently of the number of fixations.

Moreover, in a second experiment, in which the viewing time per picture was varied, Loftus found that viewing time had no influence on memory as long as the number of fixations was held constant. Finally, Loftus reports that recognition memory for pictures that received no fixations during study was essentially zero. These pictures must have fallen in the periphery of the subjects' fixations on the other member of the pair during the study phase. We know from Antes' experiment that subjects extract enough information from the periphery of a fixation to determine their next eye movement. Yet in Loftus' experiment the periphery apparently did not yield enough information to help the subjects remember pictures that received no fixations. Apparently only a limited amount of memorable information is available in the periphery.

Although Loftus' experiment suggests that the critical variable in picture memory is the number of fixations, we must be careful not to overgeneralize these results. One reason for caution is that the stimuli in the experiment contained a wealth of detail and many easily identifiable objects that made them easy to distinguish from each other. In response to such stimuli, subjects may make many eye fixations of approximately equal length in order to spot as many of the distinguishing features as possible. However, if the old slides were very similar to the new slides, subjects would have to make longer but fewer fixations in order to determine small nuance of detail.

A second reason for caution in interpreting Loftus' results is that recognition tests are only one way to assess memory performance. An alternative method is a recall test in which the subject has to produce (draw) the stimuli rather than just recognize them when they are shown. In general, recognition performance for a set of stimuli is higher than recall performance. More importantly, performance on the two types of tasks depends on which type of test the subject is expecting. Bahrick and Boucher (1968), for example, show that subjects code visual stimuli differently depending on the type of test they expect to receive. Subjects do better on the expected than on the unexpected type of test.

Obviously, a pure recall test for complex pictorial material would require subjects to have exceptional drawing skills to reproduce detailed pictures from memory. Thus Tversky (1974) used a recognition task and a variant of a picture recall task to study eye movements and picture memory. Thirty line drawings of common objects were presented for 2 seconds each during the study phase. Each drawing had the name of the object printed beneath it. Half the subjects were told that they would later have to recognize the pictures, and the other half were told that they would have to recall the names of the objects. Actually both groups of subjects performed both the recall task and then the recognition task.

Tversky predicted that subjects who expected to recall the names would fixate on the printed names more often than the drawings, while those who expected to have to recognize the drawings would look at the drawings rather than the words. However, during the study phase both groups averaged nearly four fixations on the drawings and fewer than two fixations on the names. The recall performance of subjects expecting a recall test was overall superior to that of subjects expecting a recognition test, but recall performance for both groups improved with the number of fixations made on the printed name. In both groups recall declined as the number of fixations made on the picture increased.

Following the recall test, subjects were given a recognition test in which each original picture was paired with a similar drawing of the same object (e.g., another cup of a different shape). In contrast to Loftus' results, the larger the number of fixations made on the picture during study, the poorer the subject was at recognizing it. This pattern held for both groups, although subjects expecting a recognition task showed overall better recognition than those expecting a recall task. Tversky did not analyze memory performance as a function of viewing time independent of number of fixations. Yet one suspects that increased viewing time would yield better recognition performance because very few fixations were needed to spot all the informative areas of Tversky's type of stimulus, but longer fixations would have helped subjects pick up subtleties of the stimuli. This long-fixation pattern of scanning seems to result from the nature of the drawings and not from the subjects' intentions; long fixations were made by the recognition group, who expected to have to make fine distinctions between drawings during testing, and the recall group who did not have this expectation.

From this set of experiments we conclude that memory for pictures improves as study time increases until the exposure time is long enough for all the important information to be extracted. Depending on the nature of the stimuli and the task, one of two viewing strategies will be more successful: many fixations for short periods of time each or a few fixations for longer durations.

Determinants of Memory Performance: The Role of Visual Details

Throughout our discussion of picture memory we have implicitly assumed that information about the details of a picture is helpful in remembering the picture. For example, the eye movement data collected by Antes (1974) suggest that after a highly informative region of a picture is found, detail information is obtained from further exploration of that area. The Potter, Loftus, and Tversky experiments all suggest that the more time allowed or fixations made, the more likely such details are to be extracted. However, specific detail information is not always very easy to recall initially, even though it may be useful in a later recognition test. In everyday experiences we are sometimes unable to recall details about a person or object we saw clearly, yet we are easily able to recognize the person or object from a detailed description or second presentation at a later time.

Haber and Erdelyi (1967) studied this phenomenon in an experimental situation and show that details that are not available at immediate recall may be available later. Subjects were shown a rather detailed photograph of an outdoor scene for a few seconds; they were then asked to recall as much of it as possible using both drawings and verbal descriptions. When the subject had supplied as much detail as he could, the experimenter inquired about additional details of the objects that the subject had mentioned. Objective scoring of the responses showed that although subjects could remember the theme and general organization of the scene quite well, their memory for specifics was quite poor. Subjects were then given one of two intervening tasks for 30 minutes: dart throwing or a verbal free association task. Recall for the stimulus was again assessed using the same methods as before.

Subjects who performed the verbal association task recalled significantly more details on the second test than on the first while the dart-throwers did neither better nor worse on the retest. Thus the word association task made available some details that were recorded on the initial viewing but not mentioned during the initial recall. It is possible that memory for details has a language component that might have been stimulated by the word task, thus causing better recall on the retest. We will explore such possible relationships between visual information and verbal labels in Chapter 9.

If detail information is important to memory for pictures then we might expect that pictures having large amounts of detail information might be remembered very well. This assumption led Nelson, Metzler, and Reed (1974) to compare memory performance on four types of stimuli. The basic stimuli were a set of 120 black-and-white photographs, and the three other types of stimuli were made from them (see Figure 7.4). Embellished line-drawing stimuli omitted much of the photographs' texture and background information but included the most informative parts of the photographs and some detail information. Unembellished line-drawing stimuli showed only a general outline of the informative part of the photographs. The fourth type of stimulus was a brief sentence describing the content of the photograph.

Subjects saw each of 60 stimuli of one type for 10 seconds and were tested with a two-alternative forced-choice procedure. Contrary to expectation, subjects who saw the photographs, the embellished, or the unembellished line drawings all did equally well, and all of them showed better than 85 percent correct recognition after a seven-week retention interval. The verbal descriptions were significantly harder to recall, especially after seven weeks.

A contradictory set of findings was obtained by Loftus and Bell (1975), using the same photographs, embellished, and unembellished line drawings. These investigators were particularly interested in finding out whether or not subjects were using specific detail information to recognize the pictures. They used the same type of study and test procedure as Nelson, Metzler, and Reed, but the viewing time for the study trials varied from 60 to 500 milliseconds per picture. During the recognition task, Loftus and Bell asked their subjects to indicate whether each of their recognition choices was made on the basis of some detail in the picture or solely on the basis of overall familiarity. As expected, performance on an immediate test increased as a function of the initial viewing time. Also, subjects were more likely to report having recognized a detail at the longer durations. In fact, regardless of the type of drawing the subject had seen, the recognition performance was better for pictures in which a detail had been remembered than for pictures in which no detail had been remembered, independent of exposure duration. Finally, the photographs were remembered better than either type of line drawing, but here were no differences between the two types of line drawings.

These results have been further replicated and extended by Loftus and Kallman (1979). In this experiment some subjects wrote down memorable

"A SMILING OLD MAN HOLDS A LITTLE GIRL."

Figure 7.4 Four types of stimuli used by Nelson, Metzler, and Reed (1974) and Loftus and Bell (1975): verbal descriptions, unembellished line drawings, embellished line drawings, and photographs. [Courtesy of Thomas O. Nelson. Copyright 1974 by the American Psychological Association. Reprinted by permission of the publisher and the author.]

details during the study phase, while another group of subjects did not. At the time of the test, all subjects were asked to state whether they recognized any details. In test trials in which no detail was recognized, recognition memory was quite poor for all study exposure times. In trials in which a detail was noted, the group instructed to pay attention to details at study time did significantly better than the group that did not receive such instructions. This difference was particularly evident for stimuli given long exposures (500 or 1000 milliseconds) during the original study.

The obvious procedural difference between Nelson et al.'s and Loftus' studies is that the former used 10-second study exposures, while the latter used tachistoscopic exposures of 1 second or less. Subjects in Nelson's study had time to encode all the information in all the pictures, which led to equivalent performance on all types of pictorial material. In contrast, subjects in Loftus' experiments did not have time to encode all the information in the pictures. However, information appears to be more easily extracted from a photograph than from a drawing, so that memory performance is better for photographs than drawings at short, yet equal, exposure's. Perhaps information is more easily extracted from photographs because they contain more organizational and thematic information than do line drawings.

Of course, people do not habitually notice as much detail as possible in everyday life. We can easily identify and remember many scenes and objects whose details we cannot recall. For example, try drawing the two sides of a penny. Most people remember that a penny has the head of Lincoln on one side but may forget which side of the profile is shown. When Nickerson and Adams (1979) asked people to draw a penny, subjects commonly omitted such details as the words "Liberty," "United States of America," "E pluribus unum," and "one cent." Half the subjects reversed the direction of the head and almost as many mislocated the date. Even when given the correct list of details to include, subjects made many mistakes in drawing pennies. And many subjects could not pick out a correct drawing of the face of a penny from a set of fifteen. Although all subjects would have been able to identify a penny if shown one, they had suprisingly little detail information stored in memory. Nickerson and Adams conclude that not all visual details are remembered; only details that are useful or informative in distinguishing an object from others with which it is likely to be confused are stored.

Determinants of Memory Performance:
Organization

We have thus far used two approaches in discussing the effects of visual organization. In Chapter 4 we examined Gestalt principles for the organization of simple visual patterns and the influence of this type of organization on perceptual processing. Earlier in this chapter we examined how the organization imposed by the relationships between objects in a picture affects the perceptual processing of more complex pictures. Picture memory experiments show that such organization affects memory as well as perceptual processing.

The influence of organization on memory for more complex pictures is demonstrated by a series of experiments by Mandler and Parker (1976) and Mandler and Johnson (1976). Mandler and Parker reason that there are at least three types of memory-relevant information a subject could extract from a picture, all of which might be influenced by the organization of the picture. These are (1) an inventory of the main items in the picture, (2) the physical appearance of these items, and (3) the locations of the items, including the relative spatial relationships between them. In order to find out whether the organization of a picture influences the subject's memory for these types of information, Mandler and Parker used organized and unorganized pictures of the type shown in Figure 7.5.

Subjects viewed four pictures for 20 seconds apiece during the study phase; half viewed organized pictures and half viewed the unorganized versions. Immediately following the study period subjects were tested for their memory of two of the pictures. They were tested a week later on the remaining two pictures. An object recognition test required the subject to pick out each of the eight items contained in the picture, and for each item there were eight possible choices. The distractor items differed from the correct item in size, detail, or orientation (either right or left facing). During a subsequent reconstruction test, subjects were to place the eight items they had selected in their correct spatial relationship on a blank background. Subjects were allowed to correct their object choices during the spatial reconstruction test if they thought they had made any mistakes in their original selection.

Not surprisingly, picture memory was better on the immediate tests than on the delayed tests, and memory for detail was superior to memory for either size or orientation. Performance was essentially the same for organized and unorganized pictures for detail, size, and orientation at both the im-

Figure 7.5 Mandler and Parker used both organized and unorganized scenes to test their subjects' memories for information on both the physical appearance and the spatial arrangement of the objects. [From Mandler and Parker, 1976. Copyright 1976 by the American Psychological Association. Reprinted by permission of the publisher and the author.]

mediate and the delayed tests. Organization did, however, help subjects remember the spatial information in the pictures. Subjects were significantly more accurate in their object placements if they had viewed the organized pictures. Moreover, the placements were more accurate on the vertical dimension than on the horizontal dimension in organized pictures, while the reverse was true for the unorganized pictures. Of course, the organized pictures were bound by vertical position restraints; their organization allowed subjects to use common sense about whether certain objects are likely to be in the air, on the ground, or supported by something else. Horizontal locations, however, are less likely to be dictated by positional constraints. Thus it appears that memory for detail is largely independent of memory for spatial information in pictures, and that organization helps the latter more than the former.

Physical details are one form of pictorial organization; thematic content is another. In examining a series of pictures that are thematically related and convey an overall meaning, subjects may extract the theme or meaning of the pictures rather than their details. Such processing is analogous to reading normal, connected prose. We usually remember the overall meaning of the many sentences we read, although we are unable to accurately reconstruct the exact wording of each sentence even if tested immediately after we read the passage.

The process of extracting a theme or gist has been studied using both series of related sentences and series of related pictures. An important experiment on memory for related sentences was performed by Bransford and Franks (1971). During the study phase subjects were given a series of sentences to learn, each of which expressed a part of a large, complex sentence, such as "The tall tree in the front yard shaded the man who was smoking his pipe." Subjects received sentences that contained one component (e.g., "The tree was tall," or "The man was smoking his pipe."), two components (e.g., "The tall tree was in the front yard"), or three components (e.g., "The tree in the front yard shaded the man who was smoking his pipe"). On a recognition test subjects were extremely confident in "recognizing" the complete, complex sentence—although they had never been given that sentence, only parts of it. In fact, recognition and the confidence with which it was made increased as the number of components in the test sentence increased. It appears that the information from each of the individual study sentences is integrated into an overall idea such that subjects are unable to disentangle specific original inputs during the test, although they remember well, in a general way, all the information, or the gist.

Earlier in this chapter we noted that memory for complex pictorial information is remarkably good and that subjects can make distinctions during picture recognition tests that are based on rather specific details of the material. An important question about picture memory, therefore, is whether pictures are integrated into thematic wholes (as linguistic material is) or whether picture memory is specific enough for individual pictures to be remembered. Pezdek (1978) studied this question in an experiment that is the pictorial analogue to that of Bransford and Franks.

Pezdek's stimulus materials were pictures derived from a set of standard, multiobject pictures, the pictorial equivalent of Bransford and Franks' complex sentences. Subjects viewed series of pictures that contained one, two, or three of the spatial relationships between the objects in the complex standard—but they never viewed the complete standard picture. (Samples of these stimulus types are shown in Figure 7.6.) The test consisted of 96 recognition trials on which subjects judged each test picture as old or new and gave a confidence rating for each judgment.

Pezdek's results parallel those obtained for sentence materials. Subjects gave the highest confidence ratings to the more complex pictures, and were very confident that they had seen the standard complex picture, although it had not been shown to them during study. These results indicate that memory for pictures may be quite similar to memory for linguistic material. We apparently process the pictures for theme and gist, and we do not necessarily remember the exact visual details that are necessary to distinguish between conceptually similar pictures. Thus the very good picture memory reported in many studies may result not so much from the subjects' ability to record details as from their ability to use organization, both within and between related pictures, to construct meaningful representations of integrated visual ideas.

Complex scene

Stimulus with three objects

Stimulus with two objects

Stimulus with one object

Figure 7.6 From complex scenes Pezdek composed stimuli showing one, two, or three objects. Subjects were more likely to "recognize" the complex scenes — which were not presented to them during the study phase — than to recognize the stimuli showing only one or two objects, even though those simple stimuli had been presented during original study. [From Pezdek, 1978.]

RECOGNITION OF FACES

Everyday experience shows that people vary in how well they can recognize faces. Actually, face recognition involves two separate abilities. First, one must realize that the "face is familiar," that one has seen it before. This recognition can be accomplished on the basis of a photograph or a previous meeting. In most social situations, however, one must also be able to associate the person's name with the face. Of the two recognitions, the first is the easier. Many people, those who are "bad with names," can recognize the face but do not remember the name of an old acquaintance or a person they know only slightly.

One reason that memory for faces merits a separate discussion is that the cues for processing and retaining facial information must be considerably more complex than many of the cues used to remember more conventional pictorial information. This assumption follows from the everyday observation that we are capable of distinguishing among the many individuals with whom we interact on a daily basis, yet only a minimal number of simple visual features help us to do so. Almost all faces have two eyes, a nose, a mouth, and two ears, and the physical arrangement of these features, or organizational schema, is the same for all faces. Thus we must rely on much smaller differences of shape, color, and very importantly, relative positioning of the features (e.g., narrow-set eyes).

A second reason that memory for faces requires special discussion is that this kind of memory is influenced by some variables that do not affect other types of pictorial information in the same way. We will shortly examine evidence of this "specialness" of face memory and processing, as we review experiments concerning how well facial information is remembered, how it is encoded, and what aspects of faces are used in memory.

How Good Is Memory for Faces?

Like memory for most types of visual information, memory for faces is quite good and lasts for a very long time. The striking ability most people have to remember faces for long periods of time is illustrated in a study of memory for high school classmates carried out by Bahrick, Bahrick, and Wittlinger (1975). The stimuli for each subject were the photographs of classmates taken from the subject's own yearbook. Of the 392 subjects, some were recent high school graduates (3 months since graduation) and others had graduated more than 45 years earlier. Subjects were given several memory tests to assess different aspects of their memories for their classmates. These included (1) a free recall test for the names of classmates, (2) a forced-choice recognition test in which subjects had to select a certain person's picture from among four others from their own yearbook, (3) two recognition tests in which subjects had to recognize a name or a picture of a person from their own class, (4) a matching test in which the subject had to match names with pictures, and (5) a cueing test in which subjects had to give the names of classmates shown in each of a series of pictures.

One of the most striking aspects of the results is the high level of memory performance even 10 to 15 years after graduation. Performance in the name recognition, the picture recognition, and the matching tasks was over 90 percent correct even after 14 years. Performance declined only slightly thereafter, and was 60 to 70 percent correct even after 47 years. The cueing task is the one that most closely approximates a social situation in which a person must associate a name with a face. As expected, performance on this task was worse than on the various recognition tasks, even after short retention intervals of less than a year. However, scores on this test averaged 40 to 60 percent correct for all retention intervals up through 37 years. Moreover, the results did not seem to be influenced by how often the subjects had looked at their yearbooks since graduation. Thus even face recognition did not show any significant loss of memory over a 37-year retention span.

What Is Special About Faces?

There is no reason to think that the subjects in Bahrick's study were atypical of the population as a whole. Their recognition of faces was extremely good, despite the fact that the names and faces were learned within a limited amount of time (four years or less of high school), had to be distinguished from a large number of other faces both within the subject's high school class (average class size was 300) and from other social settings, and had to be retained over long periods of time. Many possible characteristics might explain this memory performance, and to discuss these we need to examine several other experimental findings regarding face recognition.

Hochberg and Galper (1967) used a recognition test for series of pictures of human faces to demonstrate that the preferred orientation for the processing and subsequent recognition of faces is upright. When the original study series and the forced-choice recognition pair series were both presented upright, the mean percentage of errors was 2.5 percent, but when the study and test series were presented upside-down, there were seven times as many errors. When the study series was presented upside-down and the test pictures upright the error rate was 23.3 percent. It therefore seems important that faces be initially encoded from an upright position; inversion at the initial presentation does not allow the subject to process the faces well enough to recognize them later.

That such inverted faces are more difficult to recognize later does not, in itself, argue that faces are special visual stimuli. Certainly, faces are most often seen and processed in an upright orientation, and the habitual scanning and information extraction patterns for faces depend on uprightness. However, uprightness does not similarly affect the processing of other types of visual stimuli that are also commonly viewed in the upright position. For example, houses are normally viewed upright and have a limited number of characteristic features, yet Yin (1969) shows that memory for pictures of houses is less affected by inversion than memory for pictures of faces. The average error rate was 3.7 percent for faces presented upright during both study and test, and almost five times higher for inverted faces; however, it was 9.3 percent for houses in the upright condition and only 14.3 percent in the inverted condition. Thus inversion has a selective negative effect: it greatly reduces memory for faces and affects far less memory for other types of normally upright visual stimuli.

Galper (1970) shows that the use of photographic negatives during study and test also reduces facial recognition. Recognition errors were 10 times greater for photos studied and tested as negatives than for photos studied and tested in their normal positive form. Although subjects studied the negatives, they were unable to process them well enough to later recognize them, a finding that supports our earlier conclusion that transformations of faces greatly disturb the encoding of the faces. In fact, the inversion transformation has been shown to significantly impair the ability of a subject to identify even familiar and well-known faces (Rock, 1974). Clearly, such transformation affects the ability to extract enough information to make even a well-learned response.

Subjects' poor performance in recognizing transformed faces that they have studied led Carey and Diamond (1977) to suggest that subjects rely on two types of information in remembering faces. One is a simple inventory of the appearance of the various facial features, and the other is configurational information about the spatial relationships between the individual features. Carey (1978) concludes that the transformations, especially at the time of original encoding, make it more difficult for the subject to extract configural information even though visual information may be obtained about the individual features themselves. Support for this conclusion comes from a number of different sources and, as we will see, the configural, or Gestalt-like, properties of a face are extremely important to a subject's ability to remember the face in a number of different experimental tasks.

One clue to how subjects organize facial features comes from Wolff's (1933) study of facial symmetry. Although faces appear to be bilaterally symmetric, there are often subtle visual differences between the right and left sides of a face. Wolff split photographs of faces in half and constructed full-face stimuli by reproducing either the right side with its mirror-image, or the left side with its mirror image. Subjects consistently rated the face composed of two right sides as more like the original face than the stimulus composed of two left halves. This pattern is generally not reported for other types of visual stimuli.

What Do Subjects See in Faces?

In discussing eye movements, we noted that fixations tend to fall on areas of high information content for pictures, and that for faces these areas tend to be the central features such as the eyes, nose, and mouth. To determine more specifically which features are most important to subjects in remembering faces, one can assess recall for various facial features and for the configural properties of the faces. Such experiments use the Identikit and Photofit face reconstruction kits usually used by police in helping witnesses give accurate descriptions of suspects.

Ellis, Shepherd, and Davies (1975) investigated their subjects' ability to reproduce faces originally constructed from combinations of photographs of facial features in the Photofit kit. Subjects made the reconstructions both from an original present for continued viewing and from memory once the original was removed. Although subjects were more than twice as accurate in the "present" condition than in the "memory" condition, the same features seemed to be important in both tasks. Namely, the forehead was most accurately recalled in both conditions, followed by the eyes, and mouth. Neither the nose nor the chin were very accurately reported in either condition. Furthermore, although subjects remembered individual features with some degree of accuracy, the overall quality of their reproductions was poor because they failed to capture the configural or Gestalt-like aspects of the face. Even in the "present" condition the reproductions often looked strikingly different from the originals because the configural relationships between the features were reproduced inaccurately. Here again we see the importance of configural properties to face recognition.

Matthews (1978) provides further evidence for a priority of features in face processing and for the importance of configural properties. Subjects were shown two side-by-side line-drawing faces constructed from a police Identikit and were to decide whether the two were the same or different. Faces in each pair were the same or differed on one to six facial features. In general the response times were faster the more differences there were between the two stimuli. However, if the difference between the stimuli involved the hairline and forehead region, the eyes, or the chin, subjects made uniformly fast responses. Differences involving other features seemed to require that the subjects engage in a serial, top-to-bottom comparison of those features in order to determine which, if any, differed.

Matthews notes that the features noticed first are those that would help a subject generate an overall Gestalt of the face within which additional features could later be placed. That is, once the size of the forehead and chin are noted, the subject would have a general idea of the spatial relations between the features and the contour of the face. Any differences between the stimuli in these larger, configural properties of the faces were noticed immediately by the subjects. Data on the fixation patterns made by subjects in a comparison task for faces indicate that subjects do fixate first on those areas of the face that yield configural information, and only later on other features (Walker-Smith, Gale, and Findlay, 1977).

Thus experimental results show that information about individual features is insufficient for accurate comparison and reproduction of both physically present faces and faces recalled from memory. In addition, experiments using the incidental learning method show that the processing of only feature information does not yield good recognition memory (Bower and Karlin, 1974; Winograd, 1976). Winograd's subjects looked through a series of face pictures and judged each according to some physical or personality-related factor. For example, some subjects were to judge whether each face had a large nose, while others were to judge whether each face looked intelligent or friendly, or whether it looked like an actor's face. Subjects were then unexpectedly given a recognition memory test for the faces. Recognition was significantly poorer for those subjects who had paid attention to just one physical feature during the initial inspection (e.g., size of nose, straightness of hair) than for subjects who had made a personality or occupation-related judgment. Presumably subjects processed the entire configuration of features in a face in order to make the more complicated judgments, and this configural information helped them remember the faces.

A final study of recognition memory for faces also shows that information about individual facial features does not produce a good memory code. Patterson and Baddeley (1977) examined the circumstances under which subjects have difficulty in remembering faces. Subjects easily recognized a test face as one they had seen before if the test face differed from the familiar face only in regard to relatively superficial characteristics such as pose (front or profile) or expression (serious or smiling). However, when the test faces were disguised by glasses, wigs, and beards, recognition performance was quite poor. Of course, these types of disguises probably changed both the simple visual features and the configural properties of the faces, and we cannot conclude which effect is the more important.

Conceptual Influences on Face Recognition

All the factors we have thus far considered are largely based on visual information and the ease with which subjects match the features and configuration of a test stimulus with stored information in memory. However, conceptual information also affects face recognition. Bruce (1979) used a visual search task to examine the conceptual factors that influence subjects' ability to pick out a familiar face from a series of distractors. On each trial the subjects were asked to decide whether the face presented was that of one of four well-known politicians, and reaction times were measured. Bruce reasoned that at least three types of information might affect how easily subjects could detect the target or reject a distractor.

First, to observe the effect of the visual similarity between the targets and the distractors, Bruce formed one set of distractor faces that was visually similar to the targets and another set that was visually dissimilar. Second, to determine the effect of familiarity, Bruce used some distractors that were the familiar faces of other famous persons; other distractors were unfamiliar. Third, the measure the effect of the occupational category of the stimulus faces, Bruce included as distractors faces of other politicians and those of actors or media personalities.

Bruce's results confirm that visual characteristics are important in quick recognition decisions about faces. Distractors that were visually dissimilar to the targets were rejected significantly faster than distractors that were visually similar. This result indicates that subjects were able to notice large-scale configural differences more readily than less pronounced differences. Unfamiliar distractors were responded to faster than familiar distractors, suggesting that subjects obtained an initial overall impression of the familiarity of each face and immediately rejected the unknown ones. Confirming that this analysis of familiarity did not proceed beyond a rough estimation, Bruce found that the occupational category of the unfamiliar faces had no significant effect on decision times for unfamiliar faces. This result was expected because subjects cannot have conceptual information about faces they have never seen before. However, the occupational category did have a significant effect on latencies to familiar faces. Reaction times were reliably longer to faces from the same occupational category as the targets (politicians) than they were to faces from the other occupation. This result is analogous to the category effect we saw in Chapter 5 for letters and digits.

Bruce's data suggest that face recognition is carried out in such a way that visual analysis and conceptual analysis are processed in a parallel fashion. Bruce posits that both the visual analysis and the conceptual analysis send information to a decision process that keeps count of the amounts of positive and negative evidence that accumulate during processing. When either the amount of positive information exceeds some positive threshold, or the amount of negative information falls below some negative threshold, a response of one type or the other is executed. The conceptual analysis includes both an assessment of the familiarity of the stimulus and its likely occupational class. However, if the familiarity analysis yields a low value, the additional occupational analysis becomes unnecessary. This type of model predicts that the decisions that will take the longest are those in which a great deal of visual analysis must be carried out in order to counteract the positive information from the conceptual analysis. In particular, the visually similar, familiar politicians should be the most difficult to reject, and the data confirm this.

Aging: A Special Case of Configural Change

As important as constant visual features and configurations are to the recognition of faces, people can also recognize a familiar face despite large changes in the features, overall shape, and configural properties caused by aging. One reason that people are able to recognize familiar faces despite the distortions caused by aging may be that such visual changes can be described by a mathematical function that can be applied to each of the points on a facial contour. This transformation is called _cardioidal strain,_ and it has been studied extensively as a cue for aging by Pittenger and Shaw (1975) and Pittenger, Shaw, and Mark (1979).

Figure 7.7 depicts the effects of cardioidal strain. Consider the rectangular grid shown in the center of the top row. Two directions of cardioidal strain can be imposed on the points in the grid. For negative values of strain points near the top of the grid move farther away from one another in the horizontal direction, while points near the bottom of the grid move closer together. The greater the strain, the more the originally rectangular grid would appear heart-shaped (hence the term _cardioid_). Similarly, a positive cardioidal transformation tends to make the low points move farther away from one another, and the higher points move closer together. Large positive cardioidal strains transform a rectangular grid into an inverted heart.

The second row of Figure 7.7 shows what happens when cardioidal strain is applied to the profile of a human face. Negative strain yields a figure with a relatively larger forehead and skull, while positive values of strain generate profiles with a receding forehead but enlarged jaw and neck. The profiles with large negative cardioidal strain look like infants or small children, while those having a large positive strain look like older adults. Pittenger and Shaw (1975) obtained relative age estimates from subjects who were shown human profile contours that differed in cardioidal strain. The data confirm our observation that apparent age is a steadily increasing function of the amount of strain in the contour.

Moreover, it appears that cardioidal strain is a relatively universal transformation that can signal change in age for a variety of stimuli other than human faces. Figure 7.7 also shows the results of cardioidal transformations of different amounts to a standard bird's head and a standard Volkswagen. Pittenger, Shaw, and Mark (1979) obtained relative age judgments for these stimuli as a function of the amount of strain. Subjects judged stimuli having large negative strain as "younger" and those having large positive strain as "old."

It is particularly striking that the cardioidal strain transformation induces perceived differences in age even for inanimate objects, such as Volkswagens, which do not change in configuration over time. This finding indicates that our assessment of cardioidal strain is in some sense independent of our ability to extract featural information from an object or face. It is likely that at least some of the visual information we extract concerns featural invariants that allow us to recognize a familiar face no matter how much transformation has been produced by aging. Given that we have this invariant information at our disposal, we can then make use of our knowledge of the effects of cardioidal strain to predict the exact configuration and appearance of those features at any designated age. This separability of invariant features and the effects of age transformations allow us to be relatively accurate in recognizing faces in spite of aging.

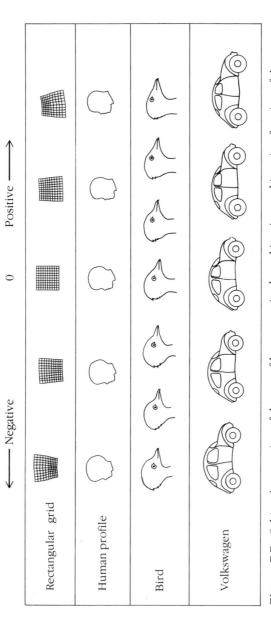

Cardioidal strain

← Negative   0   Positive →

Rectangular grid

Human profile

Bird

Volkswagen

Figure 7.7 Subjects' perception of the age of humans, animals, and inanimate objects is a function of the amount of cardioidal strain present in the drawing. [From Pittenger and Shaw, 1975. Copyright 1975 by the American Psychological Association. Reprinted by permission of the publisher and the author.]

Deficits in Facial Processing: Prosopagnosia

One type of evidence that would demonstrate that face recognition and processing are carried out by a system specialized for the task would be the existence of a face-specific processing loss. If subjects could be found who had little, if any, facial memory, and yet had no other type of memory impairment, their condition would suggest that faces are recognized by a special system that can be selectively destroyed. Clinical observers of brain-damaged patients have detected a group that shows *prosopagnosia,* the inability to recognize faces. Such patients have difficulty recognizing faces of family members, friends, and even their own face, and tend to use nonfacial physical characteristics to help them recognize people.

Prosopagnosiacs do seem able to remember some types of visual information that is not specific to face recognition, which means that prosopagnosia is not a generalized memory deficit. In fact, some prosopagnosiacs do reasonably well on face recognition tasks that involve faces of persons unknown to them. Prosopagnosia can be accompanied by other types of memory deficits, though the type of additional loss varies from patient to patient. The important point is that facial memory deficits do not result from general memory impairment, but they do not imply face-specific processing either.

Another difficulty in interpreting prosopagnosia as evidence of face-specific memory loss is that no one area of the brain seems to be solely responsible for face recognition. In the next section of this chapter we examine the role of hemispheric specialization in picture processing. However, for our present purposes we note that the right hemisphere appears to play a larger role in face recognition than the left hemisphere (Konorski, 1967; Yin, 1970). Facial-memory deficits are more likely to occur as the result of right hemisphere damage. However, such deficits can result from damage to any of a number of parts of the right hemisphere, and even from damage to the left hemisphere (see Ellis, 1975, for a review of these studies). Ellis suggests that several areas of the brain, many of them in the right hemisphere, contribute to memory for faces, and that damage to one or more of them causes prosopagnosia. This explanation would account for why different prosopagnosiacs have different accompanying memory deficits. The type of additional memory deficit would depend on the specific areas of brain damage. Ellis' explanation has important implications for the contention that face recognition is a special process. Under this conjecture, the specialness results from the joint operation of a group of cortical regions and not from the operation of one region that processes only faces. However, faces could still be considered special visual stimuli because no other patterns require that precise combination of cortical processing areas.

A Summary of Facial Recognition

Our discussion of facial recognition has emphasized two important points. First, faces have some properties that distinguish them from other types of visual stimuli. In particular, they are influenced by transformation such as inversion and photographic negative in ways that other types of stimuli are not. Second, although organization plays a major role in visual memory for all kinds of stimuli, it is particularly important for faces. In many ways, faces are the most Gestalt-like stimuli we process, and the configural properties play an even greater role in the appearance and memory for faces than for other types of visual stimuli.

HEMISPHERIC SPECIALIZATION

In our discussion of picture processing, the topic of cerebral functioning became most apparent in our examination of facial recognition. We noted that the right hemisphere is intimately involved in the ability to recognize faces. Such specialization by the right hemisphere explains why right-right composite faces look more like the original than do left-left composites, and also explains at least part of the data on prosopagnosia. However, the involvement of the right hemisphere in the processing of faces is only one aspect of that hemisphere's involvement in visual processing. Specialization of the right hemisphere for such tasks is, in turn, part of a larger organization of specialization patterns for the two cerebral hemispheres for various types of cognitive tasks. In this section we consider those aspects of hemispheric specialization that are of particular importance to visual information processing.

General Considerations

The brain consists of two hemispheres, each capable of independent cognitive functioning. As we noted earlier, the right hemisphere receives sensory input from, and controls the motor movement of, the left side of the body, while the left hemisphere controls the right side. Coordination between the two hemispheres is effected by a bundle of nerve fibers, the *corpus callosum,* that connect the two hemispheres and allow information to pass back and forth.

Although the two hemispheres are nearly physically identical, each one is specialized to perform some cognitive functions more easily than the other. In very general terms, the left hemisphere is specialized for understanding and producing language, while the right hemisphere is specialized for spatial and visual tasks. In right-handed people, the left hemisphere is the *dominant hemisphere*—because it controls the preferred hand. However, neurological and behavior tests of left-handed persons show that some have mixed dominance or left-hemisphere dominance; only about 30 percent show right-hemisphere dominance.

Studies of Split-Brain Subjects

One of the most interesting and convincing ways to determine the types of tasks each hemisphere is specialized to perform is to test a subject who has undergone commissurotomy. This operation, performed for medical purposes to relieve seizures, involves severing the corpus callosum but leaves the sensory and motor crossover points, such as the optic chiasma, intact. The patient then has two functionally independent cerebral hemispheres that can no longer communicate with each other. By presenting different types of stimulus materials to either the right or left side of the body, the experimenters can control which hemisphere is being required to perform the task, and they can assess the performance of each hemisphere independently of the other.

Gazzaniga (1967, 1970) summarizes a series of experiments in which split-brain subjects were tested with a variety of verbal and tactile stimuli. Figure 7.8 shows a sample experimental testing situation. If a subject is shown a word or picture in the right visual field, or if his right hand is given an unseen object, the information would be transmitted to the left hemisphere.

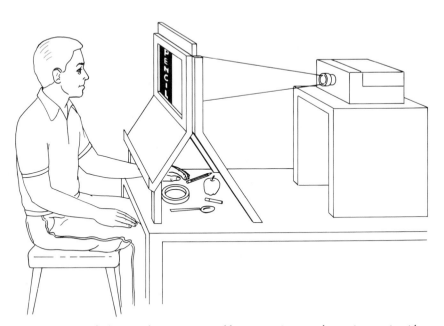

Figure 7.8 Split-brain subjects are tested by presenting words or pictures in either the right or left visual field. Subjects may be asked to respond verbally or to choose among several hidden objects with either the right or left hand. [From M. Gazzaniga, *The split brain in man*. Copyright © 1967 by Scientific American, Inc. All rights reserved.]

Split-brain subjects were able to read aloud words shown in the right visual field and to name objects felt with the right hand. However, subjects were unable to read words or name stimuli that were presented to the right hemisphere. Even a picture presented to this hemisphere failed to produce a correct naming response. These results provide support for the contention that the left hemisphere controls language and that the right hemisphere does not have access to linguistic skills.

When the right hemisphere was shown a picture of an object and its corresponding left hand was allowed to feel various objects placed out of sight, the right hemisphere was capable of matching object to picture. The right hemisphere could also identify words corresponding to concrete objects using a nonlinguistic tactile response. For example, if the right hemisphere saw the word *spoon,* the left hand could pick out the designated object by feeling several unseen objects. However, even after the right hemisphere responded in this way to a linguistic stimulus, the subject could not correctly name either the stimulus word or the held object; the right hemisphere had no means to convey the information to the left hemisphere, the source of spoken responses.

Although the left hemisphere is clearly superior at carrying out linguistic tasks, the right hemisphere appears to perform better on some types of spatial and visual tasks. Split-brain subjects copy simple line drawings more accurately with their left hand (right hemisphere) than with their right hand. Furthermore, Bogen and Gazzaniga (1965) show that the left hand can duplicate a design formed by four patterned cubes more quickly than can the right hand. This type of task requires both visual recognition of the patterns on each cube and the problem-solving ability to make the proper arrangement of these individual components. Therefore, the right hemisphere must possess considerable visual cognitive abilities independent of the linguistic abilities shown by the left hemisphere.

Studies of Normal Subjects

It is obviously difficult to study the independent abilities of the two hemispheres in normal adult subjects because the two hemispheres freely communicate across the intact corpus callosum. Thus evidence from normal subjects, which corroborates the results of split-brain studies, relies on more indirect methods of assessment. The relative superiority of the left hemisphere in processing linguistic material, for example, has been demonstrated in normal individuals using the *dichotic listening* task. In this task separate auditory stimuli are played simultaneously to each ear, and the subject's task is to identify each stimulus. When the stimuli are speech sounds, such as syllables or words, subjects are better at identifying the stimulus played to their right ear (Kimura, 1961), an effect known as the *right-ear advantage* for linguistic stimuli. Although the auditory pathways are not as completely crossed as are the visual pathways, the left hemisphere receives a larger amount of information from the right ear. Thus the right-ear advantage is really a left-hemisphere advantage for language. Because right-ear advantage does not extend to nonspeech auditory stimuli, such as tones, the conclusion is that the left hemisphere is superior in processing language.

Visual stimuli may be presented to each hemisphere by showing them to either the right or the left visual field. Which field, and hence which hemisphere, produces superior performance on visual tasks depends on the type of stimulus presented. When subjects are asked to identify letters, there is a right-field advantage (Kimura and Durnford, 1974). Since letters may be regarded as linguistic material, this corroborates the auditory findings that the left hemisphere is specialized for language. However, if an array of items is presented tachistoscopically, be they dots, geometric forms, or letters, subjects can assess the number shown more accurately using the right hemisphere (Kimura and Durnford, 1974).

Finally, a number of primarily visual tasks do not show clear superiority for either hemisphere. For example, there appears to be no difference between the hemispheres for identification of nonsense figures, patterned square matrices, or upright and inverted line drawings of common objects (Kimura and Durnford, 1974). Such visual processing abilities seem to be less lateralized than are linguistic abilities.

Hemispheric Specialization and Face Recognition

The evidence for the involvement of the right hemisphere in face recognition comes from two types of studies. The first type is the study of face recognition in subjects who have brain damage in a known portion of the brain, but whose corpus callosums are otherwise intact. Yin (1970) studied the effects of different types of brain damage on the ability to recognize upright and inverted faces and houses. Yin tested patients who had experienced damage to different cerebral regions, but the important data come from those patients having damage to the posterior region of the right hemisphere and from normal subjects.

Normal subjects showed the expected pattern of results—fewer recognition errors were made on upright faces than upright houses, and performance declined more severely for inverted faces than for inverted houses. However, the right-posterior brain-damaged subjects had nearly identical numbers of errors on the upright faces and houses, and inversion hurt performance on houses more than faces. Data from patients with other types of brain damage produced the same pattern of results as did normal subjects. Yin's experiment therefore provides strong evidence that the posterior region of the right hemisphere is critical to normal face recognition.

Yin's finding that right-posterior brain-damaged subjects were deficient in encoding upright faces but not other stimuli led Leehey et al. (1978) to posit that the portions of the right hemisphere that process complex visual patterns may not have been the regions damaged in Yin's patients. Leehey et al. reason that the right hemisphere normally processes nonverbal, visual stimuli, but that the right posterior region is critical for processing the special characteristics of upright faces. The essence of their argument is that two levels of processing are needed to recognize faces: one that is common to all complex visual patterns, and a second that is specific to upright faces. Both may well be right hemisphere functions.

To test their hypothesis with normal adult subjects, Leehey et al. used brief tachistoscopic presentation of stimuli to either the right or left visual field. The stimuli were thus initially received by either the left or the right hemisphere. The stimuli were upright or inverted faces and words presented with the letters arranged vertically. Because the words are linguistic stimuli, they were expected to, and did, show a right-visual-field advantage. Because inverted faces are complex visual patterns, they were expected to, and did, show a left-visual-field advantage. Moreover, because upright faces depend even more heavily on right hemisphere functioning than do other complex visual patterns, the left-field advantage was expected to be even greater than that obtained for the inverted faces; this result was also obtained. Leehey et al. were therefore able to support their hypothesis regarding two levels of processing by obtaining a larger left-field advantage for normal than inverted faces.

Some Conclusions on Hemispheric Specialization

Our brief discussion of how cognitive processing abilities are lateralized in the brain gives only a very oversimplified view of what is known about this topic. The evidence that the dominant left hemisphere plays a crucial role in language processing for right-handed subjects is clearly supported by the data from split-brain subjects, as well as by data from lateralized presentation of auditory and visual language stimuli to normal subjects. The experiment by Leehey et al. provides some of the clearest support for the position that the right hemisphere is superior at processing complex visual patterns and faces. Unfortunately, not all visual processing tasks yield right-hemisphere advantages (see Kimura and Durnford, 1974), nor has the left-field advantage for faces been obtained in all cases (see Ellis and Shepherd, 1975). It therefore appears that the two hemispheres are not completely complementary in their processing capacities.

Moreover, the data obtained from left-handed subjects do not always show the expected reverse pattern of hemispheric specialization. In particular, left-handed subjects frequently show a less clear pattern of specialization for language by their dominant hemispheres. In addition, male and female subjects do not appear to be lateralized to the same degree. (For further information on the role of sex and handedness in cerebral lateralization, see

Levy and Reid, 1978.) However, we have a pattern of results that characterizes a large number of subjects and represents the beginning of an understanding of brain functioning in visual processing.

SUMMARY

In this chapter we examined how human beings process and remember pictures. Throughout our discussion we observed that the organizational properties of a picture stimulus are tremendously important for all aspects of picture processing. The literature on eye movements suggests that subjects fixate on the more informative portions of a pictorial stimulus. However, the data from tachistoscopic experiments show that the amount of useful information obtained from a single fixation depends on the organization of the picture as a whole; whenever organizational constraints are violated detection and memory performance decline. The organization of a picture can help a subject distinguish one whole scene from another one and can influence how well individual aspects of the picture can be selectively attended to.

Organization also facilitates memory of both simple and complex pictures. Although the amount of detail information extracted helps subjects remember what they see, the organization within a picture and relationships between related pictures help subjects organize specific information into more memorable wholes. Perceptual processing of memory for faces provides an exceptionally good example of the role of organizational factors in visual processing: The individual features of faces form unitary wholes in which the most important aspects are the relative configural properties.

In the final section of this chapter, we saw that the right hemisphere plays a relatively larger role in processing visual stimuli than does the left hemisphere, particularly for stimuli that are faces. In concert with the perceptual and memory data, the hemispheric specialization results indicate that one role of the right hemisphere might be to process holistic, configural properties of visual stimuli.

SUGGESTED READING

Yarbus (1967) provides a very interesting and readable account of early research on eye movements. The role of organization in picture processing is covered by Biederman (1981) and other papers collected by Kubovy and Pomerantz (1981). Readers interested in pursuing hemispheric specialization will find that Requin (1978) devotes an entire group of chapters to the topic.

Chapter 8

Visual Imagery and Mental Representation

In Chapter 7 we examined many characteristics of the visual long-term memory system, but we did not specify how the visual information is represented or retained. We discussed some studies that show that the encoding of specific details is important for picture memory, but we did not consider whether such details are verbally labeled or are stored in another fashion. In this chapter, then, we must examine the form in which visual memory is represented.

Our everyday experience tells us that we need not apply verbal labels to parts of pictures in order to remember them. When asked to recall the appearance of a very familiar object, we often form a "mental picture" or image, from which we can obtain more specific information. Although not everyone is equally good at forming and using such images, almost everyone agrees that this type of memory is much different from memory in which verbal material is recalled. Indeed, images are often rich in details not easily described in words.

Psychologists make a similar distinction between two qualitatively different forms of representing information in memory. In a *propositional representation*, information is stored in terms of propositions (sometimes called *predications*) about the relationship between one or more objects, or an object and a property. For example, one could state a proposition about the appearance of a friend: "Peter has a beard." But this proposition does not exhaust all the visual properties of Peter nor even completely describe his beard. We would have to add such propositions as "The beard is short," and "The beard is black."

All this information could also be stored in memory as an *imaginal representation* (or *analog*). The mental image would likely include many more visual details and characteristics than the few preceding propositions; for example, the exact length of the beard and the exact color (completely black or with touches of grey and brown). An imaginal representation contains a great deal of detail, much of which cannot be easily expressed in propositions. However, since most people are not good at drawing, they generally convey the information contained in an imaginal representation to someone else only through verbal propositions.

The existence of imagery as qualitatively different from propositional memory is intuitively evident. Researchers have sought to obtain objective evidence for it as well. For example, during sleep rapid eye movements are associated with periods of dream imagery. Although some studies report a correlation between the direction of these rapid eye movements and the content of the dream (Dement and Wolpert, 1958), other investigators found that congenitally blind subjects also exhibit rapid eye movements even though they could not possibly be scanning visual dream images (Offenkrantz and Wolpert, 1963). Thus eye movements are not directly correlated with visual imagery during sleep, and there is little evidence of a relationship between the two during wakeful, conscious control of imagery. Antrobus and Singer (1964), for example, failed to find a correlation between eye movements and the reported vividness of the subject's images.

Another possible physiological correlate of imagery is the electroencephalogram (EEG), which shows general patterns of electrical activity in the brain. One of the characteristics of persons at rest with eyes closed is the alpha rhythm, a brain wave pattern with 8 to 12 peaks of firing per second. The alpha rhythm is suppressed when subjects report they are engaged in imagery (Lehmann, Beeler, and Fender, 1965). However, the alpha wave suppression does not directly confirm that the subject is making use of an imaginal rather than a propositional representation.

Because introspective reports and the physiological data cannot determine what type of memory representation subjects use, information processing psychologists have devised other objective, but indirect, methods for studying visual representation. In this chapter we discuss several of these methods and examine both the functional and structural characteristics of the imaginal representation. Our discussion of the functional characteristics includes several studies that give behavioral evidence showing that imagery exists and that it constitutes a system separate from the verbal, propositional memory system. Our discussion of the structural aspects of imagery focus on the nature of the imaginal representation and how it is used in a variety of tasks. We also examine individual differences in the ability to use imaginal representations. Finally, since not all psychologists support the claim that imagery is a separate representational system, we evaluate the strength of the evidence favoring imagery and consider the counterarguments.

FUNCTIONAL ASPECTS OF IMAGERY

To gather empirical evidence of the existence of imagery, researchers conduct experiments concerning subjects' ability to do any one of a number of memory and perceptual tasks. They assume that imagery functions in certain ways that would generate noticeable patterns of good or poor performance and that one can infer from the data that subjects are using imagery if no other obvious explanatory principle accounts for the pattern of performance observed. In this section we examine the performance of subjects in memory tasks to determine whether the evidence indicates that imagery is used.

Interestingly enough, some of the more convincing evidence for imagery, and for a separate imaginal representation memory system, comes from research on a task that seems unrelated to visual processing or visual memory: the paired-associate learning task. To briefly review the procedure, in a paired-associate experiment the subject is given a list of pairs of words to remember. Given the first, or stimulus, word from a pair, the subject is to supply the second, or response, member of the pair. Subjects are typically given a list of 16 or 20 such pairs, and each pair is presented individually either orally or visually. The ease of learning is assessed either by the number of trials required for the subject to master the entire list or by the number of correct responses made in a limited number of test trials.

A number of experiments suggest that imagery plays a role in a subject's ability to learn paired associates. One of the earliest experiments is Paivio's (1965), in which subjects were asked to learn lists of 16 noun pairs. Four different types of lists were constructed: CC pairs in which both nouns referred to concrete objects (e.g., pencil/tree), AA pairs in which both nouns referred to abstract concepts (e.g., health/theory), CA pairs in which the stimulus noun was concrete and the response item abstract (e.g., dress/truth), and AC pairs in which the stimulus was abstract and the response item was concrete (e.g., soul/potato). Over four test trials on these pairs, subjects averaged 11.41 correct responses on the CC pairs, 10.01 on the CA, 7.36 on the AC, and 6.05 on the AA. While subjects performed better when the response member of the pair was concrete rather than abstract, the more significant difference in performance occurs when the stimulus word is concrete.

Paivio's interpretation is that the ease of learning of a paired associate depends on there being some "conceptual peg" upon which associative links to the paired word can be hung. The best conceptual peg is imagery; concrete nouns that elicit strong images suggest many possible links to their paired associates. Subjects perform best on a paired-associate learning task when they can easily imagine the items. In particular, they must clearly image the stimulus noun so that they form a directional link from it to its response item.

To confirm this imagery hypothesis, Paivio asked another set of subjects to rate each of the nouns used in the paired-associate experiment for imagery value. Concrete nouns were rated as significantly easier to form images of than abstract nouns. However, the concrete nouns were also rated as more meaningful, in that they generated more verbal associates, and as more familiar than the abstract nouns. These data, then, do not allow us to determine whether the imagery of the concrete nouns produced superior memory performance or whether the meaningfulness or familiarity produced the result.

To separate the effects of imagery from the effects of the other factors, one must perform an experiment in which only the imagery values of the paired-associate nouns are allowed to vary while the other factors are held constant. In order to generate such lists of pairs, Paivio, Yuille, and Madigan (1968) compiled a table of imagery, concreteness, meaningfulness, and frequency (familiarity) values for each of 925 nouns. Imagery values were obtained by having a group of college students rate the nouns for their capacity to elicity "a mental picture, or sound, or other sensory picture." Paivio, Smythe, and Yuille (1968) constructed lists of high imagery–high imagery pairs (HH), low imagery–low imagery (LL) pairs, high-low (HL), and low-high (LH) pairs. The other characteristics of the four types of word lists were held constant. Correct recall was significantly higher when the stimulus noun was high in imagery value rather than low in imagery value. A smaller increase in recall was found when the response item was high in imagery value.

According to Paivio's explanation low-imagery, abstract nouns produce poorer memory performance because they elicit fewer associative links. Our experience with abstract terms is purely linguistic; because we cannot see or physically experience an abstract concept such as *soul*, we code its meaning in a largely verbal fashion. In contrast, we derive the meanings of concrete terms from both their linguistic usage and from direct visual and sensory experience. We therefore can code concepts such as *table* in terms of both visual, sensory imagery and in terms of verbal, semantic characteristics (e.g., a piece of furniture, a noun, etc.). This distinction is the essence of the *dual coding hypothesis* (Paivio, 1971). Concrete nouns can be encoded into both a verbal and an imaginal memory system at the time of presentation and, therefore, offer more opportunities for meaningful associations. Abstract nouns can be encoded only verbally.

One of the important assumptions of the dual coding hypothesis is that imagery does not simply supply an additional means of encoding the concrete nouns but rather supplies a richer source of links for forming paired associations. Bower (1970a) tested the hypothesis that forming an image is in itself not sufficient to facilitate later recall, but that an image that facilitates an interaction between the nouns in a pair does facilitate learning. All the stimuli in Bower's study were high-imagery nouns, and they were learned under one of three conditions. One group of subjects was asked to learn 30 pairs of nouns using rote repetition. Two other groups were instructed to use imagery, one by constructing an interactive scene of the two nouns, and the other by imagining each noun individually and "separated in 'imaginal space.'" Figure 8.1 gives examples of interactive and noninteractive images. After viewing each pair once for 10 seconds, subjects who used rote repetition recalled 30 percent of the paired associates; subjects who formed interactive imagery recalled 53 percent of the pairs, and subjects who formed noninteractive imagery recalled only 27 percent of the pairs.

Another way to demonstrate the relationship between associatively rich images and recall for paired associates is to provide the subjects with a picture of the stimulus and response nouns in an interacting image. Wollen and Lowry (1971) had subjects learn two lists, each containing eight paired associates. One list had high-imagery nouns, the other low-imagery nouns. One group of subjects was shown pictures of the two nouns in an interacting scene (e.g., a horse standing under a tree for the high-imagery pair horse/tree, or a flower in an open doorway for the low-imagery pair bloom/portal).

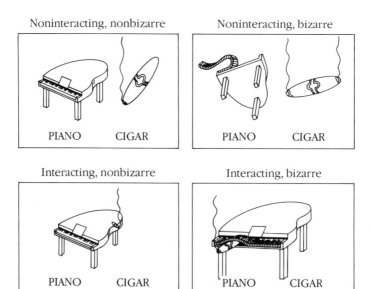

Figure 8.1 Wollen, Weber, and Lowry showed subjects pictures of the items in the paired-associate recall task. Pairs that were depicted as interacting were easier to remember than noninteracting pairs. Bizarreness of the pictures had no effect on performance. [From Wollen, Weber, and Lowry, 1972.]

A second group of subjects was shown pictures in which the words from the list were re-paired at random. The third group of subjects was not shown any pictures.

After one learning trial, high-imagery pairs were remembered significantly better than low-imagery pairs regardless of the type of pictorial information given. Moreover, subjects who saw a relevant, interacting picture remembered the pairs much better than subjects in either of the other two groups. This result confirms the hypothesis that memory is aided by the use of interactive imagery. Interestingly, subjects who viewed the randomly re-paired pictures during the learning trial did no worse than the subjects who were not shown pictures. Presumably, the former subjects were able to ignore the useless pictures and to remember pairs using the same verbal processes as the latter control subjects.

Given that associative links between the items improve recall, Wollen, Weber, and Lowry (1972) sought to determine whether more salient associative links would be more memorable. Word pairs were accompanied by pictures in which the words were shown either (1) interacting in a bizarre manner, (2) interacting in a nonbizarre manner, (3) not interacting but bizarrely drawn, or (4) not interacting and not bizarrely drawn. Examples of these pictures are shown in Figure 8.1. After one study trial of 2 seconds for each pair, pairs learned with either type of interacting picture were remembered significantly better than pairs learned with noninteracting pictures. Contrary to the original hypothesis, the bizarreness of the picture did not influence memory performance. Thus, the ability of imagery to aid memory performance depends on links between the words represented by interactive imagery, but bizarreness does not improve the subjects' retention of these links.

Imagery as a Mnemonic Device

That imagery facilitates memory has been a commonplace for centuries. One of the most famous imagery-dependent mnemonic devices is the *method of loci*, which is illustrated in the legend of the Greek poet Simonides. After Simonides had recited one of his poems at a crowded banquet, he was called outside the banquet hall—just in time to be saved when the hall collapsed, crushing the other banqueters. Although the relatives of the dead were unable to identify the crushed bodies, Simonides was able to identify each one by remembering the place where each person had been during the banquet. Thus he remembered the names of the individuals using imagery that associated the appearance of each person and the physical characteristics of each location. This associative method takes its name from the Latin word *locus*, meaning "place."

Although the story of Simonides is derived principally from legend, we know that Greek and Roman orators practiced and used the method of loci as an aid in remembering their speeches. Generally, the information to be

Visual Imagery and Mental Representation

remembered was pictured in an interactive, associative image with a set of well-known and ordered locations. By mentally proceeding from one location to another, the orator could retrieve the stored information through the imagery at each mental location. Bower (1970b) offers the pictures in Figure 8.2 to illustrate how someone could remember a shopping list using familiar locations in and around the home. Each item on the list is vividly imagined at a location one would pass on the way into the house. Hot dogs, for instance, are imagined as being large and lying on the driveway, a cat appears eating its food in the garage, and so forth. To recall the items on the list, one would simply make a mental trip from the garage into the house, noticing the item to be remembered at each location.

For such a system to work certain conditions must hold. Bower (1970b) suggests nine important conditions.

1. One must have a list of cues that one knows well. One will not be able to retrieve any associations if the cue images are not available at both presentation and recall.
2. The cues must be memory images of geographical locations.
3. Associations must be formed between the items to be remembered and the cue locations at the time of original presentation and learning.
4. The associations between the cue locations and the items must be one-to-one if the correct serial order of the items is important.

Figure 8.2 Bower suggests that these pictures might help somene use the method of loci to remember the shopping list: hot dogs, cat food, tomatoes, bananas, and whiskey. [From Bower, 1970b.]

Subjects can effectively remember several items all linked to a single cue location, but may be unable to retrieve the correct ordering of those items. Pairing one memory item with each cue location ensures that the correct ordering of items will be retained.

5. One must use imagery, especially visual imagery, to form associative links. Imagery from other sensory modalities (e.g., sound or taste) may also help memory, but visual imagery is our most vivid, and therefore useful, imagery system.

6. The image used to link the to-be-remembered item and its cue location should be interactive, though not necessarily bizarre.

7. If more than one study opportunity is given, the same cue locus should be used for a given memory item from one trial to the next.

8. The subject must be able to generate the cue locations without help during testing.

9. Any cue used during recall to retrieve memory information must be similar to the original cue used during study to learn the material.

Another mnemonic system that makes use of imagery is the *pegword method*. It is very similar to the method of loci in that the subject remembers information by forming images of the memory material with an ordered set of picturable cues. In this case, however, the cues are not geographical locations but rather nouns that are learned in the proper order by a simple rhyming verse:

> One is a bun
> two is a shoe
> three is a tree
> four is a door
> five is a hive
> six is sticks
> seven is a heaven
> eight is a gate
> nine is wine
> ten is a hen

To remember the shopping list using this method, one would form an image of the hotdogs in a bun, the cat eating out of a shoe, and so on. Bugelski, Kidd, and Segmen (1968) show that this method works for a laboratory paired-associate task as well. When subjects are allowed at least 4 seconds to form an associative image between a list item and one of the cue objects from the rhyme, they are significantly better at recalling the list items in the correct positions than if they had not used the rhyming imagery mnemonic.

As imagery helps ordinary persons remember information, it also aids some professional mnemonists and others with extraordinary memory abilities. The most famous example of an extraordinary imagery-based memory is that of S., the subject described by Luria (1968). S. could accurately reproduce from memory large tables of numbers and letters, could remember conversations or printed prose verbatim, and could solve mathematical problems using visual imagery. Luria's tests of S.'s methods showed that he was able to use the method of loci very effectively because he could picture many locations in his home city with a great deal of accuracy.

S.'s use of associative links was also greatly enhanced by synesthesia, the evocation of a sensation in one modality, say sight, from an image in another modality, such as hearing. For example, he once told a famous Russian psychologist, "What a crumbly, yellow voice you have" (p. 24). The richness and variety of S.'s imagery aided him in many memory tasks but interfered with his ability to perceive the world normally. He also had difficulty doing ordinary tasks like extracting the general meaning from a short text without memorizing it verbatim. Nevertheless, S. is another example of how an imaginal representation can enhance memory performance.

Imagery and the Visual Processing System

We have spoken of imagery as a series of mental pictures and noted that the quality of imagery, as inferred from its influence on memory performance, can be explicitly improved by presenting the subjects with pictures. In addition, the process of retrieving information coded in an imaginal form often seems to involve scanning the image in much the same way a real picture is scanned. In this section, we examine one of the consequences of the perception-like qualities of imagery: Imagery can be functionally influenced by other demands placed on the visual perceptual system.

Two studies show the interdependence of imagery and the visual processing system. Both are based on the premise that if the visual processing system is involved in maintaining a visual image in a memory experiment, then requiring the subject to process a visual stimulus during the retention interval will hurt memory performance by impairing the subject's ability to maintain the image. Atwood (1971) used a paired-associate task in which subjects were to remember 35 pairs of nouns. Subjects in one group were given noun pairs high in imagery, which were presented in short phrases that described a novel, interactive image of the two nouns (e.g., "a nudist devouring a bird"). Subjects receiving these types of pairs were asked to visualize the scene described. A second group of subjects received pairs low in imagery value, again in phrases that related the two concepts, but the phrases could not be visualized (e.g., "the intellect of Einstein was a miracle").

Some subjects in both imagery groups received one of two interfering tasks in the 4–5 second interval between each noun pair in the list. In the visual interference task subjects were shown either the digit 1 or the digit 2 during the interstimulus interval, and they were to respond by saying the name of the digit that had not appeared. Such visual processing was expected to hurt performance most for those pairs for which imagery was being used.

In the auditory interference task, the subjects heard either "one" or "two" and responded with the nonpresented number. Since this task required verbal processing of a stimulus, it was expected to interfere more with memory for low-imagery pairs being retained by verbal rehearsal. Performance on these two interference tasks was compared to the performance of a control group who received no interference task during the interstimulus intervals.

As expected, the pairs that could be remembered by using imagery were better recalled than the abstract nouns when no interference task was presented (82 percent and 70 percent respectively). When a visual interfering task was used performance on the visualized, concrete pairs dropped 24 percentage points, while performance on the verbally rehearsed abstract pairs dropped only 10 percentage points. The auditory task caused a drop of 26 percentage points for the abstract pairs and only a drop of 6 percentage points for the concrete pairs. These results indicate that when the visual processing system must be used for some other purpose a subject's ability to form and maintain an imaginal memory representation declines. This distraction of the verbal processing system has a greater negative effect on information retained in the verbal coding system than on visually coded material. Such results also provide indirect support for Paivio's dual coding hypothesis.

Brooks (1968) used similar reasoning in designing another type of experiment to show that "verbal and spatial information are handled in distinct, modality-specific manners" (p. 349). Subjects performed two types of memory report tasks. In the sentence task the subjects were given a sentence to remember, such as "a bird in the hand is not in the bush." When given a signal, the subject was to mentally scan the sentence and indicate, in order, whether each word in the sentence was a noun. Nouns were to be signaled by a yes response and other words by a no. For our sentence the correct response sequence is "no yes no no yes no no no no yes."

In the diagram task the subjects were to remember a simple block diagram of a letter, such as that shown in Figure 8.3a. At the starting signal the subject was to begin with the corner designated by the asterisk and proceed along the perimeter of the imagined figure. At each corner the subject was to signal yes if the corner was a point on the extreme top or bottom of the figure, and no otherwise. For the block letter F, the correct sequence proceeding in a clockwise manner is "yes yes yes no no no no no no yes." Subjects were timed on both tasks, and it was assumed that the easier the task, the faster the production time would be.

Brooks expected that the memory code for the sentences would be verbal and the code for the letter figures would be spatial-imaginal. He therefore devised three methods for signaling the yes and no responses, methods which were expected to differentially interfere with the two types of representation. The three methods are (1) saying yes and no aloud, (2) tapping with one hand for yes and the other for no, and (3) pointing to a Y or an N

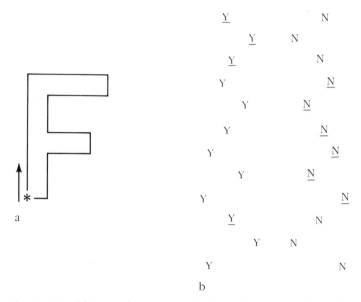

Figure 8.3 (a) A sample stimulus letter from Brooks' experiment. Subjects started at the designated corner and classified each corner as being on the letter's extremes (top or bottom) or in the middle. (b) Answer sheet for the pointing response task. The correct responses are underlined for the block letter F. [From Brooks, 1968.]

printed on a page. The first method is verbal and was expected to interfere with the sentence report task more than with the diagram report task, because speaking aloud would interfere with the verbal rehearsal process but not with visual imagery. Since tapping has neither a strong visual nor a strong verbal component, it was not expected to differentially interfere with either type of stimulus.

The pointing response, however, is primarily visual and was therefore expected to interfere with the diagram task. Figure 8.3b illustrates the visual nature of this report procedure. For the first word in the sentence, or point on the diagram, the subject was to point to either the Y or the N in the first line. The response for the next item in the stimulus was to be indicated on the next line, and so forth. Because the letters were randomly arranged on each line, the subject had to do quite a bit of visual processing in order to figure out which character to point to. This task was therefore expected to interfere with the ability to maintain an adequate representation of the stimulus diagrams but not the sentences.

Brooks obtained the expected interaction between report task and stimulus materials. Responses to the sentences took 9.8 and 7.8 seconds for the pointing and tapping methods respectively, but jumped to 13.8 seconds when verbal report was required. This result indicates that the resources of verbal memory are impaired when the verbal processing system is distracted by another task. The diagrams required 11.3 and 14.1 seconds for the verbal and tapping report respectively, but took 28.2 seconds for the pointing report. This result shows that the visual information processing system and the system that maintains imaginal memory rely on some of the same processing resources. Brooks was therefore successful in demonstrating that visual and verbal information are processed in separate, modality-specific ways.

STRUCTURAL ASPECTS OF IMAGERY

Our discussion of the functional aspects of visual imagery suggests that information about concrete objects can be stored in other than verbal form. But what is the form of an image? What is it about this form that allows images to function in the ways experimenters have observed? How does an image differ from the type of information stored in verbal memory, and how do we manipulate imaginal representations? All these questions concern the structural aspects of the imaginal representations, the topic of this section.

Imagery as a Second-Order Isomorphism

The demonstrations by Atwood and by Brooks of selective, modality-specific interference for visual and verbal memory systems show that the information in the imaginal representation system can be disrupted by incoming visual stimulation. This finding suggests a strong similarity between the structural representations used in imagery and those used in visual perception. Indeed, everyday experience may tempt us to call an image "a picture in the head." As we shall see, this analogy is a bit strong in its characterization of the similarities between perception and imagery. However, Shepard and his colleagues have developed a set of experimental findings that suggest a relationship between the two that Shepard (1978) calls a *second-order isomorphism*. A simple isomorphic relationship implies that there is a direct, one-to-one correspondence between the parts of two entities. However, according to Shepard, "the proposed equivalence between perception and imagination implies a more abstract or 'second-order' isomorphism in which the functional relations among objects as imagined must to some degree mirror the functional relations among those same objects as actually perceived" (p. 131). To fully understand this definition we must examine examples from several of Shepard's experiments.

Consider the arrangements of connected squares shown in Figure 8.4a. The task is to use the shaded square as the base and to fold the other squares along their edges until they form a cube. Once a cube has been constructed from arrangement 1, it becomes obvious that the two arrows are aligned such that their points touch. (You may wish to construct a paper replica of

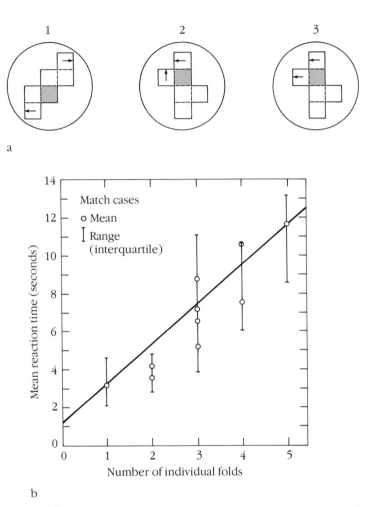

Figure 8.4 (a) Stimuli used by Shepard and Feng. In arrangements 1 and 2 the arrows will match if the squares are folded into a cube, while arrangement 3 is a mismatch. (b) The reaction times are a linear function of the number of folds necessary to make the decision. [From Shepard and Feng, 1972.]

the figure in order to verify this statement.) If you were timed from the moment you received an arrangement of squares until you decided whether the arrows met, then the longer it took you to fold the cube, the longer it would take you to decide. Folding time, in turn, would depend on the number of folds required before the arrows were in their final places. In Figure 8.4, for arrangement 1 you would have to complete the cube, but for arrangement 2 you could decide after only two folds (the three squares at the bottom of the figure are irrelevant to the decision and therefore need not be folded). Arrangement 2 therefore requires less decision time.

Most people, with varying degrees of difficulty, are able to imagine the series of folds and come to a decision about the arrows without having to fold an actual model. Mental paper folding quite obviously requires us to form an internal image of the arrangement of squares and to manipulate the squares using imagery. Whatever mental structure is used to represent the arrangement preserves the information about the relative positions of the corners, sides, and adjacent squares. Whenever some adjustment of this structural representation is made, such as a "mental paper fold," the resulting mental representation resembles the representation that would have been constructed from viewing a folded version of the arrangement. Thus the functional relationships between the perceived parts of the image are analogous to the functional relationships between the parts of an actual model. We therefore have a second-order isomorphism between the two.

If Shepard is correct in suggesting that there is a second-order isomorphism between a memory image and a perceptual image from the real world, then the same variables ought to similarly affect decisions based on either type of image. In the case of the arrow-matching task, the number of folds needed to verify a match should equally affect the physical task and the mental task. Specifically, the more mental paper folds needed to determine whether the arrows align, the longer the decision time. Shepard and Feng's (1972) data confirm this expectation. Subjects performed the mental paper-folding task for a variety of configurations of squares. The decision times were roughly a linear function of the number of folds necessary to make a decision, as shown in Figure 8.4b.

These data certainly suggest a second-order isomorphism between the imagined representation and the parts of the physical object. This particular evidence is derived from manipulations of the representations that actually change the relations between the parts. Other experiments of very different types lend additional support for the isomorphism hypothesis. Let us consider three general classes of these experiments: mental rotation, memory retrieval, and mental psychophysics.

Mental Rotation

A large number of studies supporting the hypothesis of a second-order isomorphism concern how such images are transformed and manipulated in memory. Shepard and Feng's experiment is one of these, but, as we mentioned previously, paper folding is a special case of mental transformation because each operation radically alters the relative structural relations between the parts of the stimulus. Rotation is a different type of transformation: The relative positions of the various parts of an object undergoing rotation remain constant. Shepard and Metzler (1971) did the first study of mental rotation. On each trial subjects were presented with a pair of line drawings depicting a three-dimensional arrangement of cubes (see Figure 8.5a). Subjects were to decide whether the two stimuli in the pair could be

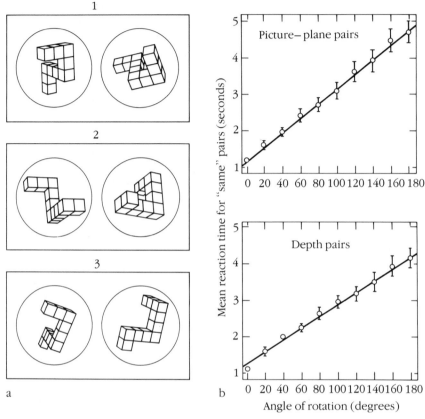

Figure 8.5 (a) Stimulus pairs from Shepard and Metzler's study; the forms in arrangement 1 are congruent when rotated in the picture plane; the forms in 2 are congruent when rotated in depth; and the forms in 3 are never congruent. (b) For pairs of the type shown in arrangements 1 and 2, reaction time is a linear function of the angle of rotation. [From Shepard and Metzler, *Science*, 1971, *171*, 701–703. Copyright 1971 by the American Association for the Advancement of Science.]

rotated into congruence with one another, and their reaction time was measured. On half the trials, the two stimuli could be rotated into congruence either by rotation in the picture plane (example 1) or rotation in depth (example 2). On the other trials, the two objects were mirror-image reversals of each other, and no amount of rotation in any direction could bring them into congruence (example 3).

To perform this task a subject was to form an image of one of the figures and mentally rotate, or transform, that image until it matched the other. A subject could discern a mismatch if a rotation that aligned one arm of the figures failed to produce perfect identity between the other parts of the figures. If imagery is isomorphic to perception, then decision time based on image rotation should be a function of the amount of rotating to be done; the greater the angular difference between the orientations of the two stimulus objects, the longer the rotation will take and the longer the decision time will be. The decision data shown in Figure 8.5b confirm this hypothesis by showing that decision times are a linear function of the angle (in degrees) through which one of the stimuli must be rotated to reach congruence with the other. The data show very little difference between rotation in the picture plane and rotation in depth.

Mental rotation can also be used to study how a mental image is constructed. Cooper and Shepard (1973), extending Shepard and Metzler's reasoning, assumed that the linear increase in decision times is a function of preparation time, that is, the time it takes to mentally rotate an image of one of the stimuli to a position in which a direct comparison can be made. Shepard and Metzler's subjects were shown a picture of the object to be imaged and rotated, but additional preparation time would be needed if subjects had to retrieve a test object from memory before their mental rotation could begin. Cooper and Shepard reasoned that if subjects had fully prepared a comparison image before the reaction-time interval began, then decision times would no longer be a function of angle of difference between the test stimulus and the image. They sought to determine how quickly subjects could retrieve and rotate an image by varying the amount of preparation time allotted and by giving subjects different types of information in advance.

To provide stimuli whose images could be retrieved from memory, Cooper and Shepard used the characters R, J, G, 2, 5, and 7. As shown in Figure 8.6a, stimulus characters appeared in either normal form or as backward, mirror-image reversals; also, the characters were either upright, or at any one of five other orientations (60°, 120°, 180°, 240°, or 300° from upright). The subject's task was to determine whether the presented character was normal or backwards, and the reaction time for this decision was measured. To perform the task, the subject would presumably have to rotate the presented stimulus to upright and then match it to a mental image of the normal character. The decision times were expected to be a function of the number of degrees of rotation through which the image had to be rotated. The results of this simple version of the experiment, the "no information" condition N, are shown in Figure 8.6b and confirm the expected dependency of latency on angle of rotation.

In condition C (combined identity and orientation information) the subject was shown a light outline of the exact test character in the exact orientation it would appear on the succeeding trial. The outline was shown for 2 seconds, follwed by a 1-second blank interval and then the test stimulus. During this 3-second period the subject could presumably construct a complete, rotated image of the test stimulus. The subsequent decision interval would therefore not be used for mental rotation, and decision times would be short and

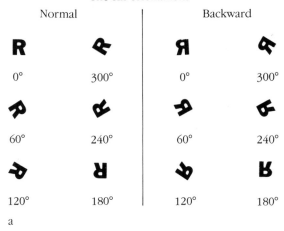

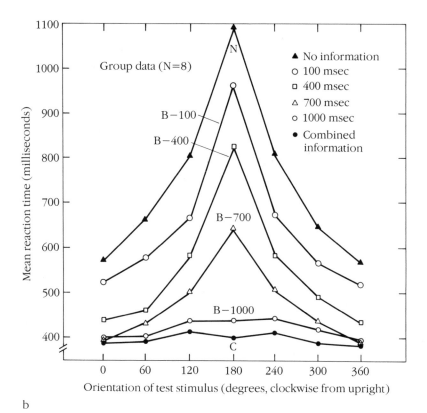

Figure 8.6 (a) Cooper and Shepard showed subjects characters and reversed characters in six orientations defined by their angle to upright. Subjects were to decide whether the character was normal or backwards. (b) Reaction times were a function of stimulus orientation when subjects did not receive previous information that enabled them to prepare the image. They became uniform when subjects were given enough time to prepare an image of the correct stimulus at the correct orientation. [From Cooper and Shepard, 1973.]

independent of the angular displacement of the stimulus. Curve C in Figure 8.6b confirms this expectation.

A similar result is expected when subjects are given separate information about the identity and the orientation of the test stimulus and sufficient time to mentally combine the information and prepare the image. In condition B-1000 (both identity and orientation information given) subjects saw an upright outline of the character to be used on that trial for 2 seconds, followed by an arrow denoting the orientation of the test stimulus, shown for 1000 milliseconds. Since the subject knew which image to retrieve from memory and had 1 second in which to rotate that image, the reaction-time curve was expected to be flat, as it was in condition C. The B-1000 condition curve in Figure 8.6b confirms this expectation.

Finally, if subjects are given less time to process the identity and orientation information and perform the mental rotation, their reaction times should show some effects of angle of orientation. The B-100, B-400, and B-700 conditions—in which the orientation information was shown for 100 milliseconds, 400 milliseconds, and 700 milliseconds respectively—confirm this expectation. In the B-700 condition, subjects were nearly fully prepared. Indeed for the smaller angles of orientation, the decision times are the same as those in the C and B-1000 conditions. However, at the larger angular disparities such as 120°, 180°, and 240°, subjects had to complete their rotation after the test stimulus appeared, and thus decision times show a small effect of angular disparity for these stimuli. As the B-100 curve in Figure 8.6b shows, 100 milliseconds of rotation time barely gives the subject any preparation advantage over having no prior information. The constant difference between the B-100 and the N curves is likely a function of subjects' knowing at least the identity of the test stimulus in advance in the B-100 condition.

Cooper and Shepard's results provide further evidence that subjects form and transform imaginal memory representations in performing certain types of cognitive tasks. The results also suggest, along with Shepard and Metzler's results, that subjects conduct a continuous rotation process once the mental image has been formed. However, this conclusion is not certain because the results do not rule out the possibility that subjects perform the rotation task by successively generating separate images of the correct object at successively larger and larger angular disparities from the original.

More direct evidence that rotation is a continuous process rather than a series of discrete steps comes from an experiment by Cooper (1976). Subjects were given a multisided nonsense form and were asked to begin to rotate the form in the picture plane. Previous testing had determined the rate at which each subject could do the rotation. At some selected time after rotation had begun, the subject was shown a test form that was either the same as the original or a mirror-image reversal of it. The subject's task was to decide which it was.

The timing of the test form was such that on some trials it appeared at the "expected" orientation; that is, the test stimulus appeared at the same orientation as the subject's image at the moment of presentation. Theoretically, the subject could directly compare his image of the normal form and the test form. Since the subject required no preparation time on these "expected" trials, reaction times were the same regardless of the orientation of the test form. On the "unexpected" trials the test stimulus appeared at some orientation other than the expected one. On these trials the subject had to continue to rotate the image until it was at the same orientation as the test stimulus. The greater the discrepancy between the test stimulus and the expected orientation, the longer the decision times were.

Cooper would have been extremely unlikely to obtain these results if the subjects were rotating their images in a series of discrete steps. It is unlikely that the size of the steps would have matched the orientations expected from continuous rotation closely enough to generate the flat reaction-time function obtained for all the expected trials. We therefore have direct evidence that rotation is carried out in a continuous fashion. We also have evidence that the nature of the image representation is continuous. The term *analog* is another way of expressing such continuity. Hence, images are often said to have an analog representation.

Memory Retrieval

In studying memory retrieval of imaginal information, Kosslyn (1973, 1975) notes that the many visual properties of concrete objects could be stored in memory in either a propositional or an imaginal form. That is, our verbal memory could hold a proposition like "A dog has four legs," and we would retrieve this proposition in order to verify properties about dogs. Alternatively, the information about the properties of a dog might be stored as a mental image of a dog. To retrieve information about properties we would scan a mental image.

Kosslyn reasons that if the memory representation for such property information is imaginal, then the type of variable that influences the perceptual verification of properties of objects in pictures should influence retrieval of property information from memory in the same way. The variable Kosslyn chose to examine was the distance that had to be scanned on an imaginal representation in order for the subject to decide whether an indicated property was true or false of a particular object.

Kosslyn (1973) had subjects view drawings of several easily imagined objects (e.g., a boat, a car, a flower). Of course, the drawings showed a number of properties of each object. During the test phase, subjects were given the name of one of the objects and, shortly thereafter, were given the name of a property that was either true or false of the object. Reaction times were measured from the time the property was given until the subject made a decision.

Each subject was run under one of four instructional conditions. Two groups were told to form an image of the designated objects on each trial and to verify the property by scanning the image to see whether the property was present. Half of these subjects, the imagery-whole group, were to imagine the entire picture; the others, the imagery-focus group, were to focus on a designated end of the stimulus image. The imagery-focus subjects were told to verify the property by shifting their focus from the end of the object and to scan until the designated property was found. The two verbal groups, the verbal-whole and the verbal-focus groups, were told to silently describe the pictures to themselves in preparation for making the property verification. The verbal-focus subjects were asked to focus their rehearsal on the properties at a designated end of the object.

The imagery groups had faster reaction times than their respective verbal groups, which indicates that imagery can be an easier representation from which to verify concrete properties. Of major interest, however, was the effect on the verification times of the position of the cued property. Subjects who imaged the whole figure were not affected by the position of the cued property, and their verification times were the same for all property locations. However, subjects who focused on one end or the other showed significantly longer times to verify those properties that were some distance away from their focus point. More specifically, properties at the focused end were verified fastest, those in the middle were verified more slowly, and those at the opposite end were slowest of all. This result offers evidence that subjects do, in fact, scan an image that is isomorphic to the perceptual representation.

In a second set of experiments Kosslyn (1975) extended his reasoning: If subjects use images, the clarity of the image—like scanning distance—should influence property verification times. The clarity of a property to be verified can be manipulated by varying the size of the object itself. In large objects, the detail of the properties is large and clear; in small objects, individual properties are difficult to see. Kosslyn (1975) therefore had subjects make images of pairs of animals. The target animal was a mouse, a collie, a cat, and so on, while the context animal was either an elephant or a fly. The subjects were to form an image of the two animals next to one another in the correct relative size. A few seconds later the subjects were given a property name and were to decide whether that property appeared on the target animal.

For example the subject might hear the animal pair "elephant/goose" followed by the property "beak." Since geese have beaks, the subject was to press a button indicating true. Had the property been "fur," the subject was to press a button for false. Subjects took 211 milliseconds longer to verify properties on animals paired with elephants than on animals paired with flies. Notice that a target animal paired with an elephant would appear very small. The longer response time presumably reflects the amount of time it took the subject to sufficiently enlarge the image of the target animal so that the property became visible.

To demonstrate that the size, rather than some other aspect of the context animals, influenced the clarity of subjects' images, Kosslyn ran a second experiment in which the relative sizes of the two context animals were reversed. Subjects were asked to imagine the target animal next to a very large fly or next to a tiny elephant. Because the target animal would be large in comparison to a tiny elephant, the properties should be easy to see and reaction times should be fast. The opposite would be true of target animals paired with a huge fly. Kosslyn's size hypothesis was again borne out; verification times were 246 milliseconds faster for tiny-elephant contexts than for huge-fly contexts.

Both of Kosslyn's studies indicate that information, such as properties of objects, can be stored and used both imaginally as well as propositionally. This conclusion is not particulary surprising in light of Paivio's original dual coding data. However, these studies show that the imaginal memory representation structurally resembles physical organization and perceptual experience.

Mental Psychophysics

A third method of establishing the relationship between the nature of the imaginal representation and the nature of perceptual experience is through the use of psychophysical techniques. As we saw in Chapter 2, these techniques are designed to estimate the magnitude or quality of a subject's internal experience of a perceptual event. Because imagery theorists claim that imagery is similar to perceptual experience, it is not surprising that to study the nature of the internal representation they use some of the same techniques as sensory psychologists.

Kosslyn (1978) carried out one such experiment to establish the "visual angle of the mind's eye." Since the eye cannot take in every object in the surrounding environment, the size of any one image must also be limited. Theoretically, one can estimate the size of the typical image in terms of the visual angle subtended by the largest clear image a subject can construct. Kosslyn asked subjects to form an image of a certain animal against a blank background. They were then told to take a "mental walk" toward the animal until the size of the animal began to exceed the size of the mental image space, that is, until the subject could no longer "see" the entire animal in the image. The apparent distance between the subject and the animal image was then assessed by a variety of techniques, including asking the subject to estimate the distance. If subjects used a very strict criterion for when the image was no longer completely visible, the visual angle of the mind's eye was estimated to be about 20°. Using a slightly laxer criterion, subjects reported being able to maintain an image of 40° to 60°.

Several characteristics of imagery are apparent from these results. First, the size of the "image space" is quite restricted—certainly much more limited than the size of a perceptual image. Second, not all the animals were originally imaged the same size by a given subject. For example, the initial image formed of a donkey was larger than that of a beaver even though both might have to subtend the same visual angle for the image to begin to exceed image space. Thus subjects have some notion of a canonical, or expected, size for well-known objects and their images take this size information into account. Finally, that different criteria exist for the boundary of image space suggests that image space is not framed like a picture. The information at the edges of a mental image is apparently fuzzy, and the loss of information at the edges is a gradual process rather than a distinct cessation at a well-defined boundary.

This last observation led Finke and Kosslyn (1980) to try to estimate the acuity of a mental image at the edges. They had subjects imagine two dots at one of three specified separations. The subjects were to image the dots in the middle of their image space and gradually turn their heads, while keeping the image of the dots stationary. Thus, the dots moved toward the periphery of the image space as the subject's head turned. Finke and Kosslyn recorded the size of the field within which dots of various separations could still be distinguished. They found that the closer together the dots were, the nearer the pair had to be to the center of the image space in order for the subject to maintain a clear image of them. The distance from the center at which the dots could be resolved increased with increasing separation of the pair.

Further, persons who have good imagery ability, as measured by a variety of imagery tasks, show similar acuity for both physically present and imagined dots. Subjects who have poorer imagery ability have more difficulty resolving imagined dots than perceived dots in the periphery. However, their acuity for the two types of stimuli follows the same pattern when plotted as a function of original dot separation. These data again show a situation in which imagery is very similar to perception.

Another useful psychophysical technique is *magnitude estimation*. This task requires subjects to assign numbers in proportion to the perceived magnitude of the stimuli. Some stimulus near the middle of the range to be judged is chosen by the experimenter to be the standard and it is given a standard value, say 100. Whenever the subject perceives a stimulus to be twice as great as the standard, the rating 200 is to be assigned; for a stimulus half as great, the rating 50 is to be assigned, and so forth. Research in sensory psychology shows that the relationship between the perceived magnitude is a power function of the actual physical magnitude. The equation describing the relationship is:

$$\psi = k\phi^{\alpha} \tag{8.1}$$

where ψ is the psychological magnitude, ϕ is the physical magnitude, and k and α are scaling constants. The value of the constant k depends on the units of measurement used, while α is a parameter that depends on the sensory dimension being evaluated and has some characteristic value for each different dimension, such as brightness, size, and weight.

Magnitude estimation was used by Kerst and Howard (1978) to examine the scales used for magnitudes in perceptual experience with a dimension and those used for magnitudes for remembered stimuli. Subjects estimated the magnitudes of the areas of the 48 continental states. One group did this while viewing a map of the United States; their estimates are therefore perceptual. Another group, the memory group, was allowed to study a map for a few minutes, but made their magnitude estimates from memory after the map was removed. Both sets of estimates were scaled as a function of the actual area of the states, and the characteristics exponent α was estimated from the data in each condition. In both cases the data were well fit by the psychophysical power function, the perceptual data having a power exponent of .79 and the memory data a power exponent of .60.

Since both the memory data and the perceptual data follow the same qualitative pattern, that of the power function, we have further evidence for the notion of an isomorphism. However, the power exponents for perception and memory are not identical, indicating that there is some quantitative difference between the two types of representations. Kerst and Howard argue that the two types are fundamentally similar and that the difference in the exponents arises from the way in which memory representations are processed. They suggest that the memory representation is based on a scaled interpretation of perceptual experience; that is, stored in the imaginal representation are not the actual sizes but the perceived sizes, which are derived from actual magnitudes by the application of equation 8.1. When the subject is asked to judge magnitudes from memory, equation 8.1 is reapplied to the previously scaled imaginal magnitudes. The resulting estimates are related to actual physical magnitudes by a power function, but the exponent of the power function is not α, but α^2. Indeed, the value obtained by Kerst and Howard is very close to this predicted value: $.79^2 = .62$ and they obtained .60.

This reperceptual hypothesis is confirmed in another experiment in which subjects estimated interstate distances. The maps supplied to the perceptual group and to the memory group showed a dot in the center of each outlined state. Estimates were to be made from center to center of various pairs of states. For distance estimates the exponent for the perceptual group was 1.04, while that for the memory group was 1.10. Because the α-value for the perceptual group is larger than 1.0 for this dimension, it is not surprising that the exponent value for the memory group, α^2, was even larger. Again the exponent for the memory group (1.10) is close to the squared value for the perceptual group ($1.04^2 = 1.08$). These data provide an interesting demonstration that the techniques subjects use to report information from their memory representations are very similar to the methods they use to report sensory experience.

One of the main contentions of imagery theorists is that the imaginal representation is continuous, that the properties of images cannot adequately be measured by a scale that marks only the relative ordering of the images (e.g., smallest, next smallest, and so forth). One way to determine the scale properties of the items stored in memory is to ask subjects to compare pairs of such items along some dimension such as size. Moyer (1973) and Moyer and Bayer (1976) used this method to determine whether concrete objects are remembered along ordinal dimensional scales or whether more continuous information about interval sizes is maintained. The ordinal method is appropriate to a discrete, propositional representation because only the order and not the exact sizes would be represented in propositions. For example, a subject might have the proposition "A bee is larger than an ant." With an ordinal representation of scale information, the absolute magnitudes of the sizes being compared would have no effect on memory comparisons.

Moyer (1973) used sets of animals that differed in size in an ordered sequence; for example, ant, bee, rat, cat, hog, cow, and elk. Subjects were asked, "Which is larger, a bee or a cat?" If subjects performed the comparison task using only propositional information, then the magnitude of the size difference between the animals being compared should make no difference. That is, subjects should be equally quick in comparing ant/bee (an ordinal position difference of 1) as ant/cow (an ordinal position difference of 5).

However, if subjects use imagery they must scan their images of the two animals, estimate the two sizes, and compare these magnitudes. Comparisons of magnitudes that are similar will take a long time because it is difficult to detect the difference between them, while magnitudes that are quite different can be compared more quickly. This inverse relationship between comparison time and size difference seems to be quite general and is reported in psychophysical experiments (Woodworth and Schlosberg, 1954), comparisons of digit magnitude (Moyer and Landauer, 1967), and comparison of letters according to alphabetic ordering (Lovelace and Snodgrass, 1971).

Moyer's results also show this inverse relationship and thus that subjects used imaginal representations in performing the task. Because the memory representations that are compared symbolize physical magnitudes, this inverse relationship between the size of images in memory and latency has come to be known as the *symbolic distance effect*. Moyer and Bayer (1976) define the symbolic distance effect thus: "The time needed to compare two symbols varies inversely with the distance between their referents on the judged dimension" (p. 230).

Moyer and Bayer (1976) also extend the generality of the symbolic distance effect. They argue that under the imagery hypothesis, reaction time should vary inversely with the sizes of the objects being compared even when ordinal distance is held constant. For example, if two pairs of objects are adjacent on an ordinal scale (e.g., ant/bee and hog/cow) and have identical ordinal difference measures, the pair having the larger size difference (hog/cow) should elicit the faster reaction time. A second concern of Moyer and

Bayer was to show that symbolic distance comparisons were similar to perceptual size comparisons. Moyer and Bayer therefore used circle stimuli in both memory and perceptual tasks.

The subjects were divided into four groups, two groups in the memory condition and two groups in the perceptual condition. One of the memory groups and one of the perceptual groups used circle stimuli that differed only slightly in diameter (11, 13, 15, and 17 millimeters), while the other two groups used circle stimuli whose diameters differed more (11, 15, 19, and 23 millimeters). Subjects in the perceptual groups compared the stimuli when cued by pictures of the actual circles. Subjects in the two memory groups were trained to associate a nonsense syllable name to each of the four circle stimuli. During testing the subjects in the memory group were asked to give relative size judgments of the circles when cued by the names of the stimulus pairs.

This task thus required subjects to make size judgments using the names of concrete objects stored in memory. Subjects had to retrieve the representations of the cued stimuli, estimate their sizes, and compare them—just like in the animal study. On the basis of the earlier data we would expect to find a symbolic distance effect. Moreover, we would expect the subjects tested with the stimuli that varied more in size to respond faster than subjects using the more uniform stimuli.

The perceptual subjects showed a distance effect; pairs more distant on the ordinal scale were compared faster than pairs closer together. Moreover, the group using the more varied stimuli responded significantly faster than the other group. The data for the memory subjects similarly replicated the distance effect and therefore support the hypothesis that imagery and perception share a second-order isomorphism.

Summary

In this section we examined in detail the claim that imagery and perception share a second-order isomorphic relationship. Three classes of experiments—mental rotation, memory retrieval, and mental psychophysics—defend this view of structural representation, and all three provide some good evidence supporting this position. In the final section of this chapter we consider some alternative views, but first we wish to examine two other aspects of the use of mental imagery.

INDIVIDUAL DIFFERENCES IN IMAGERY ABILITY

Individuals vary in the ability to form and use visual images. Although a complete discussion of how people differ in visual and spatial skills would require a book in itself, we can briefly examine two aspects of this topic.

First, we consider the nature of processing differences between subjects in mental rotation tasks that cause very different patterns of reaction-time results. Then we consider individuals whose imagery ability is far above normal—eidetic imagers.

Processing Differences in Mental Rotation and Comparison

In our review of experiments regarding the structure of the imaginal representation we discussed several tasks on which subjects differed in their ability to use imagery. For example, subjects differ in their ability to keep track of an image undergoing rotation and the speed at which they can rotate their images. Subjects might also differ in the way they compare an image to a test stimulus. Some subjects might compare the corresponding parts one by one, while other subjects might be able to match an entire image and a test stimulus all at once.

Cooper and Podgorny (1976) examined the characteristic patterns of reaction times produced by individuals using different imagery strategies. On each trial the subject was first given one of the five multisided nonsense forms shown in Figure 8.7a as the S stimuli. The standard was removed, and an arrow indicating an orientation appeared. The subject was to rotate the standard to that orientation as quickly as possible and then press a button, which allowed Cooper and Podgorny to measure RT_1, the rotation time. Then a test stimulus appeared, and the subject had to indicate whether it was the same as or different from the rotated standard; this second decision time is RT_2. As shown in Figure 8.7a, there were eight types of test stimuli: the standard (S), the mirror image reversal of the standard (R), and six forms (D1 through D6) that differed from the standard along a continuum of differentness. The D1 stimuli differed from their respective standards only slightly, while the D6 stimuli were quite different from the standards.

As the results in Figures 8.7b and c show, Cooper and Podgorny were able to divide the subjects into two groups on the basis of performance. Subjects who responded faster overall on both RT_1 and RT_2 were labeled "fast"; all other subjects were labeled "slow." Examination of RT_1 for the two types of subjects as a function of the angle of the test form shows that for both groups reaction time increased with the amount of rotation to be done. However, the fast subjects began their rotations sooner and completed their rotations more quickly. The preparation of the image completed (RT_1), the decision times for the same-or-different task (RT_2) are uniform with respect to orientation for both groups. Fast subjects, however, made these decisions more quickly and responded slightly faster when the test stimulus was the same as the standard. The slow subjects responded slower overall and did better on "different" trials than on "same" trials.

An equally interesting difference between the two types of subjects appears when we examine RT_2 times as a function of degree of difference (Figure

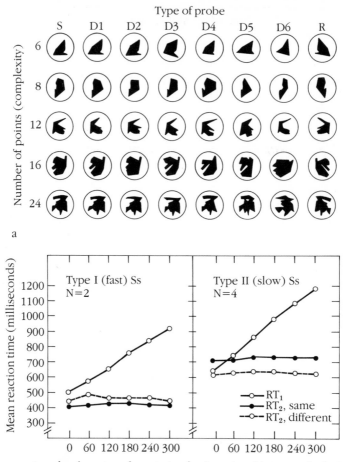

a

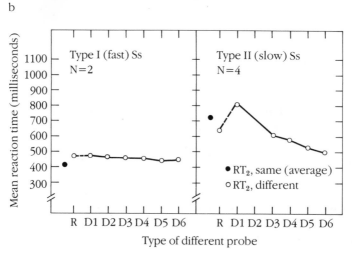

b

c

8.7c). The fast subjects respond equally quickly to all types of different stimuli, at a rate approximately equal to that for a "same" trial. For slow subjects, however, the more similar the test form is to the standard, the slower their response.

Cooper and Podgorny's results can best be explained by assuming that the two types of subjects differ with respect to how they go about comparing a mental representation to a visually presented form. The fast subjects perform holistic comparisons; their data suggest a template-matching process in which the degree of dissimilarity does not matter as long as there is a mismatch. Thus they respond to "same" and "different" stimuli equally quickly. The slow subjects seem to compare the forms part by part. When the stimulus form differs only slightly from the standard these subjects find it difficult to notice the difference, and their reaction times are slow. When there are many differences between the two, these subjects quickly notice one of the differences. Thus their RT_2 is longer on the "same" trials than on the "different" trials. A subject would respond "same" only after an exhaustive scan of all parts of the forms fails to yield any differences, while a "different" response could be made as soon as any difference was detected.

The processing differences found by Cooper and Podgorny suggest that different individuals have different preferred modes of using images. It remains to be seen how radically these preferences can be changed either by training and instruction, or by constraints imposed by the experimental task.

Eidetic Imagery

Cooper and Podgorny's subjects showed clear individual differences on the imagery task, but none of the subjects could be called unusually skilled. A few individuals, however, possess what is known as *eidetic imagery*. Eidetic imagers can accurately keep a detailed visual representation of a complex visual stimulus for minutes, hours, or days. To a person who has this ability, it seems as if the stimulus picture had never been removed; the image is still clear and remains on the original stimulus plane rather than as a memory image in the subject's head. Stromeyer and Psotka (1970) cite the example of an adult eidetic imager who could image a page of text well enough to be able to copy it quickly and accurately from bottom to top. She could also create vivid images from her imagination, such as putting a beard on a person who did not have one.

Figure 8.7 (a) Cooper and Podgorny studied individual differences in mental rotation and representation using five sets of nonsense forms (S) and seven other sets of variations on those forms. (b) and (c) Two types of processing strategies (fast and slow) were inferred from the reaction-time data. [From Cooper and Podgorny, 1976. Copyright 1976 by the American Psychological Associaton. Reprinted by permission of the publisher and the author.]

The experience of an eidetiker is similar to what we call photographic memory in that an eidetic image carries the exact details of the original scene or picture. Eidetic imagery is therefore much different from the experiences most of us occasionally have of knowing, for example, where on the page of a textbook a certain picture, fact, or graph was located. Because we do not remember the precise content and appearance, we can scarcely be said to have an eidetic image. How then can we determine whether an individual has eidetic imagery?

Haber and Haber (1964) suggest five criteria. First, an eidetic image persists longer than a conventional perceptual afterimage; Haber and Haber offer 40 seconds as a reasonable minimum for an eidetic image. Second, an eidetic image can be formed from a low-contrast stimulus, whereas conventional afterimages usually require a high-contrast stimulus. Third, an eidetic image preserves the colors of the original stimulus, as opposed to afterimages that are seen in color negative. Fourth, an eidetic image can be formed while the subject is allowed to freely scan the stimulus, while afterimages frequently require fixation on a certain portion of the stimulus. Fifth, an eidetic image is stable under eye movements: The eidetic image stays in a fixed location while the eye moves to scan it for details. Conventional afterimages, in contrast, move as the eye moves.

Haber and Haber report three other characteristics that distinguish eidetic imagers from others. Eidetikers consistently refer to their images as being "out there" in front of them. They always talk about reading the information off the image in the present tense as if it were still present. Finally, eidetic imagers say that their images disappear by fading or loss of whole fragments, rather than by blurring.

The most widely used method to study eidetic imagery is picture description and subjective report. In these studies (e.g., Jaensch, 1930; Haber and Haber, 1964; Leask, Haber, and Haber, 1969) the experimenter relies on the subject's report of what he or she is experiencing and applies criteria like those just mentioned to determine whether eidetic imagery has occurred. Tests with complex pictures are frequently preceded by simpler demonstrations of conventional afterimages in order to allow the subject to become comfortable reporting imagery. The test pictures are usually presented for a minute or less, and the subject is then questioned about the contents. Eidetic images are capable of generating accurate reports for several minutes or longer.

Results of this method, of course, are heavily dependent on the subject's ability to accurately report the eidetic experience. Experimenters sometimes use the superimposition method as a more stringent objective test for eidetic imagery. The subject is shown two pictures in succession. The pictures are such that if they are superimposed, a figure or scene emerges that was not apparent or predictable from either part individually. If a subject is able to form a true eidetic image of the first picture, then he or she ought to be able to mentally superimpose it on the second picture when it appears and thus "see" the composite scene. Figure 8.8 shows two pictures and their composite used for testing children.

Unfortunately, the nature of eidetic imagery limits the usefulness of the superimposition method. Most eidetikers report being able to maintain their images by projecting them onto a blank surface in the same position as the original picture. They have considerable difficulty maintaining the image when looking at other visual input, and most find that the image irretrievably "falls off the edge" of the projection surface if they attempt to move it. Thus some eidetikers cannot adequately maintain an image of the first picture while looking at the second, although some individuals can perform this task.

Different methods and investigations have produced widely disparate estimates of the incidence of eidetic imagery in a normal population. Both Klüver (1931) and Jaensch (1930) report estimates as variable as 0 to 90 percent among normal adults. Haber and Haber (1964) found that 8 percent of the normal school children tested had eidetic imagery on the picture-description task, while Gummerman, Gray, and Wilson (1972) found no eidetikers in their sample of normal children and adults using the same type of criteria. Although some evidence suggests that eidetic imagery might be more frequent in brain-injured individuals (Siipola and Hayden, 1965), Gummerman, Gray, and Wilson report that the only two subjects they found who showed eidetic imagery ability were retarded children who had no diagnosed brain damage. Moreover, these two subjects were unable to perform the superimposition task.

Thus the incidence of eidetic imagery seems to be extremely low throughout the population, but may be somewhat more likely among preadolescents.

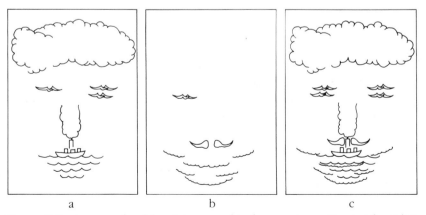

Figure 8.8 An example of the pictures used in the superimposition test for eidetic imagery by Leask, Haber, and Haber (1969). When images (a) and (b) are superimposed, a face emerges (c) that is not obvious from viewing the two component pictures individually. [Courtesy of R. N. Haber.]

Research in non-Western cultures indicates that the incidence of eidetikers may also be somewhat higher in less technologically advanced societies (Doob, 1966). These cross-cultural findings support Haber's (1969) observation that the process of verbally labeling a picture interferes with an eidetiker's ability to form an image of the picture. Perhaps language-oriented social environments hinder the development or maintenance of eidetic abilities.

One of the best-known cases of an adult eidetiker is that reported by Stromeyer (1970) and Stromeyer and Psotka (1970), which we described earlier. Because this subject reported remarkable imagery abilities, she was tested using a most difficult version of the superimposition method—fusion of random dot stereograms (see Chapter 2). In the first test she scanned the right-eye pattern for 1 minute and then waited 10 seconds before viewing the left-eye pattern. After fusing the eidetic image with the left-eye stimulus, she correctly reported the emergence of a T. The second and third tests showed that she could also maintain a right-eye dot pattern for 10 minutes after 2 minutes of viewing, or for 24 hours after 12 minutes of viewing. In each case, she was successful at reporting the correct emergent figure when she fused her right-eye eidetic image with the left-eye pattern.

Stromeyer (1970) also reports that this subject's eidetic images were accurate for color. To test this aspect of the image, Stromeyer used the Land color principle. Two black-and-white slides are made of a stimulus picture, in this case an array of different colored squares. One slide is taken through a red filter and is subsequently projected through a red filter. The other slide of the same stimulus is taken and projected through a green filter. When the two filtered black-and-white slides are superimposed, all the color information in the picture becomes apparent, even the blues, yellows, oranges, and so on. Stromeyer's eidetiker viewed one filtered slide one day and the other filtered slide the next day. By superimposing the image with the second slide, she was able to correctly report the colors of all the squares.

The experiments cited suggest that eidetic imagery exists, though it is extremely rare. And because so few people are eidetikers, researchers encounter difficulties in studying thoroughly the phenomenon. In addition, some of the best experiments, for example, the ones by Stromeyer and by Stromeyer and Psotka, have never been replicated. The evidence on eidetic imagery is therefore interesting, but weak, and the phenomenon deserves greater scientific study.

COGNITIVE MAPS

One of the primary visual activities in which everyone engages is moving about—from one room to another, from one building to another, or from one geographical region to another. Most of our trips are relatively direct; hardly anyone moves by trial and error, going randomly until happening upon the proper location. Rather we rely on our memory for information about the relative positions of where we are and where we want to be, and about possible ways of going from one to the other. This knowledge of relative spatial layout is often referred to as a _cognitive map._

Cognitive maps contain many types of information and are derived from many sources. Most of this information is derived from day-to-day visual and kinesthetic experience in getting from one place to another. After having traveled along a particular route one or more times, we begin to recognize landmarks and to know what turns to make. Thus some of any cognitive map is based on pictorial information, while other parts include labels, such as "gas station" or "school," which provide an additional method of coding map information and a convenient form for verbally conveying the information. Indeed, some individuals rely relatively more on the verbal coding strategy than on the imaginal coding strategy for representing and using spatial information. Finally, any useful cognitive map must contain information that relates different locations and routes, allowing us to figure out how to get from one place to another.

Not all the information in cognitive maps is derived from direct experience with a region or place. We learn a great deal of spatial information from cartographic maps; for example, for most of us, our knowledge of U.S. geography does not come from detailed travel in every region in the country. Rather, we often learn information about our country from maps, and even our knowledge of the layout of a city or a college campus may come from a street map.

In this section we consider several aspects of cognitive mapping that pertain to our discussion of mental imagery and representation. First, we discuss whether information about spatial relations in a cognitive map is stored imaginally, and how it is retrieved. A second concern is how the method of learning spatial information affects the structure of the resulting cognitive map. Finally, we examine how individuals differ in their ability to learn and represent spatial information.

Mental Representation of Cognitive Maps

Suppose someone asks you how far it is from one place to another, or how to get from one place to another in the city or town in which you live. To answer those questions you must retrieve information from your cognitive map. Most people say that they would mentally imagine a trip from the starting place to the goal location. If asked to give directions they would note the important landmarks and turns in their mental trip; if asked about distance, they would estimate distance on the basis of the mental trip. Although we might expect that reaction times for making decisions about distance and route information would be a function of the mental distance traversed, experimental data do not clearly support this expectation.

One challenge to the imaginal representation hypothesis for cognitive maps comes from a study by Lea (1975). The experiment was a paired-associate task in which subjects were to use the method of loci to learn a list of concrete nouns. Since the subjects were college students, the locations they were instructed to use were buildings that were in a roughly circular arrangement around the central area of their campus. After using imagery to associate each noun with one of the buildings, subjects were tested by being given the name of one of the nouns and being asked for the noun n locations away. The subjects were always to scan around the circle in a consistent direction in order to retrieve the information. Lea found that the greater the number of intervening buildings between the starting location and the goal location, the greater the retrieval time. However, the distances between buildings had no effect on the retrieval times. Regardless of whether the two adjacent buildings were close together or far apart, subjects took an equal amount of time to make one step around the circle.

A possible methodological problem with Lea's study was pointed out by Kosslyn, Ball, and Reisser (1978): Lea's subjects were instructed to go from location to location, but they were not specifically instructed to make a mental trip. Therefore, the interbuilding distances were not an integral part of the retrieval strategy. In order to show that such distances are retrieved from an analog representation, Kosslyn, Ball, and Reisser first asked subjects to learn a schematic map of an imaginary, primitive island. The island contained several specific locations designated by illustrative pictures, such as a hut, a well, and a tree. Testing consisted of a mental scanning task in which subjects were given the name of one of the locations on the island. The subject was told to focus on that location on the mental map. A few seconds later the name of a second location was given. Half of these were locations that were not on the map of the island; the other half were actual island locations. The subject was to verify the latter by scanning from the designated starting location to the target location by following an imaginary black speck moving between the two.

Under these instructions the retrieval times for actual island locations were a linear function of the distance traversed in the scan. If subjects were not instructed to base their decisions on a mental scan of the cognitive map, then retrieval times did not increase with distance. This finding confirms the contention that distance information need not be retrieved from a map unless the subject is told to do so or needs to do so.

This study and Lea's, taken together, raise the question of whether people typically use imaginal representations for their cognitive maps. If subjects have to be instructed to scan a mental map, one wonders whether their behavior during the experiment is a laboratory artifact not generalizable to everyday experience. However, Baum and Jonides (1977) provide evidence that subjects do scan an imaginal representation of map information they learned through personal visual and motor experience. Subjects were to judge, as quickly as possible, the relative distance for sets of buildings on their college campus. In the memory condition the subject was first shown the name of one building on campus, the base location. When the subject was ready, the names of two other buildings appeared, and the subject was to decide which of the two was closer to the base location. In the perceptual condition the subject was first shown a dot denoting the base location and then two other dots for the comparison locations. The task was to decide which of the comparison dots was closer to the base location.

The data were analyzed by a measure called the "distance ratio," the ratio of D_s, the shorter interlocation value, to D_l, the longer value. The symbolic distance effect would predict a positive correlation between decision times and the distance ratio. The actual correlation values for Baum and Jonides' data are .72 for the memory condition and .67 for the perceptual condition. These data suggest that people have and use an analog component in their cognitive maps.

Although these data show that cognitive maps of relatively small sets of spatial arrays have an analog component, we sense intuitively that people do not have one, continuous, analog map of all the spatial information they know. Stevens and Coupe (1978) demonstrate that subjects organize some spatial information in a hierarchical fashion, using propositions to maintain some of the relative spatial information about the parts. They examined the systematic errors subjects made in judging the relative positions of well-known locations; for example, the error "Seattle (U.S.) is farther south than Montreal (Canada)."

Stevens and Coupe explain that information about each geographical region is stored as a unit, and the relationships between different regions are stored in a hierarchy with propositions that describe those relationships. Thus, for example, information about Seattle is stored with information about the western U.S., while information about Montreal is stored as a subunit of information about Canada. The general proposition is that Canada is north of the U.S. and, therefore, any Canadian city is assumed to be north of any American city even though the curvature of the real boundary between the two nations creates many exceptions.

To demonstrate this hierarchical structure, Stevens and Coupe had subjects judge the direction of travel between pairs of geographical locations. Five location pairs were chosen such that the actual direction of travel between them differed from the relative direction relating their superordinate categories in a hierarchical representation. For each pair the subject was to draw an arrow, starting at the center of a circle, to denote the direction of travel between the locations. The diagrams shown in Figure 8.9 illustrate that subjects made systematic errors of judgment in the direction indicated by the relationship between the superordinates. Few subjects responded correctly and the deviation was always in the direction closest to the superordinate direction.

Stevens and Coupe's hierarchical results complement rather than contradict an analog interpretation. Although some elements of a hierarchical structure help organize spatial knowledge, experiments reviewed earlier show that the information about any one of the lower-level regions can be

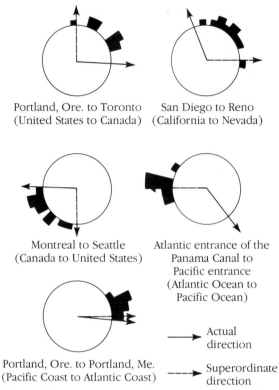

Portland, Ore. to Toronto
(United States to Canada)

San Diego to Reno
(California to Nevada)

Montreal to Seattle
(Canada to United States)

Atlantic entrance of the
Panama Canal to
Pacific entrance
(Atlantic Ocean to
Pacific Ocean)

⟶ Actual
direction

Portland, Ore. to Portland, Me.
(Pacific Coast to Atlantic Coast)

----▶ Superordinate
direction

Figure 8.9 Subjects showed systematic errors in their judgments of travel direction between pairs of locations. The errors were in the direction predicted by the relative positions of the superordinate category (given in parentheses) for each location. The frequency of subjects' responses is represented by the black bars at each circle's circumference; the longer the bar, the larger the number of responses. [From Stevens and Coupe, 1978.]

scanned imaginally. Only when areas are far apart, both organizationally and geographically, does an analog representation becomes so imprecise that propositions are more useful. The hierarchical schema proposed by Stevens and Coupe thus provides a framework within which to organize analog distance representations.

Learning Spatial Information from a Cartographic Map

Earlier we noted that people rely on two primary sources for the information in their cognitive maps: direct experience and cartographic information. Evans and Pezdek (1980) report a difference between the types of maps subjects constructed from each resource. They tested their subjects' knowledge of relative spatial positions for two kinds of items. One set of items comprised states in the U.S., the type of information most people acquire through experience with cartographic maps and almost always from maps at a fixed orientation, with north at the top. The second set of items were buildings on the subjects' college campus, the type of information derived primarily from visual and kinesthetic experience. Note that since the subjects had experienced the layout of these buildings from many different directions, it was unlikely that their cognitive representation would have any fixed orientation.

Figure 8.10 illustrates the types of trials used in this experiment. A triad of locations was spatially presented by labeled dots; the locations were either in their correct relative positions or were reversed. In addition, the overall layout of the stimuli were either aligned with common map coordinates (i.e., north at the top) or rotated 30°, 60°, 90°, 120°, 150°, or 180° from that orientation. Similar rotated and nonrotated triads were also constructed for the building locations. Subjects were to decide whether the layout was correct or reversed.

Evans and Pezdek found that the decision times for the states increased with the number of degrees of rotation in the triad presentation. This result suggests that before the subjects decided whether the relative positions were correct, they mentally rotated the configurations such that the states appeared roughly in the same orientation as they appear on a cartographic map. In contrast, for the building triads the presentation orientation did not affect decision times. Apparently, subjects did not need to rotate the stimulus in order to make their decisions, and cognitive map information acquired from direct spatial experience was accessed in an orientation-free manner.

To demonstrate that the differences between state representation and building representation were not merely a result of the difference between the sizes of the U.S. and a college campus, or an effect of any characteristic other than the method of learning, Evans and Pezdek repeated their campus experiment with subjects who were unfamiliar with the college campus. These subjects learned the locations of the buildings by studying a map that was always shown in a fixed orientation. Under these circumstances the decision times for the campus buildings linearly increased as a function of the angle of orientation. These data suggest that subjects derive only certain types of information when acquiring spatial information from a map.

Thorndyke and Stasz (1980) examined the types of procedures used by subjects as they are learning a map and the nature of individual differences in this task. Eight subjects were asked to learn the information on each of two maps. One map depicted a fictional town, and it showed roads, buildings, and natural landmarks such as a river and a park. The other map represented several fictional countries, some cities in them, roads, and natural landmarks such as rivers, lakes, and mountains. As subjects were learning this information they "thought out loud," and the verbal protocol of their thought processes was recorded and later analyzed. After each of six study periods

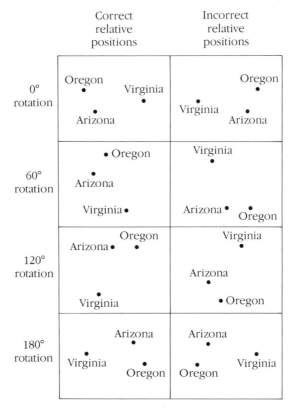

Figure 8.10 A sample triad from Evans and Pezdek's experiment in its different orientations. Subjects were to decide if the relative positions in the triad were correct or reversed. Decision time varied with degree of rotation for these triads, but not for triads of buildings on the subjects' college campus. [From Evans and Pezdek, 1980. Copyright 1980 by the American Psychological Association. Reprinted by permission of the publisher and the author.]

with each map, the subjects were tested for their recall of the various elements.

Thorndyke and Stasz examined the verbal protocols and found that subjects used four main types of processes to learn the spatial information. First, attentional processes included mentally partitioning the map into subregions for further study and focusing attention on particular areas in the map. Second, in a set of encoding operations subjects rehearsed and learned specific items by rehearsal, associations, imagery, and pattern encoding. Third, evaluation procedures allowed the subjects to retrieve previously learned material and compare it to the map itself. Finally, a set of general control procedures allowed the subjects to select procedures and switch back and forth from procedure to procedure.

On the basis of the subjects' ability to remember elements of the maps, Thorndyke and Stasz divided their subjects into good and poor learners. They found that good learners were more likely than poor learners to partition the map into subparts and to systematically study the parts. Second, the good learners were more likely to use spatial and visual encoding strategies, which implies that the analog component is very important in acquiring a good cognitive map. Finally, poor learners spent significantly longer rehearsing material they had already learned rather than trying to encode material they did not know. This finding is not surprising in that poor learners were not as accurate as good learners in remembering which items they successfully recalled on the previous recall trial.

A second experiment conducted by Thorndyke and Stasz showed that subjects' learning improved when they were given instruction in some of the skills the poor learners seemed to lack. However, individual differences were not totally erased by effective training procedures. Subjects with good spatial abilities showed relatively more improvement from their visual and spatial encoding training than did those with low spatial abilities. The training procedures were therefore more effective overall for the high-ability subjects, and those subjects showed the greatest overall improvement.

Summary

The literature on cognitive mapping shows very clearly that analog representations are not the sole form in which we store visual information. Equally important, it shows that such analog representations are extremely important to our ability to form and use cognitive maps. Although distance and positional information can be stored and retrieved using an analog representation, a good many relationships may also be specified by verbal labels and by propositions. We return to the issue of the interaction of the propositional and imaginal memory systems in Chapter 9.

ALTERNATIVES TO THE IMAGERY THEORY

We devoted most of this chapter to examining what imagery is and how it might work. Although scientific evidence that supports the imagery theory comes from a variety of sources and seems compelling, psychologists by no means agree that imaginal representations exist or that such representations would offer an adequate explanation of the phenomena we have observed. Scientists who criticize the imagery theory offer several kinds of arguments. First, they argue that imagery alone may not be adequate to explain the data accumulated thus far. Second, they suggest that the idea of a propositional representation may not be incompatible with imagery. Finally, they argue that it may not be possible to decide whether an image or a propositional representation is being used in any given case.

What Is a Proposition?

For purposes of simplicity, in this chapter we have been equating the concept of a proposition with the verbal expression of a proposition in a sentence. However, this need not be the case. Anderson (1978) outlines the three main features that characterize a proposition. First, a proposition is abstract and subsumes the exact wording of particular sentences that express it. Thus I may have some propositional knowledge about the appearance of my dog, and I may say: My dog is brown, or My dog has fur. Neither of these specific sentences, however, completely expresses the content of my propositional knowledge of what my dog looks like.

Second, a proposition is either true or false. Thus in addition to storing information in propositional form, we have a truth value associated with each proposition. In our previous example, it may be the case that my dog's fur is black. In this case, an additional "false" marker would accompany the stored proposition. Generally, however, we seem to store information in terms of true propositions, and in most communication we convey information using propositions that are true.

Third, propositions conform to a series of implicit rules that determine when a proposition is well formed. Since propositions generally assert some relationship between two or more entities, or between an entity and a property, propositional rules determine what relationships and properties are allowed for different classes of entities. An example of a poorly formed proposition is one expressed by the sentence "Chairs snore." This sentence is a nonsensical one because only living, breathing entities can snore. The propositional rule structure disallows such mismatches between an entity and the type of property it is said to have.

Clearly, any nonverbal representations that fulfill these three properties are propositions. The proposition "Dogs have fur" may be expressed equally well by an image showing a dog. Some theorists use this point as one justification for the argument that a separate imagery system is unnecessary and that propositional representations can be used to generate any set of data.

Why Is Imagery Theory "Incomplete"?

Some psychologists also argue that imagery theory is an incomplete explanation for many phenomena. Responding to subjective reports of imagery, Pylyshyn (1973) acknowledges that most people experience imagery but argues that although people report that they are using images in a particular task, people are notoriously inadequate at analyzing their own mental operations and may not be able to tell if an underlying propositional system is actually generating the image. Pylyshyn sums up this argument by saying that "while most psychologists are willing to concede that not all important psychological processes and structures are available to conscious inspection, it is not generally recognized that the converse may also hold: that what is available to conscious inspection may not be what plays the important causal role in psychological processes" (pp. 2–3).

Imagery theory is often criticized as being incomplete because not all imagery theorists agree on or even state what an image is like. Kosslyn and Pomerantz (1977) point out that thinking of an image as a mental picture is a very extreme analogy, and most imagery theorists do not hold this view. However, both Anderson (1978) and Pylyshyn (1973) note that the mental-picture analogy is certainly a dominant theme and seems to be the only clearly stated analogy used. Parallels are often drawn between the mental image and a perceptual representation, based on the modality-specific interference effects obtained by Brooks (1968) and Atwood (1971), reviewed earlier in this chapter. But if we were to assume that the mental image is a relatively raw, uninterpreted array of information, much like the information in iconic store, then an image should be subject to the same types of perceptual distortions and operations undergone by sensory images. However, the only evidence for such distortions is Kerst and Howard's (1978) data on mental size estimates.

Better agreement with the data is obtained when an image is described as being similar to the output of perceptual processing rather than to the input. Such output is generally highly interpreted and often very abstract. For example, the output of perceptual processing permits the identification of objects, the classes to which they belong, and the meaningful relationships that hold among them. These properties are the same ones that characterize propositions. Moreover, we know that the use of imagery must involve some additional propositional knowledge, as the following example from Pylyshyn (1973) illustrates. If a paired-associate task requires a subject to remember the pair child/play using imagery, the subject undoubtedly forms a mental picture of a child engaging in some play activity, such as kicking a ball. If retrieval of the response play is based on this image, how does the subject know whether to retrieve play or kick or ball? Accurate retrieval demands that the subject use a proposition to tag the relevant aspect of the picture. Although such an example does not argue against Paivio's dual coding hypothesis or the notion that imaginal and propositional representations can coexist, it does emphasize that any posited imaginal system requires a complementary system for labeling the imagery.

Further Criticisms of Imagery

Two remaining criticisms of imagery theory deserve mention. The first is that if imagery coexists with propositions, or is caused by an underlying propositional representation, then there must exist an *interlingua*, a way of translating from one representational "language" to the other. Some theorists posit a single abstract conceptual memory store to which both the visual and verbal systems have access. For these theorists this abstract memory representation would act as the interlingua. In Chapter 9 we consider more carefully this type of connection between visual and verbal memory systems; however, here we must note that if such an abstract system does not exist, then the nature of the interlingua is a problem for any theory that posits an imaginal and a propositional memory system.

The final problem in the debate is whether it is possible to distinguish imagery and propositions. Anderson (1978) makes the point that a theory about the representation of knowledge must also specify the types of mental operations (e.g., storage, retrieval, manipulation) that operate on the representation. Anderson then proves mathematically that the data produced by an hypothesized model of imaginal representation and associated operations can be completely mimicked by some propositional system and associated operations. Thus both systems would generate the exact same set of data, and no set of data could confirm one model or disconfirm the other.

Given the objections raised against imagery theory and the difficulties associated with trying to prove one representation or another, one might retreat to the conclusion that probably both representations exist. Since some types of information can be coded in both ways, and since some situations make one method superior to the other, the processing system may well be flexible. In Chapter 9 we examine how the two types of systems complement each other and interact in various tasks.

SUGGESTED READING

Kosslyn (1980) presents a very thorough account of imagery and the representation controversy. Readers interested in cognitive maps should consult Downs and Stea (1977).

_____ *Chapter 9* _____

Interactions Between Visual and Verbal Systems

We have seen that the visual processing system is very powerful and versatile. We have also examined several interactions between the visual system and the verbal system: in word recognition and reading (Chapter 6) and in dual encoding and imagery (Chapter 8). And we noted that many of the organizational principles influencing pattern perception produce arrangements of stimuli that are easily nameable (Chapter 4). All these instances reinforce our intuitive sense that visual information processing both influences and is influenced by linguistic experience.

In this final chapter we examine this interaction more closely. Of course, our discussion will be restricted in that we cannot here fully review all that psychologists and psycholinguists have discovered about how linguistic information is coded, stored, and retrieved from verbal memory. Thus we limit our presentation to only a general outline of those parts of the verbal system that relate to visual processing.

Within this limitation, however, a vast number of topics and experiments could be included in this chapter. Since an average person easily coordinates visual and verbal processing all the time, almost all activities involve some interaction between the two systems. Thus we further limit our discussion to five topics that have received a great deal of attention from psychologists. The first two topics concern interactions between the two systems during initial pattern recognition and perceptual encoding. The third topic pertains to how people coordinate visual material and verbal descriptions of visual material, in particular, how people decide that a given verbal description adequately describes a visual stimulus.

The last two topics relate to interactions between the two systems in long-term memory. We return to the dual encoding hypothesis and related hypotheses concerning the existence of a single, abstract long-term memory system that contains information obtained through both verbal and visual processing. Finally, we examine how verbal information may influence memory for events that were originally coded visually, and vice versa. This last topic has important implications for eyewitness testimony, and we review results from experiments regarding eyewitness accounts of visual events.

THE STROOP EFFECT

One of the most convincing demonstrations that the visual and verbal processing systems do not act independently comes from what has come to be known as the *Stroop effect*. Although the effect had been noted in passing in earlier experiments, Stroop (1935) published the first careful and thorough study of interference between visual and verbal processing of letter strings. Stroop demonstrated how word identification, which yields a verbal label for a stimulus, interferes with a subject's ability to make a response based on a visual characteristic of that stimulus. The stimulus in this experiment was a card on which five color terms—red, blue, green, brown, and purple—were printed many times. The 100 items were arranged in rows and columns so that each color word appeared twice in each row and twice in each column in a random order. Stroop asked subjects to read the words aloud, one after the other, scanning down and across the stimulus card, and recorded their time for reading all 100 words.

Stroop compared subjects' reading speeds under two conditions. In the control condition all the words were printed in black ink; the average reading time was 41 seconds. In the experimental condition each color name was printed in a color other than that which it named; for example, red was printed in blue ink. Thus a visual characteristic of the stimulus itself, namely the color of the ink, was at variance with the verbal response required of the subject, but this discrepancy produced only a slight increase in the average reading time, 43.3 seconds.

In Stroop's second experiment he obtained a much larger and more convincing interference effect. Subjects were to name the colors of the ink in which the stimulus items were printed. In the control condition each stimulus was a simple square printed in one of the five colors. Subjects took an average of 63.3 seconds to name the ink colors of 100 squares. In the experimental condition, however, each stimulus was a word that named a color other than its own ink color; for example, the correct response to the word red, printed in blue ink was "blue." The response of the verbal coding system in reading the letters interfered with the subject's labeling of the color of the ink. Subjects were substantially slowed in this condition, taking 110.3 seconds to respond to the one hundred stimuli on the card.

Many investigators have attempted to determine both the circumstances under which the Stroop effect is obtained and the causes of the phenomenon. Clearly, the existence of a large Stroop effect depends on the presence of competing verbal responses. Pritchatt (1968), for example, examined a situation in which subjects responded, not by naming the color of the ink aloud, but by matching the ink colors with square patches of color. In this situation the subject presumably does not have to generate the name of the ink color, so that the concurrent process of reading the word cannot interfere with the production of the correct response. Under these circumstances the magnitude of the Stroop effect is greatly reduced; however, the effect does not completely disappear. To the extent that subjects cannot suppress the tendency to name both the ink color and the response color to themselves, the color-naming responses receive some interference from the word naming. A more rigorous test of the role of verbal interference in producing the Stroop effect was made by Keele (1973). He found no interference when responses to the ink colors were signaled by key presses rather than by verbal responses.

A second characteristic of the Stroop effect is that it is not limited to stimuli that are the names of colors. In fact, interference is obtained when words that are semantically associated with the ink colors are used in the task. An example of this variation appears in an experiment by Klein (1964), who used stimuli of six different types: (1) nonsense syllables (e.g., evgjc, bhdr); (2) very infrequent English words (e.g., eft, abjure); (3) common English words that do not carry any color association or connotation (e.g., take, friend); (4) words strongly associated with colors (e.g., lemon, grass); (5) color terms that were not the names of any of the ink colors used in the printing; and (6) color words that named the colors of ink used in the printing, but that did not match the color of ink in which they were printed.

The time necessary to name the ink color of 80 stimuli of each of these six types was recorded, and was compared to the time needed to identify the ink colors of 80 asterisks (the control condition). Klein found that the magnitude of the interference effect increased as the semantic similarity between the stimulus strings and the ink colors increased. That is, nonsense syllables produced a negligible 5-second increase, while the sixth condition, the standard Stroop interference condition, produced approximately 38 seconds of interference. Words that had color-related meanings produced a significant 15.5-second interference effect.

Klein (1964) and many others since drew the conclusion that the structure of the associations between words stored in verbal long-term memory contributes to the magnitude of the Stroop effect. Several well-regarded theories of how information is represented in verbal memory are based on the principle that the associations between words that are similar in meaning are represented in verbal memory. When a word representation is used, activation spreads to the representations of semantically related words, making those associates available as responses as well. Of course, we may not be conscious of such activation, but it would explain phenomena like the Stroop effect.

In the case of Klein's color-related stimulus words, the visual information processing system simultaneously processes the ink color and indentifies the word. When the color-related word is fully identified, some such other terms as the color names closely associated with it are also activated. These terms become available as possible responses as well. Because they are produced as a sort of byproduct of the reading response, they do not interfere with the production of the ink color name as much as an actual color term. However, they do produce a significant amount of interference.

That the Stroop effect depends on the presence of competing verbal responses and that it occurs for color-related terms leads us to a further inference about the mechanisms responsible for the phenomenon. We can infer that the information processing system is capable of reading a word faster than it is capable of naming a physical factor such as the color of the stimulus. Three arguments support this hypothesis. First, if the name of the ink color were available before the name of the word, subjects would have little difficulty producing it without interference; but this is obviously not the case. Second, the reading response is so rapid compared to the naming response that even items semantically related to the originally presented word are activated before the ink color can be named. Third, we have Stroop's failure to obtain an interference effect when subjects were asked to read the words aloud. In this situation the words became available so much sooner than the ink color names that the ink colors had no chance to interfere with the correct response.

This reasoning about the relative speeds of reading and color naming led Klein (1964) to ask subjects to read a standard 100-item Stroop card by responding to each stimulus with both the word name and the color of the ink in which it was printed. In one condition subjects were to first read the word aloud and then give the ink color; in the other condition they were to give the ink color and then the word. Reading times were far longer in the second condition because a subject's response could not begin until the slower ink color name was produced and because the quicker word-naming response interfered with the subject's ability to produce the ink color. In the first condition, however, a subject could say the word name immediately after recognizing it and, with that out of the way, could produce the ink color with little trouble.

A second method for demonstrating the importance of the relative speed of reading and color naming was employed by Gumenik and Glass (1970). They reduced the legibility of the letters in a Stroop task without decreasing the quality of the color information in the ink. The interference produced by the incongruity between the word name and the ink color was greatly reduced in this situation. Apparently the visual degradation of the letters substantially increased the amount of time it took the subjects to name the words. Under these circumstances a word did not produce a competing verbal response soon enough to affect the production of the ink color name.

Since reading occurs more quickly than color naming and can therefore inhibit color naming when there is a discrepancy between the two, we can ask if there are any circumstances under which the faster reading response might facilitate the color-naming response. If our analysis is correct, when the word name and the ink color are the same the fast word-naming response should generate a quick color-naming response. Results obtained by Hintzman et al. (1972) show that word naming can, in fact, facilitate color naming of the identical ink color.

These experiments with the Stroop effect lead us to conclude that the interference arises primarily at a response selection stage. Word naming appears to be automatic—subjects do not seem to be able to avoid reading the words even when they know that this retards ink naming (Posner and Snyder, 1975). The fast processing of a word activates a memory node for the content of that word and some of its semantic associates. The slower color-naming process then activates another color node in memory, and the discrepancy concerning which is the correct response produces an interference effect.

ABSTRACTION AND GENERATION IN SHORT-TERM MEMORY

Many tasks we perform daily require that visual cues, such as color and form, be converted into a verbal form. This application of a verbal label is an example of what Posner (1969) calls *abstraction,* the process by which the system converts very specific sensory cues to progressively more general representations for stimuli. We examined another example of abstraction in Chapter 3 when we discussed the formation of prototypes from experience with multiple examples from a single category. In general, abstraction relates specific information about the physical characteristics of a stimulus to a conceptual label, often verbal, that assigns the stimulus to a general class or category. Such a label tells nothing about the precise visual characteristics of the original stimulus.

The process of converting visually coded, or analog, information into a verbal form takes place over a measureable period of time after the stimulus is presented. In a series of experiments, Posner and his colleagues (Posner and Mitchell, 1967; Posner et al., 1969; Posner, 1969, 1970) attempted to delineate how the abstraction process works. These experiments illustrate one of the ways in which the visual and verbal processing systems complement one another.

Posner and Mitchell (1967) used a reaction time task to compare subjects' ability to make abstractions that depend on physical attributes of stimuli and those abstractions that depend on the stimuli's relation to a superordinate category. Subjects were to compare two simultaneously presented letters. Under a physical identity rule the two letters were to be called "same" if they were physically identical (AA or aa), but not if they were the same letter in different cases (Aa) or were totally different (AB or Ab). Under a name identity rule, letter pairs were the "same" if they named the same letter (AA or Aa), and pairs were "different" otherwise.

The results of the physical identity and name identity trials are as follows:

	Reaction time (milliseconds)
Physical Identity Rule	
"same" trials (AA)	428
"different" trials	
dissimilar pair (Aa)	443
highly similar pair (Cc)	553
Name Identity Rule	
"same" trials	
identical pair (AA)	452
similar pair (Cc)	461
highly dissimilar pair (Ee)	523
"different" trials (EA)	556

The differences on the physical identity "different" trials suggest that a direct analog comparison of the visual characteristics takes place first. For a highly similar pair, this analog comparison can interfere with the correct response. This analog comparison, however, facilitates the response on some name identity "same" trials, in which similar pairs were recognized almost as quickly as identical pairs. Furthermore, the data from the name identity condition indicate that information about physical characteristics is available much sooner than the more abstract names. Physically identical pairs (PI) were identified 71 milliseconds faster than name-identical (NI) pairs. Apparently subjects made the "same" response on the basis of purely physical comparisons that are made quickly. However, when the physical characteristics differ, the response must wait for the process of abstraction to produce the verbal labels. Thus the data for the "same" trials under the physical identity rule and the PI "same" trials under the name identity rule indicate the use of purely visual information.

We can now trace the time course of the abstraction process. The superiority of PI over NI pairs should hold as long as visual information is available for use. Once the abstraction process finishes generating labels for the stimuli, the PI pairs will no longer enjoy an advantage because the only remaining information is verbal. On this assumption, Posner and Keele (1967) sequentially presented the letters in each pair, with a set interval— either 0, 0.5, 1.0, or 1.5 seconds—between the two. Decision times under the name identity instructions were measured for PI, NI, and completely different pairs at each of these intervals. The superiority of the PI pairs over the NI pairs was 87 milliseconds at 0-seconds delay, 58 milliseconds at 0.5-seconds delay, 47 milliseconds after 1.0 seconds, and only 19 milliseconds after 1.5 seconds. Clearly, the amount of visual information declines steadily over a 1.5-second interval until it is virtually gone.

In addition to naming, the process of abstraction includes categorization. Posner (1970) examined physical identity and name identity rules in two cases in which subjects' decisions were based on category inclusion principles. In one case, subjects were to decide whether the two characters were both vowels or both consonants; in the other, whether the two characters were both digits or both letters. When the classification was based on the vowel-consonant distinction, the items that were of the same category (e.g., AE), but were not PI or NI pairs, took 185 milliseconds longer than the PI pairs, and 59 milliseconds longer than the NI pairs. This result suggests that the process of abstracting vowel and consonant categories requires additional time beyond the naming time. However, when the classification was to be based on the digit-letter distinction, no such increase in the decision times for conceptual classifications was noted. Classification by this category rule took approximately the same amount of time as classification by name, indicating that name information does not precede digit-letter categorization. This finding, of course, further confirms the category effect discussed in Chapter 5.

Our discussion of how physical and abstract verbal codes interact would not be complete without a brief mention of the process Posner calls *generation*. Generation, the inverse of abstraction, is the process by which less abstract codes are produced from more abstract memory representations. Posner et al. (1969) show that generation can produce visual codes that are of comparable quality and utility to the physical information extracted from a visual stimulus. Subjects performed a same-different task for stimuli pairs whose first member was presented auditorally. Upon hearing the first letter name, subjects were to generate a visual representation for the corresponding uppercase character and to compare that with the visually presented second letter. After a few days of practice, response times for the PI stimuli in both this auditory-visual and a visual-visual condition were nearly identical. This result indicates that subjects became adept at converting the verbal label to a visual representation through generation.

In summary, Posner's work suggests the visual and verbal coding systems interact and complement each other even at very early stimulus-coding stages of processing. The relationship is such that information can be recoded from either system to the other with equal ease.

COMPARING SENTENCES WITH PICTURES

Our visual processing system and verbal system must interact whenever we compare or check pictorial information against a verbal description of it. To examine this interaction Clark and Chase (1972) used a *verification task,* in which the subject was given a sentence describing the relative positions of two objects and was to decide whether the sentence accurately describes the objects' positions in an accompanying picture (see Figure 9.1). Intuition suggests that the sentence is an example of a propositional representation and that the pictorial information is likely to be coded in an analog manner. How, then, does a subject discern whether the information from the two sources is identical?

Clark and Chase assume that "for a sentence and picture to be compared they must be represented, ultimately, in the same mental format" (p. 473). They posit that this format is a propositional representation, that both the sentence description and the picture arrangement are transformed into propositions containing the names of the objects and their properties, or essential relationships. From these assumptions, we can construct a model to predict reaction times for different combinations of sentence and picture types in a verification task. The method is a specific application of Donders' subtractive method for analyzing reaction times, which is presented in Appendix B. The interested reader may wish to consult that more general discussion in addition to the present example.

To analyze the verification task, consider a situation in which the subject is first shown a sentence and then looks at a picture; the reaction time is measured from the onset of sentence processing. Clark and Chase divide the reaction time into four sequentially ordered stages: (1) formation of the mental representation of the sentence (sentence encoding); (2) formation of the mental representation of the picture (picture encoding); (3) comparison of the two representations; and (4) response production. The stages are diagrammed in Table 9.1a.

Our predictions for the total reaction time depend on what our model assumes will happen at each of these stages. Let us first consider the sentence encoding. The second column of Table 9.1b provides the eight types of sentences that could describe the spatial relationship between two objects designated as A and B. The first four sentences are affirmative sentences because the relationship between A and B is expressed positively. In contrast, the negative sentences all contain the negative term "not." Based on various linguistic considerations and data from earlier experiments (e.g., Clark, 1969), Clark and Chase argue that the representation of affirmatives is less complex than that of negatives and that affirmatives are encoded more quickly during sentence encoding than negatives. Thus, every negative sentence will take longer to verify, on the average, by some amount of time which we will denote by b. The value of b in milliseconds will be estimated from the data.

Star is above plus   *

                +   **Figure 9.1**   Example of Clark and Chase's (1972) stimuli for a sentence-picture verification task.

Plus isn't above star   *

                     +

A second distinction between the sentences is that the relationship between A and B can be stated either in terms of *above* or *below*. Again, based on linguistic analysis and earlier experimental data, Clark and Chase assert that the term *above* is easier to encode than the term *below*. This assertion leads to the prediction that the sentences containing *below* will take an average of a milliseconds longer to encode than sentences containing *above*. The propositional encodings of the various sentence types are shown in the third column of Table 9.1b.

Clark and Chase's model makes a quite simple prediction about what happens in picture encoding. Quite simply, whichever relational term was used to encode the sentence will again be used to encode the picture. Therefore, if the picture $_B^A$ appears, it will be encoded as (A above B) when the preceding sentence contained *above*, and as (B below A) when the preceding sentence contained *below*. Because the picture has no linguistic content, there are no linguistic grounds for assuming any differences between these two encodings at this stage; nor are there affirmatives or negatives for picture encoding. Thus all pictures take the same amount of time to encode.

At the comparison stage, the subject must decide whether the encodings derived from the picture and the sentence match. The comparison process makes use of a *truth index*, which tells whether the response should be true or false based upon the comparisons made up to any given point (see Table 9.1a). For simplicity, the initial value of the truth index is assumed to be "true." During comparison the inner, or embedded, portions of the two encodings are compared. Because the relational term is always the same for each sentence-picture pair, a simple comparison of the subject terms in the propositions is enough to tell whether the inner propositions are identical. If these portions match, the truth index is left as it is; if the inner propositions mismatch, the truth index is changed from "true" to "false." This change of the truth index is assumed to take c milliseconds.

Following the decision on the inner propositions, the outer, or embedding, portions of the two propositions must be compared. Since the encoding of the picture always carries with it an implicit "true" in the outer proposition, a mismatch at this level will occur only for the negative sentences that have been encoded with a "false" outer proposition. Whenever such a mismatch occurs, the truth index is again changed from its current value to the other value, which requires an additional d milliseconds. Notice in Table 9.1a that

Table 9.1 (a) Clark and Chase's model for sentence-picture verification tasks. (b) Latency predictions for the task as estimated from the model. [From Clark and Chase, 1972.]

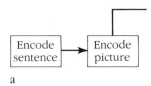

a

b

Sentence Type			Sentence	Sentence Code	Picture Code
Affirmative	True	above	A is above B.	(A above B)	(A above B)
		below	B is below A.	(B below A)	(B below A)
	False	above	B is above A.	(B above A)	(A above B)
		below	A is below B.	(A below B)	(B below A)
Negative	True	above	B isn't above A.	(false (B above A))	(A above B)
		below	A isn't below B.	(false (A below B))	(B below A)
	False	above	A isn't above B.	(false (A above B))	(A above B)
		below	B isn't below A.	(false (B below A))	(B below A)

if the truth index was "false" as a result of a mismatch at the first comparison, the second comparison changes its value back to "true."

The predicted reaction times for each of the possible sentence-picture combinations are shown as the latency components in Table 9.1b. For example, consider the second stimulus in Figure 9.1. The sentence is a true, negative sentence that uses *above*. Table 9.1b predicts that the latency first contains the term t_0, the amount of time required for all the operations common to all sentence-picture pairs: the time to read the sentence, encode an affirmative, encode the term *above*, encode the picture, do the two comparison operations, and execute a response. In addition, the prediction for the true, negative sentence includes b, the time to encode the negative in the sentence code; c, the interval during the comparison stage when the mismatch of the subjects of the inner propositions require the truth index be changed from "true" to "false"; and d, the time needed to again change the truth index because the embedding propositions do not match. Thus the predicted reaction time time for a true, negative sentence is $t_0 + b + c + d$.

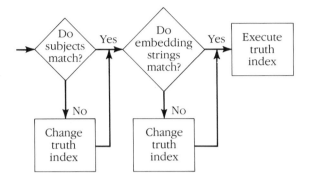

Truth Index			Latency Components		Latencies Observed	Predicted
		T	t_0		1744	1763
		T	t_0+a		1875	1856
true → false		F	t_0	$+c$	1959	1950
true → false		F	t_0+a	$+c$	2035	2043
true → false	false → true	T	t_0	$+b+c+d$	2624	2635
true → false	false → true	T	$t_0+a+b+c+d$		2739	2728
	true → false	F	t_0	$+b$ $+d$	2470	2448
	true → false	F	t_0+a+b	$+d$	2520	2541

The column of latency components in Table 9.1b illustrates three important features of the model. First, we notice that every time b is added to t_0 for encoding a negative sentence, d must be added later when that "false" in the outer string fails to match the picture's outer string. Thus b and d do not appear independent of each other. Clark and Chase refer to the quantity $b + d$ as *negation time* because it measures how much longer negatives take to process. Second, the truth or falsity of sentences is predicted to show an interaction with their affirmative or negative character. They refer to c as the *falsification time* because false affirmative (FA) sentences average c milliseconds longer than the true affirmatives (TA), and for negatives, true negatives (TN) average c milliseconds longer than false negatives (FN). Third, the predictions indicate that sentences with *above* should be overall faster than the sentences with *below* by a milliseconds.

Table 9.1b also shows the reaction times observed by Clark and Chase when testing a group of subjects. The observed latencies are very close to the pattern predicted by the model. Clark and Chase estimated the values of *a, b, + d,* and *c* as 93 milliseconds, 685 milliseconds, and 187 milliseconds respectively. The base time t_0 was 1763 milliseconds. When these values are used to generate actual numerical predictions for the reaction times, they are in close agreement with the times obtained from the subjects. This finding supports the model's accuracy as a description of the sentence-picture verification process.

Carpenter and Just (1975) simplify and extend Clark and Chase's model by examining sentence-picture verification for stimuli such as the sentences "The dots are red," and "The dots are black" and pictures of clusters of red or black dots. Like Clark and Chase, Carpenter and Just assume that both the picture and the sentences are encoded in a propositional form. Their model and examples of the encodings for TA, TN, FA, and FN sentence-picture pairs are shown in Table 9.2.

Their model, Table 9.2a, assumes that the corresponding portions of the sentence and picture encodings are retrieved and compared pair by pair. The value of the truth index is initially set at "true," but whenever portions of the encodings mismatch, the index is changed and the entire comparison process begins again. Of course, if a mismatch occurs, these portions of the encodings must be tagged so that they generate a match during the next comparison. The response that is finally executed is the value of the truth index after all parts of the two encodings have been successfully matched.

Carpenter and Just's approach to the verification task simplifies Clark and Chase's approach to reaction times by replacing *a, b, c,* and *d* with the single parameter *k,* the number of times some pair of corresponding parts of the encodings needs to be retrieved and compared. This concept of the multiple execution of a single comparison operation simplifies the model tremendously and also captures a regularity in sentence-picture verification data. Carpenter and Just noticed that negation time (*b + d* in Clark and Chase's model) is an integer multiple of falsification time (*c* in Clark and Chase's model). Although this rule only roughly approximates Clark and Chase's data, it holds very well for other sets of data in the literature (e.g., Just and Carpenter, 1971).

Carpenter and Just's *constituent comparison model* for TA, FA, FN, and TN sentences for the dots stimuli exhibit an interesting pattern. For TA sentences, comparison of both the internal and external parts of the sentence and picture representations result in matches. Thus the find-and-compare operation of the model is executed twice. For FA sentences, however, the first find-and-compare operation yields a mismatch for the internal parts. Thus the truth index is changed to "false" and these internal parts are tagged to yield a match during the next comparison. The second find-and-compare operation compares the newly tagged internal strings, and this time they match. The outer constituents are then compared, these constituents also match, and the current "false" value of the index is used as a response. Note that in this case three find-and-compare operations were executed. This logic would dictate that FN and TN sentences respectively require four and five

Table 9.2 (a) Carpenter and Just's constituent comparison model for sentence-picture verification tasks. (b) Encoding and comparison processes assumed to predict latencies. Plus signs indicate that component constituents match; minus signs indicate a mismatch. [From Carpenter and Just, 1975.]

a

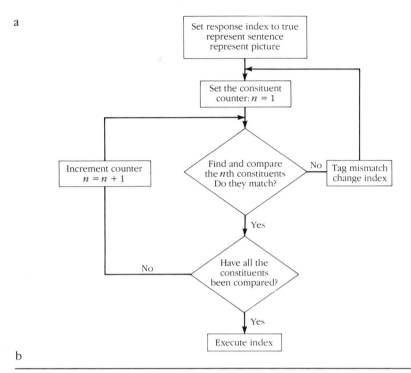

b

Stimulus and Representation	True Affirmative	False Affirmative
Sentence	The dots are red.	The dots are red.
Picture	Red dots	Black dots
Sentence representation	[AFF, (RED, DOTS)]	[AFF, (RED, DOTS)]
Picture representation	(RED, DOTS)	(BLACK, DOTS)
	+ +	− index = false
	response = true	+ +
	k comparisons	response = false
		k + 1 comparisons

	False Negative	True Negative
Sentence	The dots aren't red.	The dots aren't red.
Picture	Red dots	Black dots
Sentence representation	[NEG, (RED, DOTS)]	[NEG, (RED, DOTS)]
Picture representation	(RED, DOTS)	(BLACK, DOTS)
	− + index = false	− index = false
	+ +	− + index = true
	response = false	+ +
	k + 2 comparisons	response = true
		k + 3 comparisons

find-and-compare operations. In general, if a TA sentence requires k find-and-compare operations, then FA, FN, and TN sentences require $k + 1$, $k + 2$, and $k + 3$ operations respectively.

Notice that this model predicts the interaction previously observed between affirmative-negative and true-false characteristics. More specifically, TA sentences are predicted to be faster than FA sentences, but FN sentences will be faster than TN sentences. As Figure 9.2 shows, this prediction accurately describes subjects' performance on the verification task. The larger the number of find-and-compare operations needed to execute a response, the longer the latency. The slope of the best-fitting line through the latency data plotted as a function of the number of operations yields an estimate of the duration of each find-and-compare operation as 215 milliseconds.

The two models just reviewed are relatively simple explanations of how sentences and pictures are compared. But how general are these models? Can they be applied equally well to similar tasks? Glushko and Cooper (1978) argue that such sentence-picture comparison models are very task-specific. When they used a task that varied only slightly from Clark and Chase's and Carpenter and Just's, they obtained quite different results.

As shown in Figure 9.3, Glushko and Cooper's stimuli contained sentences and pictures that depict the relative spatial positioning of two or more shapes. These stimuli display three levels of complexity, defined by the number of propositions needed to fully describe the picture. At the beginning of each trial the subject viewed the sentence(s) alone and pushed a button when he understood the description. This reaction time for encoding the description was measured and labeled RT_1. The pushing of the button produced the picture for that trial, and the subject was to decide whether the picture was the one described by the sentences. This second reaction time for comparing the two was labeled RT_2.

RT_1 increased linearly with the complexity of the picture; that is, the more propositions there were to encode, the longer it took the subject to encode the description. Of the two models we examined before, only Clark and

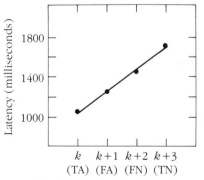

$$
\begin{array}{cccc}
k & k+1 & k+2 & k+3 \\
\text{(TA)} & \text{(FA)} & \text{(FN)} & \text{(TN)}
\end{array}
$$

Number of constituent comparisons

Figure 9.2 Carpenter and Just found that latency for a sentence-picture verification task was a linear function of the number of constituent comparison operations needed for the stimulus. [From Carpenter and Just, 1975. Copyright 1975 by the American Psychological Association. Reprinted by permission of the publisher and the author.]

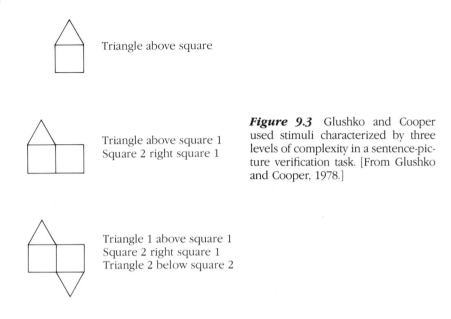

Figure 9.3 Glushko and Cooper used stimuli characterized by three levels of complexity in a sentence-picture verification task. [From Glushko and Cooper, 1978.]

Chase's model ascribes any of the differences in total verification time to encoding factors. Thus, these data argue against Carpenter and Just's contention that comparison differences account for all the variability in reaction times. Furthermore, RT_2 was constant with respect to the complexity of the figure; that is, the number of propositions in the description encoding did not affect the comparison time. This result cannot be explained by either of the earlier two models, which both assume that the comparison stage considers each portion of the encodings serially. Both models would predict that the longer the encoding of the description, the longer the comparison stage.

Taken together, the data on sentence-picture verification indicate a need for further research. On the one hand, the models proposed by both Clark and Chase, and by Carpenter and Just, are clearly supported by the data obtained in those sets of experiments. These models cannot therefore be dismissed as incorrect. On the other hand, Glushko and Cooper's results show that we cannot generalize from models based on a single type of experimental task. Further research is needed to determine when subjects will employ one kind of strategy for sentence-picture comparisons and when they will employ another.

ACCESSING PICTURES AND WORDS IN LONG-TERM MEMORY

Any discussion of how visual and verbal processes interact assumes the existence of a common format for representing both visual and verbal information. For example, the models of sentence-picture verification posited that both sources of information are represented propositionally. In general, any hypothesis about a common format involves assumptions about whether a separate, imaginally-based memory system exists for visual information, whether visual information can directly access verbal memory, or whether a modality-free conceptual memory system allows both types of information to be represented and to interact. In this section we review several naming and classification experiments that examine these issues for word and picture stimuli.

A test of whether the visual and verbal systems, as used to process pictures and words, have access to a common, abstract memory representation was carried out by Potter and Faulconer (1975). Subjects were shown either a picture of a concrete object (e.g., a chair, a coat) on the written name of such an object. In the naming condition, each stimulus was shown briefly, and the subject's latency to name the stimulus aloud was recorded. In the category condition, each trial was preceded by the name of a category. The subject was to decide whether the stimulus belonged to the designated category, and latencies were again recorded. Potter and Faulconer found that pictures took 260 milliseconds longer to name than did words. However, pictures were categorized 51 milliseconds faster than words.

Potter and Faulconer's results give us some initial information about how different types of information are stored in long-term memory. The data suggest that the pronunciation of a word is stored in a verbal, lexical information store that is directly accessed when a written word is read. The naming of pictures requires one or more extra steps. Abstract category and conceptual information is stored in a modality-free form that is slightly more accessible to the visual than to the verbal processing system. The naming of a picture requires that the visual information be processed through the abstract conceptual store, which provides access to the lexical and pronunciational information.

Several other experiments demonstrate the existence of a conceptual memory representation that is not modality-specific. Potter and Kroll (1978) investigated whether pictures of objects and written words have access to a common conceptual memory system by using both a lexical decision task and an object decision task. The lexical decision task was the same one used by Meyer and Schvaneveldt (1971), which we discussed in Chapter 6. Subjects were shown pairs of words and were to respond yes if both were English words, and no otherwise. Decision times were expected to be faster for pairs whose members were semantically related than for pairs whose members were unrelated. An analogous object decision task was constructed from line drawings of real-world objects and drawings of nonsense objects. Examples of the stimuli used in the two tasks are shown in Figure 9.4.

Several aspects of the data suggest that subjects based the two types of decisions on similar or identical information. First, the overall decision times for the two tasks were not significantly different. Examination of the reaction

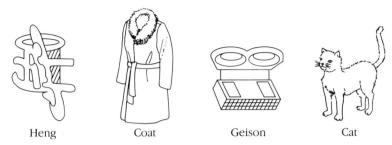

Figure 9.4 Examples of real and nonsensical stimuli used in the lexical decision and object decision tasks by Potter and Kroll (1978).

times for the thirty most frequent and the thirty least frequent stimuli in each task showed a 30-millisecond advantage for the high-frequency words in the lexical decision task and a 24-millisecond advantage for the high-frequency objects in the object decision task. Again the similarity of the data suggests a similarity in processing for pictures and words. Finally, Potter and Kroll examined the effect of semantic relatedness: related pairs were 18 milliseconds faster than unrelated pairs in the lexical decision task and 49 milliseconds faster in the object decision task. Such facilitation suggests that the relatedness effect results from information in an amodal memory store. This information can be accessed by both the verbal and the visual processing systems, but the magnitude of the facilitation suggests that it is more readily available to the visual system.

The results of the two studies by Potter and her associates support the assumptions of the memory model suggested by Nelson, Reed, and McEvoy (1977). Their two most important assumptions are that (1) words and pictures activate conceptual and pronunciational information about concepts in different orders, and that (2) pictures and words that refer to the same concept share the same conceptual and semantic information. Durso and Johnson (1979) made an explicit test of these assumptions by examining the role of stimulus repetition on both the naming and the categorization tasks. Subjects saw either a picture or a word on each trial and were to name the stimulus or to categorize it as natural or manufactured. Each concept was presented twice in the stimulus set, as either a picture or a word on each presentation.

Repetition of a stimulus item in a task like this is expected to facilitate the processing of the stimulus on re-presentation (Scarborough, Cortese, and Scarborough, 1977). The expected facilitation was observed for both the naming and the categorization tasks. In the naming task pictures were 142 milliseconds faster on the second presentation than on the first, and words were 24 milliseconds faster; in the categorization task, pictures were 39 milliseconds and words 68 milliseconds faster on the second presentation. These results are averaged across the type of initial presentation of the concept. Furthermore, in the naming task, pictures are expected to benefit more from repetition than words since words are initially faster and thus do not stand to benefit as much from repetition. Conversely, since pictures are initially superior in the categorization task, words are expected to show a more substantial improvement as a result of repetition.

A final experiment demonstrates how an amodal conceptual store might integrate complex information from sentences and pictures. Pezdek's (1977) subjects were to remember a set of presented scenes, such as those shown in Figure 9.5, originally presented as either a picture or a sentence. Embedded in the stimulus series at some point after the original stimulus, but before the memory test, was an item matched to the original. If the original was a picture, the matched intervening item was a sentence, and vice versa. The intervening item could be either relevant (as shown in the examples in Figure 9.5), or irrelevant. Test pictures probed the subject's memory for the original items. If information from the two modalities is, indeed, stored in a common conceptual memory store, then subjects should integrate relevant intervening items with the original items, and have trouble remembering the exact originals. Thus, when the intervening item is relevant, the probability of correctly identifying test items such as P_1 and S_1 in Figure 9.5 should be

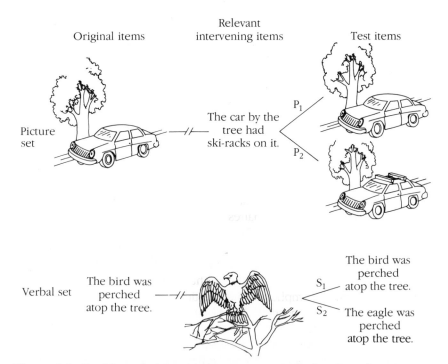

Figure 9.5 Pezdek used pictures and sentences to study the effect of intervening material on subjects' recall of visual and verbal stimuli. [From Pezdek, 1977. Copyright 1977 by the American Psychological Association. Reprinted by permission of the publisher and the author.]

low as compared to when the intervening material is irrelevant. Conversely, subjects should often falsely "recognize" test items such as P_2 and S_2 quite often after relevant intervening material. The data fit these predictions. Regardless of the modality of the original item, subjects tended to integrate semantically relevant intervening material and have a difficult time remembering the exact originals.

Taken together, the results of the studies we have discussed in this section indicate that a large amount of the conceptual information we possess about concepts is stored in a way that is accessible by either visual or verbal means. Potter and Faulconer's data and that of other experiments suggest that verbal input reaches the amodal store slightly more slowly because pronunciational information is first processed. However, the common, amodal conceptual memory store provides for the combining of information from the two modalities and the comparing of inputs from each source.

EYEWITNESS TESTIMONY

If the conclusions reached in the previous section are correct, then we know that long-term memory has both modality-specific coding mechanisms and an amodal storage mechanism. We would expect this amodal store to affect eyewitness testimony, in that the information enters the memory system primarily through the visual coding system but is reported primarily through the verbal system. In this section we review a number of experiments that show some startling effects of how subsequent linguistic experience influences how a visual event is remembered and reported.

Loftus and Palmer (1974) conducted two experiments in which subjects viewed short films showing automobile collisions. After viewing each film the subject was given a questionnaire asking specific questions about the accident. The critical question was one in which the subject was asked to estimate the speed at which the two cars were moving prior to the accident. Some questionnaires asked: "About how fast were the cars going when they hit each other?" Other questionnaires used "smashed," "collided," "bumped," or "contacted" instead of "hit." The wording of the question dramatically influenced the subjects' report: The mean speed estimates were 31.8, 34.0, 38.1, 39.3, and 40.8 miles per hour for the verbs "contacted," "hit," "bumped," "collided," and "smashed," respectively. Thus subjects' testimony depended on the presupposition implicit in the question.

Loftus and Palmer proposed two explanations of the effect of wording on the subjects' estimates. First, subjects might have been unsure about the exact speed of the cars, and a verb such as "smashed" might have biased their choice toward the upper end of their estimated range of possible speeds. Or, second, subjects knew how fast the cars were going, but their memory representations were actually modified by the verbal information contained in the question. If the second explanation is true, then we might expect to see a permanent change in a subject's report of an event after he receives a leading question.

To determine which explanation is correct, Loftus and Palmer performed a second experiment in which subjects viewed a filmed car accident and were given a questionnaire about the collision. One group of subjects were questioned about the cars' speed when they "smashed," another group about the speed when they "hit," and a third group was not questioned about the speed at all. One week later, without seeing the film again, all the subjects answered another set of questions about the accident. One of the questions in this second session was "Did you see any broken glass?" The film did not show broken glass, but Loftus and Palmer predicted that subjects originally questioned with the verb "smash" might remember the accident as being worse than it was. As predicted, only 12 percent of the control subjects and 14 percent of the "hit" subjects reported broken glass, but 32 percent of the "smashed" subjects reported glass. This result suggests that the leading question immediately after the viewing permanently influenced the subjects' memory of the film.

Loftus and Zanni (1975) show that subjects' reports are also influenced by the articles "a" or "the" in questions. Subjects viewed a film depicting a fender-bender accident and later answered questions about what they had seen. Half the subjects were asked "Did you see a broken headlight?" As Loftus and Zanni point out, this question has two parts: Was there a broken headlight? and, If there was, Did you see it? The other subjects were asked "Did you see the broken headlight?" This question presupposed that a broken headlight exists and asks only whether the subject saw it. Although the film showed no broken headlight, subjects asked about "the" headlight were more likely to report having seen one than subjects asked about "a" headlight.

Loftus and Zanni thus demonstrate that subjects will report nonexistent events in response to leading questions. Further, Loftus (1975) shows that incorrect information about nonexistent objects can be integrated into subjects' permanent memory representation of an event. Subjects viewed a videotape in which a white sportscar was involved in a traffic accident. Immediately after viewing the tape, half the subjects were asked "How fast was the white sportscar going when it passed the barn while traveling along the country road?" The other subjects were asked "How fast was the white sportscar going while traveling along the country road?" Although the videotape did not show a barn, one week later 17.3 percent of the subjects who answered the question presupposing the existence of a barn reported that they had seen one. Only 2.7 percent of the subjects who received the nonleading question reported having seen a barn.

Although we intuitively suspect that prejudicial wording would influence the nature of a witness' testimony, Loftus' experiments indicate that the effects may be more complex than we would suppose, because the information stored in memory may be altered by questioning. This result, however, is not surprising in the context of the experiments reviewed in this chapter, all of which show, that visual and verbal information can interact at all levels of processing.

SUGGESTED READING

Chase (1973) presents several interesting papers on visual processes and linguistic comprehension, including chapter 2 by Posner; chapter 7 by Clark, Carpenter, and Just; and chapter 8 by Bransford and Johnson. Posner and Snyder (1975) provide a slightly different approach to the Stroop-type interference effects we discussed. Readers interested in the problem of eyewitness testimony should consult Loftus (1979).

Appendix A

Signal Detection Theory

Throughout this book, we have discussed how well people can detect different types of visual stimuli. In Chapters 2 and 3, we examined the threshold detection of weak stimuli, sometimes in the presence of masking noise. In later chapters, we considered subjects' recognition and recall for stimuli presented during a study phase. In these cases, we were interested in knowing how effectively a subject could spot or detect the target material. Although the measure of detection ability is often expressed as the probability of subjects' recognizing the designated stimulus when it occurs, there is a better, though more complex, method for analyzing such data. The method arises from the *theory of signal detectability* (TSD), which is an account of how responses are generated in such experiments. TSD also allows an analysis of detection probability data that separates the true effects of sensitivity to the targets from shifts in the subject's response strategies. Let us clarify this concept by considering TSD within the framework of a sample experiment.

A TYPICAL DETECTION EXPERIMENT

On each trial of a typical detection experiment the subject must decide whether a designated target stimulus has been presented or not. For example, suppose the subject is asked to detect the presence of a sine-wave grating flashed briefly on a bright background. On some trials only the bright background appears, and on other trials the grating is superimposed on the background. The subject is to say yes if the grating appears and no if it does not. We refer to the bright background as the *noise*; it is the input from which the *signal*, or target, must be distinguished. In other words, on each trial the subject is to decide whether the signal and the noise have been presented, or only the noise.

Consider the trials on which the signal is presented. The subject will either make a *hit*, that is, notice the signal, or the subject will fail to detect it and make a *miss*. If the signal is extremely strong (e.g., if the sine-wave grating has high contrast), the subject should detect it almost all the time, and $P(H)$—the probability of a hit defined by the proportion of signal trials on which the signal is detected—will be quite high. Obviously, the miss rate will be low, and because each signal trial must lead to either a hit or a miss, the probabilities of the two must total 1.0.

A similar analysis can be made of the trials on which only noise is presented. On many of these trials the subject will realize that no signal has been shown and will make a *correct rejection*. However, sometimes the subject may mistakenly think that the signal was present even though it was not. Such a response is called a *false alarm*. Again, if the signal is very strong, $P(FA)$—the false alarm rate—will be quite low. In turn, the probability of a correct rejection will be very high. Again, the probability of a false alarm and the probability of a correction rejection must total 1.0 because on each noise trial either a correct rejection or a false alarm must occur. Table A.1 shows the relationship between hits, misses, correct rejections, and false alarms in terms of the events of the trial and the subject's response.

Many detection and memory experiments use $P(H)$ as a measure of subjects' performance. However, a high $P(H)$ could indicate one of two situations. One is that the subject's detection ability is quite good, that the subject is quite sensitive to the presence of the target. But, alternatively, a subject who said yes on every trial—whether the signal occurred or not—would receive a $P(H)$ of 1.0. Thus, a high $P(H)$ could merely reflect the subject's *bias* toward reporting the signal's presence.

Thus $P(H)$ alone cannot distinguish subjects who are biased toward saying yes all the time from subjects who have fine *sensitivity*, or ability to detect

Table A.1 The signal detection terms are defined by the stimulus situation on a trial and the subject's response.

| | Subject's Response | |
	Yes	No
Signal Present	Hit	Miss
Signal Absent	False alarm	Correct rejection

Probability (Hit) + Probability (Miss) = 1.0
Probability (False alarm) + Probability (Correct rejection) = 1.0

the stimulus. To make this distinction we must consider both the hit rate and the false alarm rate. Subjects who are biased in favor of reporting a signal on every trial will show a $P(H)$ of 1.0 and a $P(FA)$ of 1.0, since the subject will say yes on every signal trial and on every noise trial. In contrast, subjects who are sensitive to the target will show a high $P(H)$ and a low $P(FA)$.

ASSUMPTIONS OF THE THEORY
OF SIGNAL DETECTABILITY

TSD allows an experimenter to convert the hit and false alarm rates to standardized measures of sensitivity and bias. These measures can then be compared across experiments, or across different conditions within a single experiment, to determine which aspects of the subject's performance are influenced by the experimental factors that are being varied. Such comparisons require several assumptions about the internal effects of trials in which noise alone, or the signal plus noise, are presented. The assumptions are illustrated in Figure A.1.

The stimulus on each trial is assumed to generate a value of familiarity or _intensity_. In general, trials on which the signal is presented will seem more intense than trials on which noise alone is presented, but there is some variability in the magnitude of the subject's internal assessment of the stimulus intensity even for trials that are physically identical. The distribution of perceived intensity for noise trials is assumed to take on a normal distribution, as shown in Figure A.1. The height of the normal curve at each point along the perceived-intensity scale represents the proportion of noise trials on which noise alone produces that amount of intensity. Most trials produce relatively low values, represented by the central peak of the distribution around the mean value, $\bar{X}_n$. Relatively few trials produce subjective estimates that are quite high or extremely low.

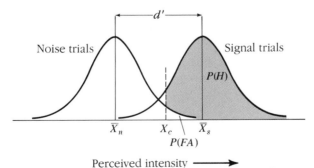

Figure A.1 The probabilities of hits and false alarms depend on the relative difference between the signal and noise distributions and the subject's response criterion along the intensity scale.

TSD makes a similar assumption about the distribution of subjective intensities for the signal trials. We again assume a normal distribution, as shown in Figure A.1, however, because the signal and the noise are present, the overall distribution for the signal trials is higher. Thus the majority of signal trials cluster around a larger value than the noise trials, and the mean of the signal trials, $\bar{X}_s$, will be greater than $\bar{X}_n$. For the sake of simplicity, TSD also assumes that the variance, or spread, of the two normal distributions is equal. However, the distance between the two distributions will depend on the intensity of the signal. If the signal is very intense, the distance between the two distributions will be large. However, if the signal is quite faint, just at threshold for example, the signal trials will not be much more intense than the noise trials, and the two distributions will nearly overlap. In TSD, sensitivity is measured by the distance between the means of the two distributions. The distance, denoted by d' is measured in standard deviate units and is therefore very much like a z-score (normal deviate score).

How does a subject decide whether a signal is present or not? On each trial the subject makes a subjective assessment of the intensity of the stimulus input. The subject is assumed to have a *criterion* value for intensity; if the perceived intensity exceeds that criterion the subject will respond yes, and if the perceived intensity falls below the criterion the response will be no. The criterion may fall anywhere along the scale. In Figure A.1, a possible criterion is indicated by the value X_c. Note that each criterion value for perceived intensity is uniquely defined by the ratio of the heights of the two curves at that point. TSD defines β, the measure of response bias, as the height of the signal distribution divided by the height of the noise distribution at the criterion value X_c.

All trials falling to the right of X_c will generate yes responses. $P(H)$, the proportion of signal trials on which a yes response is made, is represented in Figure A.1 by the area under the signal distribution that falls to the right of X_c. Similarly, any trial from the noise distribution falling to the right of X_c will also generate a yes response, but these responses are false alarms. $P(FA)$ is therefore the area under the noise distribution that lies to the right of X_c, as shown in Figure A.1.

Because $P(H)$ and $P(FA)$ correspond to areas under the two distributions, these values can be used to compute d' for a set of data. To compute d', we have to discover how many normal standard deviates lie between $\bar{X}_n$ and $\bar{X}_s$. This calculation is the same as computing the z-score X_c would have if it were part of the noise distribution. Let us assume that $P(H) = .75$ and $P(FA) = 0.10$. We can determine the z-score value of X_c on the noise distribution because we know what proportion (the false alarm rate) of all the noise trials lie to the right of X_c. Using a table of the normal distribution, we find that a z-score of 1.28 leaves 0.10 in the area under the tail of the noise distribution to the right of it. Next, we compute the z-score distance between X_c and $\bar{X}_s$. From $P(H) = .75$ we know that 75 percent of the signal distribution lies to the right of X_c, which means that X_c is approximately .68 standard deviations below $\bar{X}_s$. To compute d' we simply add the two standard deviate scores and obtain $d' = 1.96$. β is quite easy to compute because we now know the z-score values for X_c on each of the distributions. Using a table of the height of the normal curve at each of these scores, we find that the height of the noise distribution at $X_c = .176$, and the height of the signal distribution at $X_c = .317$. Dividing .317 by .176, we find $\beta = 1.80$.

CHANGING SENSITIVITY AND BIAS

As noted earlier, the subject's sensitivity and bias determine the values of $P(H)$ and $P(FA)$ for that subject. We can now vary sensitivity (d') and observe the effect on $P(H)$ and $P(FA)$. The graphs in Figure A.2 show values of d' from 0 to 2.0 when c is constant. When $d' = 0$ the signal and noise curves are identical and $P(H) = P(FA)$. As d' becomes larger, the signal curve shifts to the right. Although $P(FA)$ remains the same, progressively larger amounts of the signal curve lie to the right of X_c and $P(H)$ increases.

Figure A.3 illustrates the effect of the subject's criterion when sensitivity remains constant, that is, when d' remains constant. If the subject is completely unbiased, then the criterion will fall at the point at which the signal and noise curves are of equal height, the point halfway between the means of the two distributions. Figure A.3 shows this point as C_4, with a β-value of 1.0. However, if the subject's responses are biased in the direction of reporting signals even when the subjective intensity of a trial is weak, then we can express this bias as a criterion value of C_3, C_2, or even C_1 in Figure A.3. If the criterion lies far to the left, the height of the signal curve, especially in relation to the height of the noise curve is extremely small, and β approaches 0. Thus, β-values that are less than 1.0 indicate a bias toward reporting a signal present.

Conversely, if a subject is extremely conservative and will not respond yes unless he is extremely sure, we can express this bias as a criterion value of C_5, C_6, or even C_7 in Figure A.3. In these cases the height of the noise curve is rapidly approaching 0, which causes the value of β to become extremely large. Large values of β therefore indicate a bias against reporting a signal. Notice that as β changes, both $P(H)$ and $P(FA)$ change. At C_7 both probabilities are quite small, but as β approaches 1.0 $P(H)$ increases faster than $P(FA)$. As β decreases below 1.0, $P(FA)$ grows dramatically with little increase in $P(H)$.

THE RECEIVER OPERATING CHARACTERISTIC CURVE

The experimental conditions prevailing in a given experiment or within one condition of an experiment greatly affect the values of d' and β observed

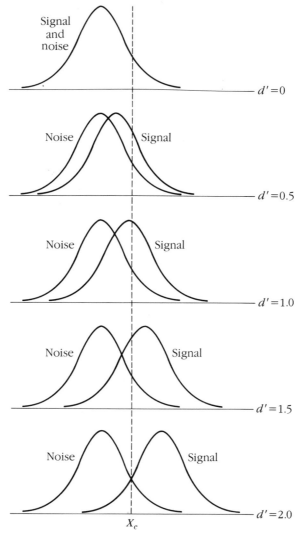

Figure A.2 The effects of subject's sensitivity, d', on performance. Note that the hit rate increases as d' increases even though the criterion X_c remains the same.

under those conditions. Of course, both sensitivity and bias are influenced by characteristics of the subject as well, but the more interesting fluctuations in the sensitivity and bias parameters are generally those brought about by the nature of the stimuli and the nature of the task. Generally, the nature of the stimuli will bring about changes in d', and it is this measure of the subject's detection ability, uncontaminated by response bias, that yields the best estimate of stimulus effects. However, experimenters can manipulate

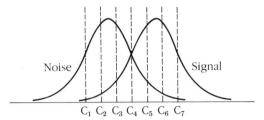

Figure A.3 Effect of subject's response criterion, or bias, on hit rate and false alarm rate.

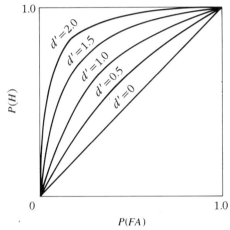

Figure A.4 Receiver operating characteristic curves for different values of d'.

the value of β by encouraging the subject to respond in a biased way. For example, if the subject is to be paid a large amount for each signal detected, the subject would tend to respond yes whenever there was the slightest chance that a signal had occurred. This experimental condition would thus create a bias toward reporting a signal and β would be quite small. Another way to bias subjects toward reporting many signals is to have many more signal trials than noise trials.

By manipulating bias in ways such as these, we can observe sensitivity, or d', under several bias conditions. For each of these conditions we can plot the data as a single point with $P(FA)$ as its x-coordinate and $P(H)$ as the y-coordinate. If we plot a whole series of experimental conditions under which d' remains constant, but β shifts, we find that the points fall on a bow-shaped curve of the type shown in Figure A.4. If $d' = 0$, the curve will be a straight line, the diagonal running from the origin to the point (1,1) in the coordinate space. To the extent that d' is greater than 0, the curve will bow away from this straight line, with the largest values of d' generating curves that approach the upper left corner of the coordinate space. Points that are generated by very high values of β are on the lower left portion of each curve, and low values of β fall on the upper right portion of each curve. The curve of $P(H)$ plotted as a function of $P(FA)$ is called a *receiver operating characteristic* curve and is a convenient way of summarizing detection data from several conditions at once.

SUMMARY

The theory of signal detectability provides a useful framework within which to analyze a subject's ability to detect or recognize a designated stimulus. It allows the experimenter to separate out the effects of response biases from the factors that affect a subject's sensitivity, or ability to perform a task. The hit rate and the false alarm rate can be used to determine standard measures of sensitivity (d') and bias (β), which can then be compared across experiments or conditions within an experiment.

Analysis of Reaction Times

One of the primary measurements useful for studying information processing is reaction time. Several types of conclusions can be drawn about underlying cognitive processes from analyses of the amount of time a subject takes to respond appropriately to a stimulus. At the simplest level, if one type of stimulus requires longer to generate a response than another, then we can assume it is more complex or harder to process. However, if we want to determine _why_ one stimulus is easier than another, we must generate some working hypothesis about the information processing events that are executed and the delays caused by the more difficult stimulus. These hypotheses are very often serial-stage models of the type outlined in Chapter 1, and they frequently involve the repeated application of one or more mental operations, as do the sentence-picture verification models in Chapter 9. Testing such models requires estimating the duration of each of these component stages and positing what occurs at each stage. In this discussion we examine some of the procedures for analyzing reaction times that allow these types of inferences to be made.

DONDERS' SUBTRACTION METHOD

Measuring the duration of a single stage, or mental operation, is difficult because such operations are usually executed so quickly that we cannot reliably time a single stage and because a single stage usually cannot be executed in isolation from other stages in processing. Suppose, for example, we want to measure the duration of the component stages of a meal. For convenience we could divide the entire task into three serially ordered stages:

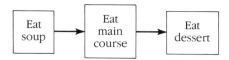

Suppose, further, that our timing devices are not precise enough to measure the individual durations of each of the three component stages, but that we can measure the amount of time taken to eat the entire meal. How could we determine the duration of the second stage, eating the main course? According to the logic suggested by Donders (1868, [1969]), we would measure the duration of the entire meal-eating task twice, once with the main course included and once without the main course. By subtracting the second time from the first, we could estimate the amount of time necessary to execute the second stage. This *subtraction method* can be be used to measure the duration of a component mental operation whenever we can create two tasks that differ only in the presence or absence of that one component operation.

Donders used the subtraction method to estimate the amount of time necessary to select a response in a choice reaction time task. In one condition subjects were required to respond to only one of a set of possible stimuli. In another condition they were to respond differently to each of the stimuli. In both conditions the subjects had to execute a stimulus identification operation to determine which stimulus had been presented. However, the second condition required subjects to execute an additional response-selection stage in order to pick the appropriate response. The difference in the reaction times for the two conditions was taken to be the duration of the response-selection stage.

ADDITIVE STAGE DURATIONS

Sternberg (1969) points out one of the difficulties of Donders' subtraction method: Donders assumed that the insertion of an additional processing stage leaves the other stages completely unchanged, which is not necessarily true. In the dinner-eating task, for example, the insertion of the main course might reduce the amount the subject would eat at dessert and would therefore influence the duration of the dessert-eating stage. To avoid such interference, one could devise experimental tasks in which the stages remain unchanged, but the tasks vary in the number of stages or how many times each stage is executed. This approach has come to be known as the *additive stage method*.

The additive stage method can best be explained by reviewing a sample experiment. Sternberg (1969) performed a short-term memory scanning experiment in which subjects were given a small set of items to remember on each trial. The items in some experiments were digits or letter names, while in others nonsense forms or pictures of faces were used. Let us consider the data from the face experiment. Following the presentation and removal of the memory set, the subject was given a single item and was to press one button if the stimulus had been part of the memory set, and another button otherwise. Reaction times were measured from the time the test stimulus appeared to the time the response button was pressed.

We can easily divide the memory scanning task into the component operations needed to execute the task on each trial. First, during the stimulus encoding stage the subject identifies the stimulus being shown. Next, the identified stimulus is compared to the items in the memory set. As we will soon see, the data indicate that this comparison stage takes longer when the memory set has many members (five or six, for example) than when it has just a few (two or three). In fact, the subjects appear to sequentially compare the stimulus to each member of the memory set. Thus the memory comparison operation involves the repeated execution of a single basic comparison operation between the stimulus and each individual memory set item. The number of these comparisons depends on the number of items in the memory set. Following the comparison stage, the subject selects a response and executes it.

This type of experiment has all the necessary characteristics for the application of the additive stage method. The stimulus encoding, comparison, and response execution stages are all executed on every trial, which means that the task is qualitatively the same each time. However, by manipulating the number of items in the memory set, we can control the number of separate times a comparison must be made between the stimulus and a memory item. Figure B.1 shows the reaction times plotted as a function of the size of the memory set. Note that the points fall almost exactly along a straight line. The reaction time intercept of this line—that is, the point at which it crosses the *y*-axis—reflects the amount of time needed to carry out the operations that are the same for all memory set sizes, namely the encoding and response stages. However, the data also show that for each additional item in the memory set, the reaction time for performing the task increased by 56 milliseconds. Thus the duration of a simple comparison between a stimulus face and a single face in the memory set requires 56 milliseconds.

The additive stage method can also be used to determine which stages are influenced by changes in the stimulus or response characteristics. Consider the following example from another experiment performed by Sternberg (1969). Sternberg wanted to determine how memory scanning would

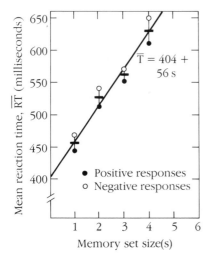

Figure B.1 Sternberg showed that short-term memory scanning times were a linear function of the memory set size. [From Sternberg, 1969, and Anne M. Treisman.]

be affected by visual degradation of the test stimuli. The memory set items and stimuli were digits, and reaction times were obtained for different memory set sizes for both the standard test stimuli and stimuli visually degraded by a superimposed checkerboard of dots. Sternberg suggested that the visual degradation could slow reaction times in one of two ways. One possibility is that degradation would merely slow down the encoding operation; subjects would take longer to identify the stimulus on each trial because it was not clearly visible. If this were the case then the main difference between the standard and degraded stimulus conditions would be seen in the intercept of the reaction time line function.

The other possibility is that visual degradation could slow down the memory comparison operations. This could happen if the subject remembered the memory set items using a visual code and attempted to compare the test stimulus using a kind of template matching. If the test stimulus is degraded, such a matching operation would take longer to carry out, and this added time would be reflected in an increased memory comparison time for degraded, as opposed to standard, stimuli.

The data show that visual degradation influences memory scanning in both of these ways. Stimulus degradation increased the intercept values from 372 milliseconds in the intact condition to 439 milliseconds in the degraded condition. It also increased the memory comparison time from 36 to 43 milliseconds. On the basis of these data Sternberg concluded that the encoding process creates a stimulus representation that includes many of the physical attributes of the stimulus, including degradation when it is present. Thus it is harder to compare the degraded stimulus with the memory set items. This means that although degradation does slow the encoding process, encoding does not eliminate the effects of degradation on later stages.

SUMMARY

In this discussion we reviewed two methods frequently used in the analysis of reaction-time data. By applying these methods to carefully selected tasks, an experimenter can determine the presence of, and duration of, mental processing stages that are unmeasurable by direct methods. Furthermore, by using a method such as Sternberg's, an experimenter can locate the stages at which different experimental manipulations affect information processing. From these findings inferences can be made about the nature of processing operations at those stages that makes them susceptible to variations in task variables.

References

Adelson, E. H. Iconic storage: The role of rods. *Science,* 1978, *201,* 544–546.

Anderson, J. R. Arguments concerning representations for mental imagery. *Psychological Review,* 1978, *85,* 249–277.

Antes, J. R. The time course of picture viewing. *Journal of Experimental Psychology,* 1974, *103,* 62–70.

Antrobus, J. S., and J. L. Singer. Eye movement accompanying daydreaming, visual imagery and thought suppression. *Journal of Abnormal and Social Psychology,* 1964, *69,* 244–252.

Attneave, F. Some informational aspects of visual perception. *Psychological Review,* 1954, *61,* 183–193.

Attneave, F. Transfer of experience with class schemata. *Journal of Experimental Psychology,* 1957, *54,* 81–88.

Attneave, F. *Applications of information theory to psychology: A summary of basic concepts, methods, and results.* New York: Holt, 1959.

Atwood, G. An experimental study of visual imagination and memory. *Cognitive Psychology,* 1971, *2,* 290–299.

Averbach, E., and A. S. Coriell. Short-term memory in vision. *Bell System Technical Journal,* 1961, *40,* 309–328.

Averbach, E., and G. Sperling. Short-term storage of information in vision. In C. Cherry (Ed.), *Information theory.* London: Butterworth, 1960.

Bahrick, H. P., P. O. Bahrick, and R. P. Wittlinger. Fifty years of memory for names and faces: A cross-sectional approach. *Journal of Experimental Psychology: General,* 1975, *104,* 54–75.

Bahrick, H. P., and B. Boucher. Retention of visual and verbal codes of the same stimuli. *Journal of Experimental Psychology,* 1968, *78,* 417–422.

Banks, W. P., and W. Prinzmetal. Configural effects in visual information processing. *Perception & Psychophysics,* 1976, *19,* 361–367.

Baron, J., and I. Thurston. An analysis of the word superiority effect. *Cognitive Psychology,* 1973, *4,* 207–228.

Baum, D. R., and J. Jonides. Cognitive maps: Comparative judgments of imagined vs. perceived distance. Paper presented at the meeting of the Psychonomic Society, Washington, D.C., November 1977.

Beardslee, D. C., and M. Wertheimer (Eds.). *Readings in perception.* Princeton, N. J.: Van Nostrand, 1958.

Beck, J. Effect of orientation and of shape similarity on perceptual grouping. *Perception & Psychophysics,* 1966, *1,* 300–302.

Becker, C. A. Semantic context and word frequency effects in visual word recognition. *Journal of Experimental Psychology: Human Perception and Performance,* 1979, *5,* 252–259.

Becker, C. A., and T. H. Killion. Interaction of visual and cognitive effects in word recognition. *Journal of Experimental Psychology: Human Perception and Performance,* 1977, *3,* 389–401.

Berkley, M. A., and J. M. Sprague. Striate cortex and visual acuity functions in the cat. *Journal of Comparative Neurology,* 1979, *187,* 679–702.

Berlyne, D. E. The influence of complexity and novelty in visual figures on orienting responses. *Journal of Experimental Psychology,* 1958, *55,* 289–296.

Biederman, I. Perceiving real-world scenes. *Science,* 1972, *177,* 77–80.

Biederman, I. On processing information from a glance at a scene: Some implications for a syntax and semantics of visual processing. In S. Treu (Ed.), *User-oriented design of interactive graphics systems.* New York: ACM, 1977.

Biederman, I. On the semantics of a glance at a scene. In M. Kubovy and J. R. Pomerantz (Eds.), *Perceptual organization.* Hillsdale, N.J.: Lawrence Erlbaum Associates, 1981.

Biederman, I., and S. F. Checkosky. Processing redundant information. *Journal of Experimental Psychology,* 1970, *83,* 486–490.

Biederman, I., A. L. Glass, and E. W. Stacy, Jr. Searching for objects in real-world scenes. *Journal of Experimental Psychology,* 1973, *97,* 22–27.

Biederman, I., J. C. Rabinowitz, A. L. Glass, and E. W. Stacy, Jr. On the information extracted from a glance at a scene. *Journal of Experimental Psychology,* 1974, *103,* 597–600.

Bjork, E. L., and W. K. Estes. Detection and placement of redundant signal elements in tachistoscopic displays of letters. *Perception & Psychophysics,* 1971, *9,* 439–442.

Blake, R., and E. Levinson. Spatial frequency- and orientation-specificity of binocular neurons in the human visual system. *Experimental Brain Research,* 1977, *27,* 221–232.

Blakemore, C., and F. W. Campbell. On the existence of neurons in the human visual system selectively sensitive to the orientation and size of retinal images. *Journal of Physiology,* 1969, *203,* 237–260.

Blakemore, C., and J. Nachmias. The orientation specificity of two visual aftereffects. *Journal of Physiology,* 1971, *213,* 157–174.

Bodis-Wollner, I. Visual acuity and contrast sensitivity in patients with cerebral lesions. *Science,* 1972, *178,* 769–771.

Bogen, J. E., and M. S. Gazzaniga. Cerebral commissurotomy in man: Minor hemisphere dominance for certain visuo-spatial functions. *Journal of Neurosurgery,* 1965, *23,* 394–399.

Bower, G. H. Imagery as a relational organizer in associative learning. *Journal of Verbal Learning and Verbal Behavior,* 1970a, *9,* 529–533.

Bower, G. H. Analysis of a mnemonic device. *American Scientist,* 1970b, *58,* 496–510.

Bower, G. H., and M. B. Karlin. Depth of processing pictures of faces and recognition memory. *Journal of Experimental Psychology,* 1974, *103,* 751–757.

References

Bransford, J. D., and J. J. Franks. The abstraction of linguistic ideas. *Cognitive Psychology*, 1971, *2*, 331–350.

Brooks, L. R. Spatial and verbal components of the act of recall. *Canadian Journal of Psychology*, 1968, *22*, 349–368.

Bruce, V. Searching for politicians: An information-processing approach to face recognition. *Quarterly Journal of Experimental Psychology*, 1979, *31*, 373–395.

Bugelski, B. R., E. Kidd, and J. Segmen. Image as a mediator in one-trial paired-associate learning. *Journal of Experimental Psychology*, 1968, *76*, 69–73.

Burns, B., B. E. Shepp, D. McDonough, and W. Wiener-Ehrlich. The relation between stimulus analyzability and perceived dimensional structure. In G. H. Bower (Ed.), *Learning and motivation*. Vol. 12. New York: Academic Press, 1978.

Campbell, F. W., and L. Maffei. The tilt aftereffect: A fresh look. *Vision Research*, 1971, *11*, 833–844.

Campbell, F., and L. Maffei. Contrast and spatial frequency. *Scientific American*, 1974, *231*(5), 106–114. (Offprint 1308.)

Carey, S. A case study: Face recognition. In E. Walker (Ed.), *Explorations in the biology of language*. Montgomery, Vt.: Bradford Books, 1978.

Carey, S., and R. Diamond. From piecemeal to configurational representation of faces. *Science*, 1977, *195*, 312–314.

Carpenter, P. A., and M. A. Just. Sentence comprehension: A psycholinguistic processing model of verification. *Psychological Review*, 1975, *82*, 45–73.

Cattell, J. McK. *Philosophical Studies*, 1885, *2*, 635–650.

Cattell, J. McK. The inertia of the eye and brain. *Brain*, 1885–1886, *8*, 295–312.

Chase, W. G. (Ed.). *Visual information processing*. New York: Academic Press, 1973.

Clark, H. H. Linguistic processes in deductive reasoning. *Psychological Review*, 1969, *76*, 387–404.

Clark, H. H., and W. G. Chase. On the process of comparing sentences against pictures. *Cognitive Psychology*, 1972, *3*, 472–517.

Coltheart, M. Iconic memory: A reply to Professor Holding. *Memory & Cognition*, 1975, *3*, 42–48.

Cooper, L. A. Demonstration of a mental analog of an external rotation. *Perception & Psychophysics*, 1976, *19*, 296–302.

Cooper, L. A., and P. Podgorny. Mental transformations and visual comparison processes: Effects of complexity and similarity. *Journal of Experimental Psychology: Human Perception and Performance*, 1976, *2*, 503–514.

Cooper, L. A., and R. N. Shepard. The time required to prepare for a rotated stimulus. *Memory & Cognition*, 1973, *1*, 246–250.

Cooper, R. M. The control of eye fixation by the meaning of spoken language: A new methodology for the real-time investigation of speech perception, memory, and language processing. *Cognitive Psychology*, 1974, *6*, 84–107.

Davelaar, E., M. Coltheart, D. Besner, and J. T. Jonasson. Phonological recoding and lexical access. *Memory & Cognition*, 1978, *6*, 391–402.

Dement, W. C., and E. Wolpert. The relation of eye movements, body motility, and external stimuli to dream content. *Journal of Experimental Psychology*, 1958, *55*, 543–553.

De Valois, R., and De Valois, K. Spatial vision. *Annual Review of Psychology*, 1980, *31*, 309–341.

Diamond, I. T. Organization of the visual cortex: Comparative anatomical and behavioral studies. *Federation Proceedings*, 1976, *35*, 60–67.

Donders, F. C. Over de snelheid van psychische processen. Onderzoekingen gedaan in het Psysiologisch Laboratorium der Utrechtsche Hoogeschool, 1868–1869, Tweede reeks II, 92–120. Translated by W. G. Koster in W. G. Koster (Ed.), *Attention and performance II, Acta Psychologica*, 1969, *30*, 412–431.

References

Doob, L. W. Eidetic imagery: A cross-cultural will-o'-the wisp? *Journal of Psychology,* 1966, *63,* 13–34.

Downs, R. M., and D. Stea. *Maps in minds.* New York: Harper & Row, 1977.

Durso, F. T., and M. K. Johnson. Facilitation in naming and categorizing repeated pictures and words. *Journal of Experimental Psychology: Human Learning and Memory,* 1979, *5,* 449–459.

Ellis, H. D. Recognizing faces. *British Journal of Psychology,* 1975, *66,* 409–426.

Ellis, H. D., and J. W. Shepherd. Recognition of upright and inverted faces presented in the left and right visual fields. *Cortex,* 1975, *11,* 3–7.

Ellis, H. D., J. W. Shepherd, and G. Davies. An investigation of the use of the Photofit technique for recalling faces. *British Journal of Psychology,* 1975, *66,* 29–37.

Erdman, B., and R. Dodge. *Psychologische Untersuchungen über das Lesen auf experimenteller Grundlage.* Halle, Germany, 1898.

Eriksen, C. W., M. D. Pollack, and W. E. Montague. Implicit speech: Mechanism in perceptual encoding? *Journal of Experimental Psychology,* 1970, *84,* 502–507.

Eriksen, C. W., and T. Spencer. Rate of information processing in visual perception: Some results and methodological considerations. *Journal of Experimental Psychology,* 1969, *79* (2, pt. 2), 1–16.

Estes, W. K. Interactions of signal and background variables in visual processing. *Perception & Psychophysics,* 1972, *12,* 278–286.

Estes, W. K. The locus of inferential and perceptual processes in letter identification. *Journal of Experimental Psychology: General,* 1975a, *2,* 122–145.

Estes, W. K. Memory, perception, and decision in letter identification. In R. L. Solso (Ed.), *Information processing and cognition: The Loyola Symposium.* Hillsdale, N.J.: Lawrence Erlbaum Associates, 1975b.

Estes, W. K., E. L. Bjork, and E. Skaar. Detection of single letters and letters in words with changing versus unchanging mask characters. *Bulletin of the Psychonomic Society,* 1974, *3,* 201–203.

Estes, W. K., and H. A. Taylor. A detection method and probabilistic models for assessing information processing from brief visual displays. *Proceedings of the National Academy of Sciences of the United States of America,* 1964, *52,* 446–454.

Estes, W. K., and H. A. Taylor. Visual detection in relation to display size and redundancy of critical elements. *Perception & Psychophysics,* 1965, *1,* 9–16.

Estes, W. K., and D. L. Wessel. Reaction time in relation to display size and correctness of response in forced-choice visual signal detection. *Perception & Psychophysics,* 1966, *1,* 369–373.

Estes, W. K., and G. L. Wolford. Effects of spaces on report from tachistoscopically presented letter strings. *Psychonomic Science,* 1971, *25,* 77–80.

Evans, G. W., and K. Pezdek. Cognitive mapping: Knowlege of real-world distance and location information. *Journal of Experimental Psychology: Human Learning and Memory,* 1980, *6,* 13–24.

Felfoldy, G. L. Repetition effects in choice reaction time to multidimensional stimuli. *Perception & Psychophysics,* 1974, *15,* 453–459.

Finke, R. A., and S. M. Kosslyn. Mental imagery acuity in the peripheral visual field. *Journal of Experimental Psychology: Human Perception and Performance,* 1980, *6,* 126–139.

Franks, J., and J. Bransford. Abstraction of visual patterns. *Journal of Experimental Psychology,* 1971, *90,* 65–74.

Frisby, J. P. *Seeing: Illusion, brain, and mind.* Oxford: Oxford University Press, 1980.

Galper, R. E. Recognition of faces in photographic negative. *Psychonomic Science,* 1970, *19,* 207–208.

Gardner, G. T. Evidence for independent parallel channels in tachistoscopic perception. *Cognitive Psychology,* 1973, *4,* 130–155.

References

Garner, W. R. *The processing of information and structure.* Potomac, Md.: Lawrence Erlbaum Associates, 1974.

Garner, W. R. Interaction of stimulus dimensions in concept and choice processes. *Cognitive Psychology,* 1976, *8,* 98–123.

Garner, W. R. Selective attention to attributes and to stimuli. *Journal of Experimental Psychology: General,* 1978, *107,* 287–308.

Garner, W. R., and G. L. Felfoldy. Integrality of stimulus dimensions in various types of information processing. *Cognitive Psychology,* 1970, *1,* 225–241.

Gazzaniga, M. S. The split brain in man. *Scientific American,* 1967, *217*(2), 24–29. (Offprint 508.)

Gazzaniga, M. S. *The bisected brain.* New York: Appleton-Century-Crofts, 1970.

Gibson, E. J. Learning to read. *Science,* 1965, *148,* 1066–1072.

Gibson, E. J., A. D. Pick, H. Osser, and M. Hammond. The role of grapheme-phoneme correspondence in the perception of words. *American Journal of Psychology,* 1962, *75,* 554–570.

Gibson, E. J., F. Shapiro, and A. Yonas. Confusion matrices of graphic patterns obtained with a latency measure. *The analysis of reading skill: A program of basic and applied research.* Final report project No. 5-1213. Cornell University, 1968, 76–96.

Gilchrist, A. Perceived lightness depends on perceived spatial arrangements. *Science,* 1977, *195,* 185–187.

Gilinsky, A. S. Orientation-specific effects of patterns of adapting light on visual acuity. *Journal of the Optical Society of America,* 1967, *58,* 13–18.

Gleitman, H., and J. Jonides. The cost of categorization in visual search: Incomplete processing of targets and field items. *Perception & Psychophysics,* 1976, *20,* 281–288.

Gleitman, H., and J. Jonides. The effect of set on categorization in visual search. *Perception & Psychophysics,* 1978, *24,* 361–368.

Glushko, R. J., and L. A. Cooper. Spatial comprehension and comparison processes in verification tasks. *Cognitive Psychology,* 1978, *10,* 391–421.

Goldiamond, I., and W. F. Hawkins. Vexierversuch: The log relationship between word-frequency and recognition obtained in the absence of stimulus words. *Journal of Experimental Psychology,* 1958, *56,* 457–463.

Gottwald, R. L., and W. R. Garner. Effects of focussing strategy on speeded classification with grouping, filtering, and condensation tasks. *Perception & Psychophysics,* 1972, *11,* 179–182.

Gregory, R. L. *Eye and brain.* New York: McGraw-Hill, 1966.

Gross, C. G., C. E. Rocha-Miranda, and D. B. Bender. Visual properties of neurons in inferotemporal cortex of the macaque. *Journal of Neurophysiology,* 1972, *35,* 96–111.

Gumenik, W. E., and R. Glass. Effects of reducing the readability of the words in the Stroop color-word test. *Psychonomic Science,* 1970, *20,* 247–248.

Gummerman, K., C. R. Gray, and J. M. Wilson. An attempt to assess eidetic imagery objectively. *Psychonomic Science,* 1972, *28,* 115–118.

Guzman, A. Decomposition of a visual scene into three-dimensional bodies. In A. Grasselli (Ed.), *Automatic interpretation and classification of images.* New York: Academic Press, 1969.

Haber, R. N. Eidetic images. *Scientific American,* 1969, *220*(4), 36–44. (Offprint 522.)

Haber, R. N., and M. H. Erdelyi. Emergence and recovery of initially unavailable perceptual material. *Journal of Verbal Learning and Verbal Behavior,* 1967, *6,* 618–628.

Haber, R. N., and R. B. Haber. Eidetic imagery: I. Frequency. *Perceptual and Motor Skills,* 1964, *19,* 131–138.

Haber, R. N., and L. G. Standing. Direct measures of short-term visual storage. *Quarterly Journal of Experimental Psychology,* 1969, *21,* 43–54.

Handel, S., and S. Imai. The free classification of analyzable and unanalyzable stimuli. *Perception & Psychophysics,* 1972, *12,* 108–116.

Harmon, L. D. The recognition of faces. *Scientific American,* 1973, *229*(5), 70–82. (Offprint 555.)

Harris, J. R., M. L. Shaw, and M. Bates. Visual search in multicharacter arrays with and without gaps. *Perception & Psychophysics,* 1979, *26,* 69–84.

Hawkins, H. L., G. M. Reicher, M. Rogers, and L. Peterson. Flexible coding in word recognition. *Journal of Experimental Psychology: Human Perception and Performance,* 1976, *2,* 380–385.

Hemenway, K., and S. E. Palmer. Organizational factors in perceived dimensionality. *Journal of Experimental Psychology: Human Perception and Performance,* 1978, *4,* 388–396.

Hess, R. F., and E. R. Howell. The threshold contrast sensitivity function in strabismic amblyopia: Evidence for a two-type classification. *Vision Research,* 1977, *17,* 1049–1055.

Hess, R. F., and G. Woo. Vision through cataracts. *Investigative Opthamology and Visual Science,* 1978, *17,* 428–435.

Hintzman, D. L., R. A. Carre, V. L. Eskridge, A. M. Owens, S. S. Shaff, and E. M. Sparks. "Stroop" effect: Input or output phenomenon. *Journal of Experimental Psychology,* 1972, *95,* 458–459.

Hochberg, J., and R. E. Galper. Recognition of faces: I. An exploratory study. *Psychonomic Science,* 1967, *9,* 619–620.

Hochberg, J., and E. McAlister. A quantitative approach to figural "goodness." *Journal of Experimental Psychology,* 1953, *46,* 361–364.

Hochberg, J., and A. Silverstein. A quantitative index of stimulus-similarity: Proximity vs. differences in brightness. *American Journal of Psychology,* 1956, *69,* 456–458.

Holding, D. H. Sensory storage reconsidered. *Memory & Cognition,* 1975, *3,* 31–41.

Houlihan, K., and R. W. Sekuler. Contour interactions in visual masking. *Journal of Experimental Psychology,* 1968, *77,* 281–285.

Hubel, D. H., and T. N. Wiesel. Receptive fields, binocular interaction, and functional architecture in the cat's visual cortex. *Journal of Physiology,* 1962, *160,* 106–154.

Hubel, D. H., and T. N. Wiesel. Receptive fields and functional architecture of monkey striate cortex. *Journal of Physiology,* 1968, *195,* 215–243.

Huey, E. B. *The psychology and pedagogy of reading.* New York: Macmillan, 1908.

Jaensch, E. R. *Eidetic imagery and typological methods of investigation.* O. Oesser, translator. New York: Harcourt, Brace, 1930.

Johansson, G. Visual motion perception. *Scientific American,* 1975, *232*(6), 76–88. (Offprint 564.)

Johnston, J. C., and J. L. McClelland. Visual factors in word perception. *Perception & Psychophysics,* 1973, *14,* 365–370.

Johnston, J. C., and J. L. McClelland. Experimental tests of a hierarchical model of word identification. *Journal of Verbal Learning and Verbal Behavior,* 1980, *19,* 503–524.

Jonides, J., and H. Gleitman. A conceptual category effect in visual search: O as letter or as digit. *Perception & Psychophysics,* 1972, *12,* 457–460.

Julesz, B. *Foundations of cyclopean perception.* Chicago: University of Chicago Press, 1971.

Julesz, B. Experiments in the visual perception of texture. *Scientific American,* 1975, *232*(4), 34–43. (Offprint 563.)

Just, M., and P. Carpenter. Comprehension of negation with quantification. *Journal of Verbal Learning and Verbal Behavior,* 1971, *10,* 244–253.

Kaufman, L. *Sight and mind.* New York: Oxford University Press, 1974.

Keele, S. W. *Attention and human performance.* Pacific Palisades, Calif.: Goodyear, 1973.

Kerst, S. M., and J. H. Howard, Jr. Memory psychophysics for visual area and length. *Memory & Cognition,* 1978, *6,* 327–335.

Kimura, D. Cerebral dominance and the perception of verbal stimuli. *Canadian Journal of Psychology,* 1961, *15,* 166–171.

Kimura, D., and M. Durnford. Normal studies and the function of the right hemisphere in vision. In S. J. Dimond and J. G. Beumont (Eds.), *Hemispheric function in the brain.* London: Elek Science, 1974.

Kinchla, R. A., and J. Wolf. The order of visual processing: "Top-down," "bottom-up," or "middle-out." *Perception & Psychophysics,* 1979, *25,* 225–231.

Kinney, G. C., M. Marsetta, and D. J. Showman. Studies in the display symbol legibility, Part XII. *The legibility of alphanumeric symbols for digitalized television.* Bedford, Mass.: Mitre Corporation, 1966.

Kleiman, G. M. Speech recoding in reading. *Journal of Verbal Learning and Verbal Behavior,* 1975, *14,* 323–339.

Klein, G. S. Semantic power measured through the interference of words with color-naming. *American Journal of Psychology,* 1964, *77,* 576–588.

Klüver, H. The eidetic child. In C. Murchison (Ed.), *A handbook of child psychology.* Worcester, Mass.: Clark University Press, 1931.

Konorski, J. *Integrative activity of the brain.* Chicago: University of Chicago Press, 1967.

Kosslyn, S. M. Scanning visual images: Some structural implications. *Perception & Psychophysics,* 1973, *14,* 90–94.

Kosslyn, S. M. Information representation in visual images. *Cognitive Psychology,* 1975, *7,* 341–370.

Kosslyn, S. M. Measuring the visual angle of the mind's eye. *Cognitive Psychology,* 1978, *10,* 356–389.

Kosslyn, S. M. *Image and mind.* Cambridge, Mass.: Harvard University Press, 1980.

Kosslyn, S. M., T. M. Ball, and B. J. Reisser. Visual images preserve metric spatial information: Evidence from studies of image scanning. *Journal of Experimental Psychology: Human Perception and Performance,* 1978, *4,* 47–60.

Kosslyn, S. M., and J. R. Pomerantz. Imagery, propositions, and the forms of the internal representations. *Cognitive Psychology,* 1977, *9,* 52–76.

Krantz, D. H., and A. Tversky. Similarity of rectangles: An analysis of subjective dimensions. *Journal of Mathematical Psychology,* 1975, *12,* 4–34.

Kubovy, M., and J. Pomerantz (Eds.). *Perceptual organization.* Hillsdale, N.J.: Lawrence Erlbaum Associates, 1981.

Kuffler, S. W. Discharge patterns and functional organization of the mammalian retina. *Journal of Neurophysiology,* 1953, *16,* 37–68.

Kulikowski, J. J., R. Abadi, and P. E. King-Smith. Orientational selectivity of grating and line detectors in human vision. *Vision Research,* 1973, *13,* 1479–1486.

Kulikowski, J. J., and D. J. Tolhurst. Psychophysical evidence for sustained and transient detectors in human vision. *Journal of Physiology,* 1973, *232,* 149–162.

LaBerge, D., and S. J. Samuels. Toward a theory of automatic information processing in reading. *Cognitive Psychology,* 1974, *6,* 293–323.

Landauer, T. K. Rate of implicit speech. *Perceptual and Motor Skills,* 1962, *15,* 646.

Lea, G. Chronometric analysis of the method of loci. *Journal of Experimental Psychology: Human Perception and Performance,* 1975, *1,* 95–104.

Leask, J., R. N. Haber, and R. B. Haber. Eidetic imagery in children: II. Longitudinal and experimental results. *Psychological Monograph Supplement,* 1969, 3 (3, whole No. 35).

Leehey, S., S. Carey, R. Diamond, and A. Cahn. Upright and inverted faces: The right hemisphere knows the difference. *Cortex,* 1978, *14,* 411–419.

Lehmann, D., G. W. Beeler, Jr., and D. H. Fender. Changes in patterns of the human electroencephalogram during fluctuations of perception of stabilized retinal images. *Electroencephelography & Clinical Neurophysiology*, 1965, *19*, 336–343.

Lehmkuhle, S., and R. Fox. Effect of depth separation on metacontrast marking. *Journal of Experimental Psychology: Human Perception and Performance*, 1980, *6*, 605–621.

Lennie, P. Parallel visual pathways: A review. *Vision Research*, 1980, *20*, 561–594.

Levy, J., and M. Reid. Variations in cerebral organization as a function of handedness, hand posture in writing, and sex. *Journal of Experimental Psychology: General*, 1978, *107*, 119–144.

Lockhead, G. R., and M. C. King. Classifying integral stimuli. *Journal of Experimental Psychology: Human Perception and Performance*, 1977, *3*, 436–443.

Loftus, E. F. Leading questions and the eyewitness report. *Cognitive Psychology*, 1975, *7*, 560–572.

Loftus, E. F. *Eyewitness testimony*. Cambridge, Mass.: Harvard University Press, 1979.

Loftus, E. F., and J. C. Palmer. Reconstruction of automobile destruction: An example of the interaction between language and memory. *Journal of Verbal Learning and Verbal Behavior*, 1974, *13*, 585–589.

Loftus, E. F., and G. Zanni. Eyewitness testimony: The influence of the wording of a question. *Bulletin of the Psychonomic Society*, 1975, *5*, 86–88.

Loftus, G. R. Eye fixations and recognition memory for pictures. *Cognitive Psychology*, 1972, *3*, 525–551.

Loftus, G. R., and S. M. Bell. Two types of information in picture memory. *Journal of Experimental Psychology: Human Learning and Memory*, 1975, *1*, 103–113.

Loftus, G. R., and H. J. Kallman. Encoding and use of detail information in picture recognition. *Journal of Experimental Psychology: Human Learning and Memory*, 1979, *5*, 197–211.

Loftus, G. R., and N. H. Mackworth. Cognitive determinants of fixation location during picture viewing. *Journal of Experimental Psychology: Human Perception and Performance*, 1978, *4*, 565–572.

Lovelace, E. A., and R. D. Snodgrass. Decision times for alphabetic order of letter pairs. *Journal of Experimental Psychology*, 1971, *88*, 258–264.

Luria, A. R. *The mind of a mnemonist*. New York: Avon, 1968.

Mackworth, N. H., and A. J. Morandi. The gaze selects informative details within pictures. *Perception & Psychophysics*, 1967, *2*, 547–551.

Mandler, J. M., and N. S. Johnson. Some of the thousand words a picture is worth. *Journal of Experimental Psychology: Human Learning and Memory*, 1976, *2*, 529–540.

Mandler, J. M., and R. E. Parker. Memory for descriptive and spatial information in complex pictures. *Journal of Experimental Psychology: Human Learning and Memory*, 1976, *2*, 38–48.

Marr, D. Early processing of visual information. *Philosophical Transactions of the Royal Society of London*, 1976, *275*, 483–524.

Mason, M. Reading ability and letter search time: Effects of orthographic structure defined by single-letter positional frequency. *Journal of Experimental Psychology: General*, 1975, *104*, 146–166.

Massaro, D. W., R. L. Venezky, and G. A. Taylor. Orthographic regularity, positional frequency, and visual processing of letter strings. *Journal of Experimental Psychology: General*, 1979, *108*, 107–124.

Matthews, M. L. Discrimination of Identikit constructions of faces: Evidence for a dual processing strategy. *Perception & Psychophysics*, 1978, *23*, 153–161.

Mayzner, M. S., and M. E. Tresselt. Tables of single-letter and digram frequency counts for various word-length and letter-position combinations. *Psychonomic Monograph Supplements*, 1965, *1*, 13–32.

References

Meyer, D. E., R. W. Schvaneveldt, and M. G. Ruddy. Functions of graphemic and phonemic codes in visual word-recognition. *Memory & Cognition,* 1974, *2,* 309–321.

Mezrich, J. J. The word superiority effect in brief visual displays: Elimination by vocalization. *Perception & Psychophysics,* 1973, *13,* 45–48.

Miller, G. A. The magical number seven, plus or minus two: Some limits on our capacity for processing information. *Psychological Review,* 1956, *63,* 81–97.

Miller, G. A., J. S. Bruner, and L. Postman. Familiarity of letter sequences and tachistoscopic identification. *Journal of General Psychology,* 1954, *50,* 129–139.

Monahan, J. S., and G. R. Lockhead. Identification of integral stimuli. *Journal of Experimental Psychology: General,* 1977, *106,* 94–110.

Morton, J. A. Interaction of information in word recognition. *Psychological Review,* 1969, *76,* 165–178.

Morton, J. A. A functional model of memory. In D. A. Norman (Ed.), *Models of human memory.* New York: Academic Press, 1970.

Moyer, R. S. Comparing objects in memory: Evidence suggesting an internal psychophysics. *Perception & Psychophysics,* 1973, *13,* 180–184.

Moyer, R. S., and R. H. Bayer. Mental comparison and the symbolic distance effect. *Cognitive Psychology,* 1976, *8,* 228–246.

Moyer, R. S., and T. K. Landauer. Time required for judgments of numerical inequality. *Nature,* 1967, *215,* 1519–1520.

Navon, D. Forest before trees: The precedence of global features in visual perception. *Cognitive Psychology,* 1977, *9,* 353–383.

Neisser, U. Decision-time without reaction time: Experiments in visual scanning. *American Journal of Psychology,* 1963, *76,* 376–385.

Neisser, U., and R. Becklen. Selective looking: Attending to visually specified events. *Cognitive Psychology,* 1974, *7,* 480–494.

Nelson, D. L., V. S. Reed, and C. L. McEvoy. Learning to order pictures and words: A model of sensory and semantic encoding. *Journal of Experimental Psychology: Human Learning and Memory,* 1977, *3,* 485–497.

Nelson, T. O., J. Metzler, and D. A. Reed. Role of details in the long-term recognition of pictures and verbal descriptions. *Journal of Experimental Psychology,* 1974, *102,* 184–186.

Nickerson, R. S., and M. J. Adams. Long-term memory for a common object. *Cognitive Psychology,* 1979, *11,* 287–307.

Offenkrantz, W., and E. Wolpert. The detection of dreaming in a congenitally blind subject. *Journal of Nervous and Mental Disorders,* 1963, *136,* 88–90.

Olson, R. K., and Attneave, F. What variables produce similarity grouping? *American Journal of Psychology,* 1970, *83,* 1–21.

Paivio, A. Abstractness, imagery, and meaningfulness in paired-associate learning. *Journal of Verbal Learning and Verbal Behavior,* 1965, *4,* 32–38.

Paivio, A. *Imagery and verbal processes.* New York: Holt, Rinehart and Winston, 1971.

Paivio, A., P. C. Smythe, and J. C. Yuille. Imagery versus meaningfulness of nouns in paired-associate learning. *Canadian Journal of Psychology,* 1968, *22,* 427–441.

Paivio, A., J. C. Yuille, and S. Madigan. Concreteness, imagery, and meaningfulness values for 925 nouns. *Journal of Experimental Psychology,* 1968, *76*(1, Pt. 2).

Palmer, S. E. The effects of contextual scenes on the identification of objects. *Memory & Cognition,* 1975, *3,* 519–526.

Palmer, S. E. Hierarchical structure in perceptual representation. *Cognitive Psychology,* 1977, *9,* 441–474.

Parker, D. M. Contrast and size variables and the tilt aftereffect. *Quarterly Journal of Experimental Psychology,* 1972, *24,* 1–7.

Patterson, K. E., and A. D. Baddeley. When face recognition fails. *Journal of Experimental Psychology: Human Learning and Memory,* 1977, *3,* 406–417.

Pettigrew, J. The neurophysiology of binocular vision. _Scientific American,_ 1972, _227_(2), 84–95. (Offprint 1255.)

Pettigrew, J. D., T. Nikara, and P. O. Bishop. Binocular interaction of single units in cat striate cortex: Simultaneous stimulation by a single moving slit with receptive fields in correspondence. _Experimental Brain Research,_ 1968, _6,_ 391–410.

Pezdek, K. Cross-modality semantic integration of sentence and picture memory. _Journal of Experimental Psychology: Human Learning and Memory,_ 1977, _3,_ 515–524.

Pezdek, K. Recognition memory for related pictures. _Memory & Cognition,_ 1978, _6,_ 64–69.

Pierce, J. Some sources of artifact in studies of the tachistoscopic perception of words. _Journal of Experimental Psychology,_ 1963, _66,_ 363–370.

Pittenger, J. B., and R. E. Shaw. Aging faces as viscalelastic events: Implications for a theory of nonrigid shape perception. _Journal of Experimental Psychology: Human Perception and Performance,_ 1975, _1,_ 374–382.

Pittenger, J. B., R. E. Shaw, and L. S. Mark. Perceptual information for the age level of faces as a higher order invariant of growth. _Journal of Experimental Psychology: Human Perception and Performance,_ 1979, _5,_ 478–493.

Polyak, S. L. _The vertebrate visual system._ Chicago: University of Chicago Press, 1957.

Pomerantz, J. R., and W. R. Garner. Stimulus configuration in selective attention tasks. _Perception & Psychophysics,_ 1973, _14,_ 565–569.

Pomerantz, J. R., and S. D. Schwaitzberg. Grouping by proximity: Selective attention measures. _Perception & Psychophysics,_ 1975, _18,_ 355–361.

Posner, M. I. Abstraction and the process of recognition. In G. Bower and J. T. Spence (Eds.), _Psychology of learning and motivation._ Vol. 3. New York: Academic Press, 1969.

Posner, M. I. On the relationship between letter names and superordinate categories. _Quarterly Journal of Experimental Psychology,_ 1970, _22,_ 279–287.

Posner, M. I., S. J. Boies, W. H. Eichelman, and R. L. Taylor. Retention of visual and name codes of single letters. _Journal of Experimental Psychology Monographs,_ 1969, _79,_ 1–16.

Posner, M. I., R. Goldsmith, and K. E. Welton, Jr. Perceived distance and the classification of distorted patterns. _Journal of Experimental Psychology,_ 1967, _73,_ 23–38.

Posner, M. I., and S. W. Keele. Decay of visual information from a single letter. _Science,_ 1967, _158,_ 137–139.

Posner, M. I., and S. W. Keele. On the genesis of abstract ideas. _Journal of Experimental Psychology,_ 1968, _77,_ 353–363.

Posner, M. I., and R. F. Mitchell. Chronometric analysis of classification. _Psychological Review,_ 1967, _74,_ 392–409.

Posner, M. I., and C. R. R. Snyder. Attention and cognitive control. In R. L. Solso (Ed.), _Information processing and cognition: The Loyola Symposium._ Hillsdale, N.J.: Lawrence Erlbaum Associates, 1975.

Potter, M. C. Short-term conceptual memory for pictures. _Journal of Experimental Psychology: Human Learning and Memory,_ 1976, _2,_ 509–522.

Potter, M. C., and B. A. Faulconer. Time to understand pictures and words. _Nature,_ 1975, _253,_ 437–438.

Potter, M. C., and J. F. Kroll. Lexical and object decisions: Accessing memory for words and things. Paper presented to the Psychonomic Society, San Antonio, Tex., November, 1978.

Potter, M. C., and E. I. Levy. Recognition memory for a rapid sequence of pictures. _Journal of Experimental Psychology,_ 1969, _81,_ 10–15.

Prinzmetal, W., and W. P. Banks. Good continuation affects visual detection. _Perception & Psychophysics,_ 1977, _21,_ 389–395.

References

Pritchatt, D. An investigation into some of the underlying associative verbal processes of the Stroop color effect. *Quarterly Journal of Experimental Psychology,* 1968, *20,* 351–359.

Prytulak, L. S. Good continuation revisited. *Journal of Experimental Psychology,* 1974, *102,* 773–777.

Pylyshyn, Z. W. What the mind's eye tells the mind's brain: A critique of mental imagery. *Psychological Bulletin,* 1973, *80,* 1–24.

Reed, S. *Psychological processes in pattern recognition.* New York: Academic Press, 1973.

Reicher, G. M. Perceptual recognition as a function of meaningfulness of stimulus material. *Journal of Experimental Psychology,* 1969, *81,* 275–280.

Requin, J. *Attention and performance.* Hillsdale, N.J.: Lawrence Erlbaum Associates, 1978.

Rock, I. The perception of disoriented figures. *Scientific American,* 1974, *230*(1), 78–85. (Offprint 557.)

Rosch, E., and C. B. Mervis. Family resemblances: Studies in the internal structure of categories. *Cognitive Psychology,* 1975, *7,* 573–605.

Rosch, E., C. B. Mervis, W. Gray, D. Johnson, and P. Boyes-Braem. Basic objects in natural categories. *Cognitive Psychology,* 1976, *8,* 382–439.

Rubenstein, H., S. S. Lewis, and M. A. Rubenstein. Homographic entries in the internal lexicon: Effects of systematicity and relative frequency of meanings. *Journal of Verbal Learning and Verbal Behavior,* 1971, *10,* 57–62.

Rumelhart, D. E. A multicomponent theory of the perception of briefly exposed visual displays. *Journal of Mathematical Psychology,* 1970, *7,* 191–218.

Rumelhart, D. E., and P. Siple. The processes of recognizing tachistoscopically presented words. *Psychological Review,* 1974, *81,* 99–118.

Sakitt, B. Locus of short-term visual storage. *Science,* 1975, *190,* 1318–1319.

Scarborough, D. L., C. Cortese, and H. S. Scarborough. Frequency and repetition effects in lexical memory. *Journal of Experimental Psychology: Human Perception and Performance,* 1977, *3,* 1–17.

Schneider, W., and R. M. Shiffrin. Controlled and automatic human information processing: I. Detection, search, and attention. *Psychological Review,* 1977, *84,* 1–66.

Schuberth, R. E., and P. D. Eimas. Effects of context on the classification of words and nonwords. *Journal of Experimental Psychology: Human Perception and Performance,* 1977, *3,* 27–36.

Selfridge, O. G. Pandemonium: A paradigm of learning. In *The mechanization of thought processes.* London: Her Majesty's Stationery Office, 1959.

Selfridge, O. G., and U. Neisser. Pattern recognition by machine. *Scientific American,* 1960, *203,* 60–68.

Shaw, M. L. A capacity allocation model for reaction time. *Journal of Experimental Psychology: Human Perception and Performance,* 1978, *4,* 586–598.

Shaw, P. Processing of tachistoscopic displays with controlled order of characters. *Perception & Psychophysics,* 1969, *6,* 257–266.

Shepard, R. N. Attention and the metric structure of the stimulus space. *Journal of Verbal Learning and Verbal Behavior,* 1964, *1,* 54–87.

Shepard, R. N. Recognition memory for words, sentences, and pictures. *Journal of Verbal Learning and Verbal Behavior,* 1967, *6,* 156–163.

Shepard, R. N. The mental image. *American Psychologist,* 1978, *33,* 125–137.

Shepard, R. N., and C. Feng. A chronometric study of mental paper folding. *Cognitive Psychology,* 1972, *3,* 228–243.

Shepard, R. N., and J. Metzler. Mental rotation of three-dimensional objects. *Science,* 1971, *171,* 701–703.

Shepp, B. E., B. Burns, and D. McDonough. The relation of stimulus structure to perceptual and cognitive development: Further tests of a separability hypothesis.

In F. Wilkening, J. Becker, and T. Trabasso (Eds.), *The integration of information by children*. Hillsdale, N.J.: Lawrence Erlbaum Associates, 1980.

Shiffrin, R. M., and G. T. Garner. Visual processing capacity and attentional control. *Journal of Experimental Psychology,* 1972, *93,* 72–82.

Shiffrin, R. M., D. P. McKay, and W. O. Shaffer. Attending to forty-nine spatial positions at once. *Journal of Experimental Psychology: Human Perception and Performance,* 1976, *2,* 14–22.

Shiffrin, R. M., and W. Schneider. Controlled and automatic human information processing: II. Perceptual learning, automatic attending, and a general theory. *Psychological Review,* 1977, *84,* 127–190.

Sigel, I. E. The development of pictorial comprehension. In B. S. Randhawa and W. E. Coffman (Eds.), *Visual learning, thinking, and communication.* New York: Academic Press, 1978.

Siipola, E. M., and S. D. Hayden. Exploring eidetic imagery among the retarded. *Perceptual and Motor Skills,* 1965, *21,* 275–286.

Smith, F. *Understanding reading.* New York: Holt, Rinehart and Winston, 1978.

Sperling, G. The information available in brief visual presentations. *Psychological Monographs,* 1960, *74*(11, Whole No. 498).

Sperling, G. A model for visual memory tasks. *Human Factors,* 1963, *5,* 19–31.

Sperling, G. Successive approximations to a model for short-term memory. *Acta Psychologia,* 1967, *27,* 285–292.

Spoehr, K. T. Phonological encoding in visual word recognition. *Journal of Verbal Learning and Verbal Behavior,* 1978, *17,* 127–142.

Spoehr, K. T., and E. E. Smith. The role of syllables in perceptual processing. *Cognitive Psychology,* 1973, *5,* 71–89.

Spoehr, K. T., and E. E. Smith. The role of orthographic and phonotactic rules in perceiving letter patterns. *Journal of Experimental Psychology: Human Perception and Performance,* 1975, *1,* 21–34.

Sternberg, S. Memory-scanning: Mental processes revealed by reaction-time experiments. *American Scientist,* 1969, *57*(4), 421–457.

Stevens, A., and P. Coupe. Distortions in judged spatial relations. *Cognitive Psychology,* 1978, *10,* 422–437.

Stromeyer, C. F., III. Eidetikers. *Psychology Today,* November 1970, pp. 76–80.

Stromeyer, C. F., III, and J. Psotka. The detailed texture of eidetic images. *Nature,* 1970, *225,* 346–349.

Stroop, J. R. Studies of interference in serial verbal reactions. *Journal of Experimental Psychology,* 1935, *18,* 643–662.

Thompson, M. C., and D. W. Massaro. Visual information and redundancy in reading. *Journal of Experimental Psychology,* 1973, *98,* 49–54.

Thorndyke, P. W., and C. Stasz. Individual differences in procedures for knowledge acquisition from maps. *Cognitive Psychology,* 1980, *12,* 137–175.

Townsend, J. T. Theoretical analysis of an alphabetic confusion matrix. *Perception & Psychophysics,* 1971, *9,* 40–50.

Townsend, J. T. Issues and models concerning the processing of a finite number of inputs. In B. H. Kantowitz (Ed.), *Human information processing: Tutorials in performance and cognition.* Hillsdale: N.J.: Lawrence Erlbaum Associates, 1974.

Treisman, A. M., and G. Gelade. A feature-integration theory of attention. *Cognitive Psychology,* 1980, *12,* 97–136.

Turvey, M. T. On peripheral and central processes in vision: inferences from an information-processing analysis of masking with patterned stimuli. *Psychological Review,* 1973, *80,* 1–52.

Tversky, B. Eye fixations in prediction of recognition and recall. *Memory & Cognition,* 1974, *2,* 275–278.

References

Tzeng, O., and H. Singer (Eds.). *Perception of print: Reading research in experimental psychology.* Hillsdale, N.J.: Lawrence Erlbaum Associates, 1981.

Vernoy, M. W. Masking by pattern in random element stereograms. *Vision Research,* 1976, *16,* 1183–1184.

von Wright, J. M. On the problem of selection in iconic memory. *Scandanavian Journal of Psychology,* 1972, *13,* 159–171.

Walker-Smith, G. J., A. G. Gale, and J. M. Findlay. Eye movement strategies involved in face perception. *Perception,* 1977, *6,* 313–326.

Ware, C., and D. Mitchell. The spatial selectivity of the tilt aftereffect. *Vision Research,* 1974, *14,* 735–738.

Weisstein, N., and C. S. Harris. Visual detection of line segments: An object superiority effect. *Science,* 1974, *186,* 752–755.

Werner, H. Studies in contour: I. Qualitative analysis. *American Journal of Psychology,* 1935, *47,* 40–64.

Wertheimer, M. *Principles of perceptual organization.* In D. C. Beardslee and M. Wertheimer (Eds.), *Readings in perception.* Princeton: Van Nostrand, 1958.

West, R. F., and K. E. Stanovich. Automatic contextual facilitation in readers of three ages. *Child Development,* 1978, *49,* 717–727.

Wheeler, D. D. Processes in word recognition. *Cognitive Psychology,* 1970, *1,* 59–85.

Winograd, E. Recognition memory for faces following nine different judgments. *Bulletin of the Psychonomic Society,* 1976, *8,* 419–421.

Winston, P. H. Learning structural descriptions from examples. Report MAC TR-76. Massachusetts Institute of Technology, 1970.

Winston, P. H. *Artificial intelligence.* Reading, Mass.: Addison-Wesley, 1977.

Wolff, W. The experimental study of forms of expression. *Character and Personality,* 1933, *2,* 168–176.

Wolford, G. Perturbation model for letter identification. *Psychological Review,* 1975, *82,* 184–199.

Wolford, G., and S. Hollingsworth. Lateral masking in visual information processing. *Perception & Psychophysics,* 1974a, *16,* 315–320.

Wolford, G., and S. Hollingsworth. Retinal location and string position as important variables in visual information processing. *Perception & Psychophysics,* 1974b, *16,* 437–442.

Wollen, K. A., and D. H. Lowry. Effects of imagery on paired-associate learning. *Journal of Verbal Learning and Verbal Behavior,* 1971, *10,* 276–284.

Wollen, K. A., A. Weber, and D. H. Lowry. Bizarreness versus interaction of mental images as determinants of learning. *Cognitive Psychology,* 1972, *3,* 518–523.

Woodworth, R. S., and H. Schlosberg. *Experimental psychology.* New York: Holt, Rinehart and Winston, 1954.

Yarbus, A. L. *Eye movements and vision.* New York: Plenum, 1967.

Yin, R. K. Looking at upside-down faces. *Journal of Experimental Psychology,* 1969, *81,* 141–145.

Yin, R. K. Face recognition by brain-injured patients: A dissociable ability. *Neurophsychologia,* 1970, *8,* 395–402.

Author Index

Author Index

Subject Index

ABCDEFGHIJKLMNOPQRSTUVWXYZ

ZYXWVUTSRQPONMLKJIHGFEDCBA

ZYXWVV

ZYXWVUTSRQPONMLKJIHGFEDCBA